The Last
Best League

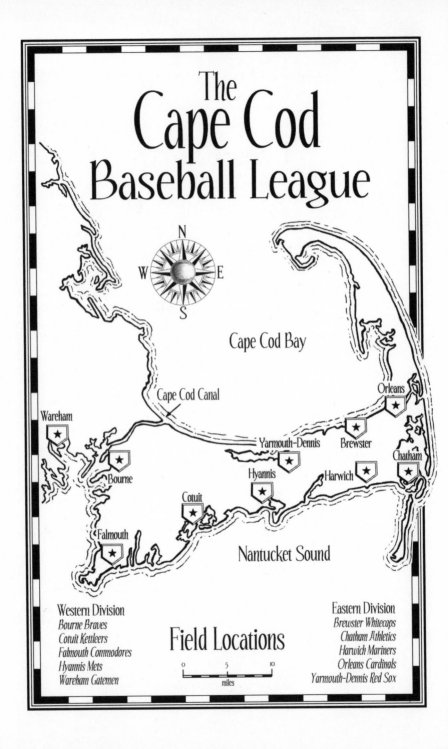

The Last Best League

10TH ANNIVERSARY EDITION

*One Summer, One Season,
One Dream*

JIM COLLINS

Da Capo Press
A Member of the Perseus Books Group

Designed by Brent Wilcox
Typeset in New Caledonia

Cataloging-in-Publication data for this book
is available from the Library of Congress.

First Da Capo Press edition 2004
Paperback edition 2005
ISBN: 978-0-306-82310-7 (paperback)
ISBN: 978-0-306-82311-4 (e-book)

Published by Da Capo Press
A Member of the Perseus Books Group
http://www.dacapopress.com

Da Capo Press books are available at special discounts for bulk purchases
in the U.S. by corporations, institutions, and other organizations.
For more information, please contact the Special Markets Department at
the Perseus Books Group, 2300 Chestnut Street, Suite 200, Philadelphia,
PA, 19103, or call (800) 810-4145, ext. 5000, or e-mail
special.markets@perseusbooks.com.

10 9 8 7 6 5 4 3 2 1

FOR KRISTEN

Contents

Preface

I FIRST HEARD OF THE CAPE COD BASEBALL LEAGUE when I was an infielder at Dartmouth College in the early 1980s. Players didn't use the league's formal name, but, rather, talked wistfully about "playing on the Cape," as if some kind of aura surrounded the geography, itself. The league was the best of the NCAA summer leagues. We didn't know much about it or how someone went about getting into it—that was part of the Cape's mystique—but we knew that most of us had been team captains and all-stars and most valuable players in high school, and none of us was good enough to play there.

I spent my first college summer back home in Walpole, New Hampshire, playing on a team that attracted the most serious players within an eight- or ten-town radius, players who had gone on, mostly, to small northeastern colleges. Some noncollege guys played on the team as well. They worked their full-time jobs around the games, brought beer in the trunks of their cars, gave the eight-team league a rough, townie edge. I'd been aware all along of the sorting taking place around me, and now I felt the pinch.

I had played with or against many of the players in Walpole before—we stood at the tip of a local pyramid whose base stretched across a broad rural area, our talent or drive having lifted us higher than almost everyone we'd played with on the way up. The winnowing, at the lower levels, had been clear, relatively painless, usually self-selected. Millions of kids start out dreaming of being big-league ballplayers. Most of them, at early ages, admit they don't have what it takes, or decide the game isn't worth the effort, or find some other passion to replace it. Dreams are fragile. But I had fallen in love with the game at eight years old, and from then on I wanted nothing more than to play second base for the Boston Red Sox.

Wanting to be a baseball player differed from wanting to be an astronaut or a policeman. I could actually work at becoming a baseball player, and I grew up believing I could will myself to the majors by working harder than anybody else. I was the kid who slept with his baseball glove, who shoveled snow off the driveway so I could play catch in the winter. I talked my parents into letting me go to baseball camps. My father, a Brit, didn't understand the sport. My mother knew only a little about it, but she loved watching my games, and both of them respected how much I wanted to be good at it. They bought me baseball books, reassured me, without really knowing, that I had a chance. When I was twelve years old I saw an ad in the back of a *Baseball Digest* and wrote away for information about how to become a major league ballplayer. I pored over the thick binder that arrived, memorizing the mimeographed pages of tips and exercises and descriptions of what scouts looked for in a prospect. Fortunately, I had a knack for the game. At each higher level I stood out, got picked for all-star teams.

And baseball changed me. I lived for the game, and made decisions based on how they'd affect my playing. I ate differently than the rest of my family—no soda, no junk food. I went to bed early without being told. I was a shy kid. I didn't like drawing attention to myself, except on a baseball field. There I took charge, felt the confidence that comes from being looked up to, admired, singled out.

Only one other talented player in my class shared the same dream. Jeff Hubbard and I had pushed each other ever since Little League. We practiced endlessly—I threw balls at his feet, he hit grounders just beyond my reach, to make me dive. Before games, we dressed together at Jeff's house, getting psyched up to the thump of Tom Petty and the Heartbreakers. We weren't alike. I thought he was cocky, and I couldn't understand why he turned everything into a competition. I was quiet, serious, brooded over small failures. But we were best friends. His dad, who had been a star pitcher at the University of New Hampshire before throwing snowballs ruined his arm, took both of us to Winter Haven, Florida, each March to watch the Red Sox train for their upcoming season—and to prepare us for ours. We stayed at the same hotel as the Red Sox players, ate in the same restaurants. In the evenings Jeff and I sneaked onto a perfectly groomed red-clay infield at the minor league complex and practiced fielding ground balls over and over and over until it became too dark to see them. We hopped the fence of an orange orchard beyond the outfield of Chain O' Lakes Park and chased down home-run balls. We kept a milk crate's worth so we could take our own batting practice with the real thing.

Jeff and I both played in college—a rare occurrence for athletes from our small town—but I knew, that first year, that Jeff had stepped out from the local pyramid and entered a much larger one. He was our best player and perennial all-star shortstop, and the only one missing from my summer team. He'd gone to the University of North Carolina on a baseball scholarship. In the summer he was playing on the Cape.

THE SUMMER BEFORE WE STARTED college was a powerful one, and I remember the way it ended.

My dream of playing professional baseball felt very close. I had been named the outstanding player in the previous year's state American Legion tournament. I played second base for the strongest Legion team in the district, and Jeff played shortstop; the papers called us the best double-play combination in the state in years. Our coach told me that major league scouts had been asking about both of us.

I had gone on my first date with the smartest girl in my class, someone I'd had a crush on for a long time. We'd driven an hour to a theater at Dartmouth, where I was headed that fall. We'd watched a performance of *Richard III*, and later, at her front door, we'd kissed goodnight. The next day, on a sunny, hot, glorious afternoon, feeling invincible, I hung in too long turning a double play. Jeff was pitching in a tense, close game. The groundball up the middle got hung up in our shortstop's glove. I floated over to the bag, planted my left leg, and waited until he found the ball and shuffled it to me. It arrived as the baserunner lowered his shoulder and crashed into the side of my left leg.

Something in my trajectory ripped apart as my knee's ligaments tore, and I sensed in the hospital that any chance I'd had of playing in the pros had disappeared. The surgeon prepared me for half a year of rehab, just to play again with a bulky knee brace.

At Dartmouth I worked year-round, as hard as ever, and started on the varsity as a freshman. I had romantic notions about being discovered on an unlikely ball field in northern New England, but I knew now they were fantasies, and reality gradually smothered them altogether. Looking back, I wonder whether I didn't know the truth even earlier, when I tossed out recruiting letters I'd received from Division I schools, including North Carolina, and chose an Ivy League school close to home for its academics. At the time, I simply created a story that my dream could fit into: If I were good enough, I'd be seen no matter where I played. I didn't look deeply enough to see the fear.

At every earlier level I had excelled, and expected to excel. But after the knee injury I lost my quickness in the field, and then my confidence at bat, and I never again felt the absolute sureness that I'd felt the summer I was eighteen. For the first time I couldn't tell where I stood. I was just another player on a mediocre team in a mediocre baseball conference. Working hard and getting plenty of sleep didn't make any difference. Disoriented, hungry to experience college, I quit playing after my junior season, just as Jeff Hubbard was heading back to the Cape, a year before the Baltimore Orioles drafted him.

Having been defined and changed by a boy's game, I put it away and found a full life waiting. My world lost a center and became bigger at the same time.

IN THE SUMMER OF 2001, researching an article for *Yankee* magazine, I spent a few days on the lower Cape with my wife and young daughter. I'd written features for several national publications and dozens more for *Yankee* by then, including a profile of Bill Lee, an eccentric pitcher called Spaceman whom I'd loved watching during those spring trainings in Winter Haven, Florida. I'd come back to the game as a fan, though not a serious one. The Red Sox radio broadcasts still soothed me. I occasionally glimpsed a high school game while I was driving and pulled over to watch an inning or two. But I'd become busy with work, with restoring an old farmhouse, eventually with family. Over time my circle of friends included fewer and fewer athletes, more people whose interests leaned to canoeing or back-country skiing or gardening.

On the Cape, we meandered one evening down Route 28 to the village of Chatham, and watched the Chatham A's play the Falmouth Commodores in a Cape Cod League baseball game. The soft June air carried wisps of fog over the dark brown dirt and lush grass. The field glowed under the lights, seemed alive. The players, smooth, graceful, beautiful, drew my eye. I felt old longings rise. I recognized the players in an instant. They weren't dispassionate, nearly robotic, major leaguers. Nor were they hard-edged minor leaguers fighting for survival. These were kids, full of life—some of them laughing, some scared, some swaggering with the absolute sureness of invincibility. And they were phenomenally talented.

I registered all of it instinctively, in a way that, probably, only a former player could. If not for a knee injury, or more size, or a streak of cockiness, or different parents, or a different school, or a thin margin of talent, that could have been me out there, once.

From my vantage point I could tell, even better than they could, what kind of sorting was going on, what was at stake. About half of the players on the field that night would take the next step—from the top level of the best amateur pyramid in the country to the bottom of the much smaller pyramid of the pros. A handful would make it all the way to the top. The question hanging in that soft summer air was *who*. And a more complex one: Why those and not the others?

I saw a human story at every position. I wondered what it must feel like to be a twenty-year-old all-star on Cape Cod. To spend ten weeks around the sun and sand and blue water, standing out among the finest college players in the country. Or to be in that same bucolic landscape but struggling, doubting yourself for the first time, suddenly questioning whether you had what it took to make it. I pointed out the scouts to my wife, Kristen. We could see them sitting behind the home-plate backstop with their digital stopwatches and radar guns that looked like black plastic blow dryers. A dozen guns lifted in unison every time a pitch sped toward the plate.

I wondered what my friend Jeff would see watching these same players. He'd lasted five years in the minors with three different organizations before washing out at the age of twenty-six. For a while after that he'd become a coach with a minor league team. But the constant travel drained too much time away from his growing family. After years of running a fitness club, he'd recently become restless, missed the game. He was trying to find a way back in. He'd looked for a stepping stone, and had found one. I didn't know it that evening, but Jeff was back in the game, coaching in Wareham in the Cape Cod Baseball League.

For the better part of a year I couldn't get that Chatham game out of my head—the wispy fog, the beautiful players, the radar guns behind home plate, the kids playing catch into the dark next to the brightly lit field. The following June I moved my family to Cape Cod to witness the most crucial summer of some young men's lives. The Cape League would be at their center, and I wanted to be there to watch. It wasn't only the baseball I was interested in, but what happened to their dreams.

The Cape, then, in early summer, held an especial clarity of light, imparting a first-day-of-Creation feeling, like the opening movement of Beethoven's Ninth Symphony. The leaves of the honey locusts shone yellow-green in the sun against the clean blue of the sky. Everything so brimmed with youth that it held the power to peel back the years and restore the excitements of childhood to us older persons. The heat of summer had not yet tired the countryside; meadows were white with daisies, yellow with coreopsis, purple with vetch. The dunes glowed golden with poverty grass in bloom. Little white boats tossed on the bay, shining in their new coats of paint. This moment of clear joy was preciously transient. It would never more exist until the following June.

Clare Leighton,
"The Rituals of Summer"

Prologue
The Call

A MOMENT ARRIVED IN EVERY player's story when the stakes suddenly changed. For Jamie D'Antona, that moment came in the dim fluorescent light of a batting cage in suburban Connecticut.

At the beginning, the hitting lessons focused on drills: thirty dry hacks with the bottom hand, then thirty with the top hand, whipping the bat at imaginary balls coming low and outside, in high and tight. Then off a batting tee, thirty with both hands, then thirty with each hand again. Then another series with the old man crouching off to his side, softly tossing baseballs toward the strike zone of the four-teen-year-old boy. Finally, a machine arm flung a pitch, and another, and another, and for twenty minutes more Jamie D'Antona swung, with Joe Benanto watching and barking corrections.

All this happened a long time ago, to D'Antona's way of regarding time, in a batting cage at Joe Benanto's laboratory, the B&B Indoor Training Center in Shelton, Connecticut. He'd seen the best players from other schools taking lessons there, too. Shelton, a nondescript mill town, drew hopeful kids from five or six surrounding suburban towns, along with parents who had ambitions for them.

Over time, D'Antona internalized near-perfect mechanics, converted them into solid line drive after solid line drive. Drills and tee-work took up less of each session. Benanto offered him more advanced skills—recognizing pitches, anticipating, working the strike zone. Then he simply turned the boy loose in the cage.

Benanto was one of those guys who sit low down in the vast infrastructure of the professional baseball world. He had coached for forty years. He'd won 200 games in high school, then gone up the turnpike from Shelton and won nearly 250 more at Yale. In retirement he'd started a little baseball school with six batting cages. He had an eye for talent and a knack for nurturing it. He charged fifty bucks for a sixty-minute hitting lesson, and was overbooked.

In between lessons, D'Antona worked seven days a week at the batting cages. He loaded the machines with balls, fiddled with dials to adjust the pitching arms, picked up and swept the place. Soon he was helping teach the younger kids, and he caught for Joe Benanto while Benanto taught the older ones. By that time, Jamie was excelling on all-star teams, hitting with power and consistency rarely seen in hard competition.

At seventeen, an age when some American teenagers lose their taste for work, D'Antona tore out of the school parking lot each day in his '97 ragtop Mustang, dropped his younger sister at home, cruised over to Shelton, and worked until nine. On Saturdays and Sundays he worked mornings. It wasn't so much that he liked to work—he hardly considered it working when he was at the cages. And he didn't need the money. He lived in Trumbull, in Fairfield County, one of the wealthiest counties in the entire country. His parents, who both commuted to teaching jobs in Greenwich—where the serious money was—were well enough off to own a big house in a nice neighborhood and a twenty-six-foot off-shore fishing boat that they moored at a yacht club on Long Island Sound. Joe and Karin D'Antona had encouraged their son to take the job at the batting cage. They supported his baseball, and they liked Joe Benanto's influence. They also liked that the job kept Jamie busy. D'Antona was the kind of kid who could get into trouble—he was impulsive, took chances, wanted to experience life at a hundred miles an hour. He fishtailed his Mustang on ice just to scare his sister. He blasted hard rock music. Hitting a baseball focused his attention, channeled all that energy. D'Antona put in overtime at the batting cages because he threw himself hard into everything he loved, and he loved hitting a baseball more than anything.

Some weekend mornings he let himself into the cages extra early to hit for a down hour with nobody around. Hit from the stances of his favorite major leaguers. Switch over and hit left-handed. Move up and see how near he could get to the pitching machine before it blew the ball past him—stand ten or twelve feet away from it, with almost no time to react—and still hit. Hit, for the way it made him feel proud, and for the joy of it, for the feel in his hands when he struck a ball so solidly that he thought it might tear through the mesh netting at the back of the cage.

Every week from October to March, during the cold New England off-season, Jamie D'Antona took two thousand, three thousand swings in the cages. He came to know every nuance of his swing—his stance, the loading, timing, weight transfer, the rotation of his hips and upper body, whip of his hands, his follow-through. He came to understand his swing unconsciously, so that he could put every part of it together in the two blinks of an eye it took a distant ninety-mile-an-hour fastball to cross the plate. He could clear his mind of every distracting thing; he could hit without thinking. It was considered the single most difficult thing to do in all of sports—something experts had endlessly, elegantly dissected into its many components—but Jamie D'Antona simply saw the ball and crushed it. Balls exploded off his bat.

Early on, Benanto realized he was working with an extraordinary talent, a once-in-a-lifetime talent. He stopped taking payments from big Joe D'Antona, who had attended every one of his son's lessons before Jamie had gotten his driver's license. Benanto considered it a privilege just to watch the boy hit.

One afternoon late in his senior year at Trumbull High School, D'Antona was pulled aside by his coach. A major league scout, Matt Merullo of the Arizona Diamondbacks, had called to say he was coming to watch D'Antona play. D'Antona couldn't believe the news, though he shouldn't have been surprised. He'd grown up starring in a baseball-obsessed town. Trumbull had upset Taiwan in the Little League World Series in 1989, a few years before Jamie came through. The victory had made Trumbull something of a legend throughout Little League baseball. Townspeople fussed over the best players from a young age.

D'Antona had batted varsity cleanup since his sophomore year—the power position in the line-up, the one carrying the highest expectations and pressure. As a junior he'd batted .623—amazingly, almost two hits for every three times at bat. He'd been the youngest ever to play for Team USA/New England's junior team in international competition. He'd led his state's under-eighteen Amateur Athletic Union (AAU) team to a national championship, and had won the Most Valuable Player award in that tournament's world series. The insider's bible, *Baseball America*, called him the top high school player to watch in Connecticut.

But he resisted taking his talent seriously. He had gone to a couple of major league tryouts but felt awkward at them, didn't know what he was doing there. He played best when baseball was fun. He liked challenging himself, liked winning. As the adults and newspapers got more serious about his prospects, he himself seemed to get less serious about his playing. He joked with opponents during games, rolled his eyes or laughed at errors he made at third base. He hardly ever talked about baseball away from the field, and especially not about his future. "I'm more of a here-and-now-type person," he'd say. People watching him—unaware of the hours he'd spent in the batting cage mimicking his heroes—might have wondered whether D'Antona even cared about how well he did.

He tried desperately to keep the game from getting too intense. He'd only grudgingly started talking about the possibility of playing in college. But, told that a scout would come to watch *him*, he found himself taking batting practice with a new purpose. As he hit line drive after line drive, he let himself think, for the first time, that he might someday play in the majors. He could actually get paid—

maybe hundreds of thousands of dollars, maybe millions of dollars—
to hit a baseball. The thought thrilled him.

At two years old Tim Stauffer picked up a football and hurled
the thing with a perfect spiral. His aunts and uncles laughed. One of
his uncles called him Spike, and from then on everybody in the family knew the kid had a gift for throwing.

At seven years old he dreamed of pitching in the major leagues.
He lost a game in Little League and was so upset that he cried inconsolably. His father put a pitcher's rubber in the family's back yard
in Saratoga Springs, New York. Rick Stauffer had once appeared in
Sports Illustrated's "Faces in the Crowd" for his American Legion
pitching statistics. As a pitcher at St. Joseph's University in Pennsylvania, he had attracted the looks of big league scouts before an arm
injury ended his career. He knew the game and saw the talent in his
only son.

The back yard was hidden from neighbors by trees in a new, leafy
development not far from the Hannaford Supermarket that Rick
Stauffer managed, just north of the race track and the Skidmore College campus and Saratoga Springs' grand old Victorian downtown.
Tim played catch with his dad most nights before dinner, sometimes
after dinner, too, and always with a purpose. They called one of their
games "What If?"

"What if there are runners on first and second and no outs?" the
father would ask. "Where would you throw the ball if it's hit to you?"

"What if you've got an oh-two count on a hitter, and you've thrown
him two fastballs down and in? What do you want to throw on the
next pitch?"

They played the game incessantly. More than once, they played
"What If?" during the family's entire seven-hour drive to an uncle's
beach house on the Delaware shore.

The boy learned to command his pitches. He wasn't flashy, not a
kid anyone looked at and thought *This one's special*. Except that

throwing is an unnatural motion. And even in Little League—in *Little League*, where ten-year-olds are still working out the coordination to throw a baseball *near* home plate—Timmy Stauffer threw strikes. He had an easy, loose motion to his arm and a feel for situations that eluded most older players.

In fifth grade he wrote a poem entitled "Timothy" that included the lines "I am baseball / thoughtful, in control." (His mom put the poem, framed in a little piece of glass, on the window ledge above the kitchen sink, and it sits there today, stained and worn, the glass frame cracked.) He devoured the sports pages of *The Saratogian*, memorizing statistics, registering each rise and fall of his favorite team, the Boston Red Sox. He plastered his bedroom wall with baseball posters. Every Christmas morning he delightedly unwrapped a new complete set of Topps baseball cards. He studied the game, grew to love its complexity and the way each inning offered brand-new challenges and surprises.

Between nine and fourteen, he added a shoe size each year. By high school he was up to size-fourteen cleats, stood six foot two, weighed 190 pounds, and threw three kinds of pitches, each at several speeds and all with uncanny accuracy. He stopped throwing to his father off the rubber in the back yard. His father could no longer catch him. In his senior year he led his team—serious, tiny, unassuming Saratoga Central Catholic High School—all the way to the New York class C finals. He won thirteen games that spring and lost none. He struck out 173 batters and walked only fifteen. Some long-standing friendships drifted because Stauffer cared more about baseball than about partying and being one of the guys. (Years later, he told his parents why those friendships had ended, but not then. He had felt an allegiance to his friends, and honored it.) He was a quiet, extremely private teenager, dutiful around adults, an altar server at church. He knew he could pitch well, but he aspired to a higher standard. He drove himself harder than any parent or coach could have. Nobody could recall a local pitcher with better control.

The Baltimore Orioles selected him in the 2000 Major League Baseball First-Year Player Draft. They dangled $60,000 in front of him to induce him to begin his professional career in the Orioles' farm system. It might have been a heady, gratifying proposition for most kids who had been aiming for so long at such a small opening. Of every two hundred high school seniors playing organized baseball that year, only one got the chance to turn pro. But it didn't go to Stauffer's head. All along his parents had insisted he go to college. He accepted a scholarship from the University of Richmond over other offers, including one from the Naval Academy in Annapolis.

He knew that fate and injury lurked beyond his control. Throwing a baseball put tremendous stress on still-developing elbows and shoulders. Major league teams drafted high school pitchers carefully for that reason. Drafted high school pitchers were only half as likely as college pitchers to make it to the big leagues. Young pitchers were racehorses, fine and unpredictable.

Stauffer never said so, but even as he turned down the Orioles' offer, he knew he might be passing up the best chance he'd ever get.

His father told him he'd get an even better opportunity in a few years—if he stayed focused.

Thomas Pauly's turning point came later than usual. He'd stood out at a private school in Jacksonville, Florida, playing outfield and pitching. He was named captain and MVP and twice all-city. But every high school in the country had players with credentials like that. Unlike the brightest stars, Pauly never played in "Area Code Games" or on select AAU teams. He skipped baseball camps and major league showcases. What he'd really excelled at was swimming. He had top-sixteen finishes in both the hundred-yard and fifty-yard freestyle in the toughest division of Florida's state competition. In high school he surfed and worked as a lifeguard and spent more time at the beach and the pool than on a diamond.

He'd grown up in a household that valued education. His mother, Marta, born in Cuba, had been a freshman at Jacksonville University xxiv ° THE LAST BEST LEAGUE

when she'd met Tom Pauly, a young first-year philosophy instructor. Tom, tall and fit, was from a Milwaukee German family, and his son Thomas had inherited his long arms and long legs. In high school, Pauly stood six foot two but wore thirty-seven-and-a-half-inch sleeves. Classmates called him "Orangutan Arms."

Pauly's coach, a former major league baseball player named Joel Davis, saw promise in those long limbs and the strong outfield throwing arm, and converted Pauly to a sidearming pitcher during his junior year. Davis knew about his player's grades and high SAT scores and made a call to a former big league teammate, Scott Bradley, coach of the baseball program at Princeton University. Bradley flew down to Florida, and he saw the promise too.

Starting at Princeton, Pauly wasn't sure he belonged on a Division I field, even in the Ivy League, which was known for its academics and lacrosse and rowing, not baseball. Ivy schools didn't even offer athletic scholarships.

Pauly, hiding his anxiousness, pretended he didn't care whether he failed or not. He had an unusually deep sense of humility, which he translated into acting dumb, making fun of himself. The team's "kangaroo court" fined him more often than any other player for seemingly clueless behavior.

In his first college appearance, in March 2001, Oklahoma State rocked him for ten runs in just two and two-thirds innings. Between innings Pauly punched a bathroom stall and popped a blood vessel in his right hand. He sulked through much of the season, acting angry or disinterested, especially when he didn't perform well. But Bradley patiently nurtured him. He told Pauly that college freshmen often struggled against juniors and seniors—that was when bodies changed, filled out, when boys turned into men. Pauly weighed just 175 pounds.

Bradley changed Pauly's pitching motion from sidearm to overhand. Pauly learned how to pitch on the job, and slowly he bought in to Bradley's teachings. Bradley was quietly, ambitiously, building a very good program. The Ivy League occasionally sent players on to the pros, but in the past few years, the highly drafted players had come from Princeton.

Bradley brought Pauly into a crucial situation against Dartmouth with the league championship on the line, and Pauly saved the win. In the NCCA tournament, Pauly pitched four innings against Central Florida, a team ranked seventh in the nation, and gave up just one run. He soaked up all the advice and instruction he could get, becoming the kind of athlete that Bradley called a "sponge."

For the first time in his life, he became serious about pitching.

The summer between freshman and sophomore years, Pauly went back to Florida to lifeguard and to work out with his younger brother William. They lifted weights, ran, and threw "long-toss"—something pitchers do to strengthen throwing muscles and reinforce good mechanics. Throwing a baseball a long way requires concerted work from the legs, lower back, trunk, and arm.

Back at Princeton in the fall, Pauly continued the regimen. At a place noted for hard work, Pauly's work ethic was extraordinary. He wore his teammates out—he threw farther and farther, backing them up across the field until they ran out of field. By the time he threw off the mound at the start of his sophomore season, he had, incredibly, increased the speed of his fastball from a middling eighty-four to a major league ninety-four miles per hour. He'd worked up a sharp-breaking slider to go with the fastball. He threw the slider low and hard, and when it wasn't working he simply fired fastballs past hitters. He knew then he could pitch in the Ivy League.

On the way back from Princeton's spring trip, Bradley sat next to Pauly at an ice cream shop and told him to start thinking about whether he'd remain at Princeton for all four years. He told Pauly that he was not only good enough to pitch at Rice, Stanford, and Arizona, but that he had what it took to pitch in the pros.

Pauly couldn't believe that was true. He hadn't grown up dreaming of playing major league baseball. He was pulling good grades in a tough chemical engineering major, thinking he might find fun, well-paying work at Bacardi back home in Florida. But the idea of his talent taking him all the way to the big leagues got inside his head. He couldn't shake it. He didn't set it as a goal—he was too practical for that. He didn't believe making the majors was the kind of goal someone could set for himself and then achieve. He believed a person was either blessed with the ability, or he wasn't. But if he had the talent in him, he vowed to bring it out and see how far he could go with it.

During his sophomore season he carried himself differently on the field. He realized he was working toward something bigger than he'd ever let himself imagine.

THE PLAYERS CAME TOGETHER on two sheets of lined paper John Schiffner kept in a battered brown briefcase. Schiffner managed the Chatham Athletics—the Chatham A's—of the Cape Cod Baseball League, one of nine summer leagues certified by the National Collegiate Athletic Association. It was the best college summer league in the country, the most exclusive amateur baseball league in the world. Schiffner penciled in the players' names in neat block letters, along with their positions and their colleges. They came from Illinois, Maine, Tennessee, Spokane. They came from families that valued hard work and families that hoped to one day get rich off them. They came from schools where baseball was a religion and they came from Podunk. Every name came with a different story but the same dream.

Some of the names had been on Schiffner's lined paper for a couple of years. Some had just been added. Almost all had been recommended by professional scouts and college coaches who understood what this league demanded of and meant to a young player. In this most heavily recruited-for profession in the country, which identified prospects as early as sixth grade, which plucked élite athletes from playing fields in Asia, the Caribbean, and Latin America, one out of every six major league baseball players still rose through this single league on Cape Cod. It had helped launch many of the sport's biggest stars: Todd Helton, Nomar Garciaparra, Jeff Bagwell, Frank

Thomas, Albert Belle, Mo Vaughn, Robin Ventura, Tino Martinez, Craig Biggio, Matt Anderson, Darin Erstad, Tim Salmon, Jeff Kent, Barry Zito—household names, all, to anyone who follows the game.

Schiffner was one of the gatekeepers of the Cape Cod Baseball League. He taught history and social studies at a high school in Plainfield, Connecticut—hadn't switched jobs in twenty-four years—but his life's work was coaching the Chatham A's. He'd coached in the league longer than had the other nine current field managers combined. He spent a lot of time recruiting his players. He worked more than a season ahead, getting a bead on high school seniors destined to star in college. He cultivated contacts until his network reached into every corner of organized baseball. He was a master of telephone conversations that stretched over years, and he knew how to treat people well. Some kinds of genius in this world win the Pulitzer or Nobel prize. Others get you great baseball players. In his nine seasons as manager John Schiffner had led Chatham to eight play-off appearances, five division titles, and two league championships.

The list of potential 2002 Chatham A's in Schiffner's briefcase rested alongside a copy of the league's policies and guidelines, a directory of NCAA athletic departments, an old beat-up three-ring vinyl address book, a cell phone, and ten years' worth of loose sheets on which he'd built his earlier teams. "Once in a while I even have some school stuff in there," he mused. Time and handling had tattered and smudged many of the pages. Some of his working pages, full of cross-outs and circles and substitutions, looked ridiculous. But you could still make out the names. More than seventy-five of Schiffner's former players now played professionally.

Getting called to play in the Cape Cod Baseball League didn't guarantee a brilliant professional career, just as getting into Juilliard, West Point, or Harvard Business School didn't automatically mean musical, military, or managerial greatness. Such launching pads dampen as well as enliven dreams. Every major league team sent its scouts to evaluate Cape League prospects, and from them there was no hiding. A year or more of college ball remained between Schiffner's players and the major league draft. They would have another chance to audition, in other words—but no other showcase would be as revealing as a summer on the Cape. The stakes included fame and fortune—the average major league salary had climbed above two million dollars—or, alternatively, the dawning prospect of a career in sales, maybe, or in the family cement business.

At the same time, something more personal was at stake, something more human. On Cape Cod's level fields, players sorted out from the uneven landscape of American college baseball discovered exactly where they stood. They glimpsed how their dreams might end.

JAMIE D'ANTONA GOT THE CALL early, at Wake Forest University. His coach, George Greer, an old friend of Schiffner's, pulled him aside during afternoon practice near the end of D'Antona's freshman year and asked, "How would you like to play on the Cape? I'd like you to go to Chatham—not this summer, but next summer, after your sophomore year." D'Antona knew about the Cape, but the first thing that came into his mind was *Summer Catch*, the soon-to-be-released Warner Bros. film that had used the Chatham A's as a backdrop. "Sweet!" he said.

Tim Stauffer got the call later that summer in Keene, New Hampshire, while playing in the New England Collegiate Baseball League. He'd expected the call; Schiffner had already talked with Jimmy Howard—the Orioles scout who had hoped to sign Stauffer out of high school—with Stauffer's parents, and with his coach at the University of Richmond. Schiffner made a gentle pitch for Chatham, letting his team's reputation do the selling.

Stauffer was unusually thoughtful for an athlete at this stage, when career decisions are increasingly controlled by adults. He was on the verge of blossoming into one of the best college pitchers in the nation. He knew that the summer prior to his junior year would be crucial—it would be the last before he became eligible, again, for the major-league draft. He feared committing to anything too early. He mulled over the call for a couple of weeks. At the end of August Schiffner's cell phone rang in Kalamazoo, Michigan, where Schiffner and his wife, Martha, vacationed. Stauffer told the coach he'd given it a lot of thought. He would be happy to play in Chatham the next summer.

Thomas Pauly didn't get the call until the following April, just two months before the 2002 Cape Cod baseball season would begin. That spring Schiffner had lost two pitchers on his short list to arm injuries, and another to academic ineligibility, and one more looked certain to go in the June draft. Schiffner called around, working off his long list, looking for available arms. Pauly was pitching in baseball obscurity at Princeton, beneath the gaze of most Cape League coaches, but he was having a breakout year. That spring he would be named the only All-America player from the Ivy League. His coach, Scott Bradley, thought Pauly was the sort of player who benefited most from playing on the Cape. The exposure to major-league scouts would put him on the national map, give him a higher profile than he could ever cut at Princeton. And Pauly would face tougher competition than he'd ever seen.

Pauly had been planning to return to Florida, to lifeguard and work out again with his younger brother. Bradley urged him to go to Cape Cod instead. Reluctantly, Pauly agreed. He wasn't sure he belonged in that league.

SCHIFFNER'S RECRUITS FOR THE 2002 Chatham A's understood much about what a summer in the Cape Cod Baseball League meant, even if only intuitively. The players knew that for those not big or fast or talented enough to go on, the summer on the Cape would stand as the height of their achievement, the nearest to professional they would experience. There was no place left after this except the solace of fantasy camps, beer leagues, and fast-pitch softball. And for those who did move up the professional ranks, the game would soon become a business, lose its innocence, some of its fun. Except for the rarest of players who went on to star in the minors or the major leagues, Cape Cod would be the last place these athletes would ever stand above the heads and shoulders of their peers. What they didn't know, couldn't possibly know, was who among them would make the cut.

Schiffner knew at least one more thing that would come clear later: They would never again have a season like the one they'd experience with him. They would never again be twenty years old, playing baseball on Cape Cod, with their entire lives and all the sky in front of them.

Many of the players, both the ones who stopped here and the ones who climbed further, would look back at this as the last, best summer of their playing careers.

ONE

Chatham

F OR JOHN SCHIFFNER THE SUMMER of 2002 began at four
o'clock on the eighth of June. Strolling onto Veterans Field in
Chatham, Massachusetts, he wore a blue Chatham A's windbreaker
tucked into pinstriped uniform pants, a crisp new Chatham A's cap.
A sloping mustache and a paunch set him apart from the lean, fresh-
faced college athletes on the field with him, but he looked at home
in baseball clothes. He had the stocky frame of a third baseman,
which is what he'd been in his time. His face had turned ruddy from
the season just past, coaching his high school team back in Plainfield.
He was juggling his work in Chatham with the end of the school year
in Connecticut, surviving for ten more days on coffee and No-Doz.
But he was here now, where he felt most alive. At forty-seven,
Schiffner had coached in Chatham since before these players were
born. He gathered the first-arriving members of this year's team
around him and welcomed them to Cape Cod.

He couldn't run a full-scale workout with just seven players, and
didn't try. Some coaches on the Cape scrambled to bring in temporary
players for a few scrimmages before the real games began. Schiffner
believed forty-four games were enough for any summer league.
Southern Cal and North Carolina and most of the other programs
from which he picked his players ran with fierce intensity. Unlike the
other coaches in the league, Schiffner had played on the Cape himself—for Harwich, over three summers back in the seventies, back

I

when he starred at Providence College and had dreamed of playing in the major leagues. He understood the need for a breather between the baseball season just ending and the one about to begin. He let his players drift in on their own timetables, which varied with differing school semesters and the logistics of travel. Most had played fifty to sixty games since early February. Tim Stauffer's Richmond Spiders were still playing in the Super Regionals, just a step away from the pinnacle of the NCAA baseball season, the eight-team College World Series in Omaha, Nebraska. Richmond had ended Jamie D'Antona's spring early when it knocked off Wake Forest in the first round of the post-season tournament. D'Antona was en route to Chatham, but had stopped in Connecticut for a couple of days to squeeze in a visit with his parents and sister. His father was recovering from cancer treatments. Schiffner knew where his players were coming from.

Raw, rainy weather on the Cape had chilled the first week of June, made the air sharp, more like November than summer. But now the sun shone brightly on the A's. The breeze smelled fresh, of cool grass, almost of mint. A boxy wooden press box, newly painted gray, sat above rows of aluminum bleachers that traced the hill behind home plate. A tall, dark stand of pines loomed behind the field's electronic scoreboard, framing the chain-link fence in left field. Beyond center and right fields, a grassy embankment swept up to a quiet paved street and the weathered, shingled buildings of Chatham's police and fire departments. The topography set the field in a shallow bowl, a natural stadium without walls. Schiffner loved this field, though in truth it didn't compare to the lavish, minor-league-quality palaces in which many of the A's had spent their spring.

He stood in front of the third-base dugout and squinted into the sun through the red lenses of his Oakley sunglasses. He told his early arrivers that they'd use these first few practices for knocking some rust loose, getting some running in, getting acquainted. He was seeing many of the players for the first time in person. He knew each year that at least a few of them would surprise him. No matter how carefully he recruited, no matter how highly recommended the player, it was tough to judge a kid's character from a distance. He looked at the faces around him and wondered if he'd made any mistakes.

THE PLAYERS STOOD QUIETLY, each of them tightly pulled knots of cool, anticipation, and nervousness. It was easy to sort out the strands. The league attracted a certain kind of swagger, and also justified it. These athletes were studs—studs' studs—and had been handpicked for the most select summer league in the country. Besides, fine athletes were often a little aloof, especially young men taking each other's measure. Yet the early arrivers were as anxious as they were cocky. They came from low-profile programs, the ones whose seasons had ended earlier than the rest: Princeton, Siena, Bryant, Gonzaga. These players had something to prove. Thomas Pauly was one of them. He had driven to Chatham over the past two days, wearing the same lifeguard jacket, shorts, and sandals he'd worn since leaving Florida's heat. He'd pulled into a gas station a few miles from town and stepped out into the breezy, fifty-degree air. He called his mother and said he'd made it to the Cape, but told her it was freezing. "It will get warmer," she said. "Don't worry."

But Pauly did worry. He felt out of place. He'd never played on an élite team before. He'd lucked into a spot here as a last-minute alternate, not a first choice. He'd read the bios of his teammates and realized how thin his pedigree was in comparison. Coming from Princeton implied a certain sophistication, but *school* differed from *baseball*. He'd never even been away from home in the summer. He still half wished he'd stayed in Florida to do his own thing.

Like the others around him Pauly had tracked the names of his new teammates on the Internet, names from U.S.C. and Baylor, names that showed up in *Baseball America* and *Collegiate Baseball*. That charged the anticipation, to see how good Tim Stauffer really was— Stauffer, who had burst into the college limelight that spring and won fifteen games, more than any other pitcher in Division I; *Stauffer*, who suddenly ranked on some lists as the best college pitcher in the whole country. Or *Jamie D'Antona—the* Jamie D'Antona—the all-everything from Wake Forest, the Atlantic Coast Conference leader in home runs and runs driven in, the 2001 NCAA freshman player of the year. Those credentials could intimidate a guy from Princeton who had pitched, essentially, for only three or four years. Pauly had driven into Chatham feeling the same uneasiness he'd felt upon entering Princeton, the same vague sense that—despite his straight A's in high school, despite his 1400 College Board scores, he didn't belong on an Ivy campus. Only after he'd received his first-semester grades had he begun to feel confident in the classroom.

While Schiffner greeted the players, Pauly stood next to a teammate from school, pitcher Scott Hindman. Hindman was funny, easy to be around, socially adept. He slipped effortlessly into new surroundings. Hindman didn't act like a replacement pick, although, just like Pauly, that's what he was. He didn't seem daunted by the knowledge that Ivy League players rarely were invited to the Cape. He came from a rich family in a Chicago suburb and had a view of the world based, in part, on a sense of entitlement. He was a history major, a talker, curious about social structures, full of ideas and theories. He liked zany, sophomoric humor. For the Chatham A's team brochure, he'd listed his off-field interests as "tap dancing and cooking candlelight dinners."

Pauly was a realist, analytical, a chemical engineering major from a home with immigrant-family values. Tanned, dark-haired, with round, dark eyes and the lean body of a swimmer, he told people he came from Atlantic Beach, Florida, a section of town on the water, because he identified with the beach. But in fact he came from Jacksonville proper. His family had only recently moved to the beach, because the city's serious crime had reached the edge of their old neighborhood on the St. John's River. For whatever reason, Pauly had more respect for teammates who had started with a little less than Hindman, maybe, who didn't talk so much about themselves, who needed to work harder at developing their talent. Still, the two of them bonded over goofiness, and hung out occasionally at Princeton. In Chatham, Pauly found comfort in familiarity. He felt more confident just standing next to Hindman.

But Hindman had worries of his own. He felt the lingering pain of reconstructed ligaments in his left elbow. The pain kept him from fully straightening his arm, even at rest. Hindman had missed all of his sophomore year following the surgery, and this past spring he'd thrown just seven innings. But he stood six foot three, and he could do something only a handful of amateur left-handed pitchers in the country could do: throw a baseball ninety miles an hour. Earlier that week the Anaheim Angels had risked a twenty-second-round pick on him in the 2002 major league draft. Hindman sensed that his elbow hadn't recovered but told Anaheim he'd need at least six figures to sign, far more than clubs typically paid draft picks from such a low round. The Angels wanted to monitor his progress over the summer before extending an offer, a variation on an arrangement the clubs called a "draft-and-follow." The Angels, understandably, weren't eager to invest a lot of money on the strength of seven innings of Ivy League pitching.

Pauly and Hindman looked around as Schiffner welcomed the team. Arriving at the field earlier that afternoon, the two of them each had the same thought: *This? This was the ball field of the Chatham A's, the class of the vaunted Cape Cod League? It looked high-schoolish.*

A massive brick school building next to the field had been closed following the construction of a new school outside the village, and with it had gone the showers and locker rooms once used by the A's. The players had to show up in their uniforms or change in the parking lot. Three port-a-johns stood in a line behind the first-base dugout. The local high school team did in fact use the field. So did a town soccer team, for that matter. Its painted field markings occasionally marred the pristine surface of the diamond.

The field would be transformed on sultry summer nights when bright lights bathed the green grass, and two thousand people colored the embankments with lawn chairs and picnic blankets—when the air itself felt electric. Pauly and Hindman hadn't experienced it yet, but they would. Sitting next to each other in the bullpen, they'd look out and say it was an awesome field. They were used to playing before only a couple of hundred fans at Princeton, while an entire campus bustled around them, unaware.

The character of the field suited the town. Chatham, a burnished summer resort on the outer bend of Cape Cod, had grown affluent in part from the appeal of toney understatement. Art studios, bookstores, old-fashioned shops, and high-end boutiques fronted the town's long, tree-shaded Main Street. It had the feel of a college town. The wooden signs hanging by the village's Mobil and Getty stations had been gilded in gold leaf. Off Main Street, white-clapboard and cedar-shingled houses lined narrow lanes that ran to hidden oceanfront estates and unmarked boat landings. Bed-and-breakfasts drew tourists away from the generic strip development that crowded other parts of the Mid- and Upper Cape. Chatham's year-round population of seven thousand quadrupled during the months of July and August, the narrow roads became crowded with Land Rovers and Mercedes SUVs. Summer money, tourists, and well-heeled retirees had not only sanded the edges of the town's old fishing and boat-building trades, they'd laid a veneer over them.

SCHIFFNER LEFT TWO hitters taking batting practice with his assistant coach, Matt Fincher, and followed the pitchers down the left-field line to the bullpen, an open area with two raised pitching mounds and two home plates backed by a large mesh screen. Billowy clouds blew across a luminous blue sky. The old sound of a wooden bat hitting a baseball rang out over the field, carried above the low hum of distant motors and wind in the trees. The annual rhythms commenced.

Each pitcher threw off the mound for several minutes, slowly at first, then with more steam. Schiffner stood off near the foul line, just out of earshot, with his hands in his back pockets. He looked in at

Adam Yates, a tall, broad-shouldered right-hander from Ole Miss.
Yates threw a couple of hard fastballs that cracked into the catcher's
mitt like rifleshot. "Oh, my," said Schiffner. He whistled softly watching Eric Everson's lively, three-quarter-arm fastball. Under his breath
he said, "*I'm* impressed." Everson—small for a pitcher—looked
shorter than the five foot eleven at which he'd been advertised. He
had a funky delivery. He seemed to sling the ball straight out of his
armpit. He'd closed games for Gonzaga University in eastern Washington State, a second-rate place for baseball. Schiffner had trusted
the Gonzaga coach's high appraisal, though, and a rival coach out
there (who'd once played for Schiffner) had corroborated it. They'd
said that Everson's fastball touched ninety-two miles per hour.
Schiffner watched the pitcher throw three weak, slow-breaking curve
balls in a row. "Ooooo-kay," Schiffner muttered, to no one. "He
doesn't have a curve ball. He has no *idea* how to make a ball curve."

Behind Schiffner's back, the other pitchers scattered around the
outfield, shagging batting practice while waiting their turns on the
mound. Thomas Pauly stood way out by the 357-foot marker in
right-center field and loosened his arm by throwing long-toss with
infielder Blake Hanan, standing near the left-field line. One of
Pauly's throws sailed over Hanan's head, nearly hitting Schiffner.
Schiffner walked a few steps farther away. Pauly's next throw nearly
hit the bullpen catcher. "Hey!" Schiffner yelled to Pauly. "Move it
somewhere else!" He caught the eye of Scott Hindman and said,
"They teach you that at Princeton?"

"He's added ten miles to his fastball since he started throwing
long-toss," Hindman answered. "Eighty-four to ninety-four."

"That kid's crazy," said Schiffner. But Pauly's throws had traveled
close to 350 feet on the fly—a tremendous distance—and he was
throwing mostly with his arm.

At the end of the workout Schiffner brought his players together
in front of the third-base dugout. Blake Hanan, a dark-haired shortstop from Siena College, couldn't stop talking. He wanted Everson
to show him how they taught the change-up grip at Gonzaga. He

asked Simon Williams, an outfielder from the University of Maine, if he would be lifting weights over the summer. The banter eased his anxiety.

Hanan had more reason than most to feel nervous about being there. He stood five foot eight and played at a small school with an undistinguished baseball program where the head coach spent most of his time as assistant athletic director and parents had to raise money for the team's spring trip. Hanan had one bona fide credential. One summer he and Tim Stauffer had helped take a New York State select team called the South Troy Dodgers all the way to the Connie Mack World Series in Santa Fe. The team had finished as runners-up against some of the best competition in North America. Hanan had started at shortstop and sparked the top of the batting order. But scouts and Division I recruiters had all but ignored him, probably because of his size.

He'd chosen Siena under the guidance of Jimmy Howard, the Oriole scout who had tipped off Schiffner about Tim Stauffer. Howard, a Siena alum who'd played in the Toronto Blue Jays' farm system, had advised Hanan that standing out in a small program, where he could start right away, would help his pro prospects more than taking a chance at a big-deal school. Hanan eagerly took Howard's advice, and who could blame him? The scout was Hanan's only link to professional baseball, and he clung to it.

Jimmy Howard had recommended Hanan to John Schiffner, as well. Schiffner had honored the recommendation, even though Hanan was small and his numbers only so-so at Siena. Schiffner had told Hanan up-front that he'd be a reserve and would probably get into just fifteen or twenty games. Hanan's coach at Siena had warned Schiffner against quick judgments about his infielder. "By the end of the season," he'd said, "I guarantee Blake will have found a way into your starting lineup."

On his Chatham A's player questionnaire Hanan had written "batting practice" as his favorite thing to do when he *wasn't* playing baseball. For years he'd repeated a mantra to himself whenever things got hard—*Against All Odds*. He wrote *A.A.O.* inside his baseball hats in felt-tipped marker. He was thinking of having the letters tattooed on the small of his back. For as long as he remembered he had been proving himself to people who considered him too small to play at a high level.

Hanan had come with a five-pound container of protein supplement and a sore knee he wanted to keep secret. Other players who came early usually were bored at home, their college seasons long over. Hanan showed up early because he always showed up early, and because this was the Cape Cod Baseball League. This league was his chance, and he knew it.

Schiffner kept the tone light. "We'll get you pitchers on a running program once our pitching coach is here," he said. "For now, do what you've been doing. Do what you have to do. I'd like to ask, though, that you do your running right here on the field. Not that we don't trust you. It's just that . . . we don't trust you." The boys chuckled.

"Okay, you position players," he said to Hanan and Williams. "Let's get your running in. All two of you . . . in groups of three!" More chuckles.

Hanan sprinted to the outfield to be the first in line.

IN THE ATTACHED one-car garage at Charlie Thoms's house, racks of neatly pressed uniform tops hung in four groups: Chatham's home white shirts with blue pinstripes, away grays, and two versions of bright blue mesh, one for games, the other for pregame practice. On a separate rack hung thirty nylon Chatham A's baseball jackets. Boxes of stiff, blue wool baseball caps, sorted by size, lined one wall, next to neatly arranged bins of sanitary socks, baseball stockings, cotton belts, extra-large duffel bags, batting helmets, bottles of pine tar, pine-tar rags, rock rosin bags, catcher's gear, dozens of baseballs, and a case of Cutter bug spray. The baseballs, made by Diamond, displayed the Cape Cod Baseball League logo in green ink. Sixteen boxes of Louisville Sluggers, each box holding six new wooden bats, stood stacked next to the doorway alongside a smaller number of bats made by the Barnstable Bat Co., a boutique wooden-bat company located not far from Chatham. That company's owner, Tom Bednark, had burned the logo of Cape Cod Potato Chips (a big sponsor of the league) into all of the bats, both his own and the Louisvilles.

The Chatham A's gear crowded out everything else in Charlie Thoms's garage and hinted at his obsession with the team. It also revealed how well the Chatham Athletic Association treated its players. You wouldn't find this kind of stash at many Division I colleges, let alone summer leagues.

Dozens of volunteers, both men and women, devotedly served their baseball teams in the Cape Cod League. Thoms, the Chatham A's volunteer general manager, couldn't articulate what drove him, other than to say it was fun. It was a kick to do things in style. But he clearly enjoyed his association with the ballplayers. He loved talking about them, telling baseball stories from the inside. Sports psychologists might see some basking in reflected glory, "BIRGing," at play. Thoms's position gave him a seat on the field and a place in the lives of some kids who went on to be famous. His involvement bordered on the fanatical. In addition to overseeing the uniforms and equipment, he arranged contracts, plane tickets, scheduling, umpires, housing, postgame meals. A sandy-haired contractor who'd done well enough to own a sailboat and dabble in out-of-town real estate, Thoms had also built the new dugouts at Veterans Field and had remodeled the press box, mostly from his own pocket. The previous spring he'd driven two thousand miles in eight days to personally welcome the players coming to Chatham. A few weeks earlier he'd flown out to California and caught up with some former A's before they graduated from college. On the campuses he gave away Chatham A's hats and T-shirts as if they were salesmen's samples. At the start of each season, it was usually Thoms who picked up players at the airports in Boston and Providence, each two hours away.

He and his partner, Ginor Hayes (everybody pronounced her name "Jenna"), had a full house with two teenage boys, but they opened it up to the players every summer, turning it into an unofficial team gathering place. Thoms wanted the players to feel comfortable, to have a place where they could relax, especially during their first few days in town. Every night of the week before the season, he or Ginor put steaks or burgers on the grill, or baked a big pan of lasagna. Next to the baseball bats in the garage, a spare refrigerator cooled cases of beer and soda, and a commercial-grade icemaker chugged away. Free food in quantity would always bring a group of college boys together.

Charlie and Ginor put up three or four players each summer in their basement apartment. Cape League players lived with host families for the ten-week season. The NCAA, vigilantly patrolling the line between professional and amateur status, made sure that college-eligible athletes received no financial reward for their playing. The A's gave their players a travel stipend of up to $250 for getting to Chatham, and reimbursed them for gas money for driving to away games, but that was as far as the money went. The league's teams required players to pay a weekly rent of around fifty dollars to their host families. Given the often-deluxe accommodations in Chatham—waterfront views, separate guesthouses, in-ground pools, landscaped gardens, tennis courts—the rent amounted to a token gesture.

In addition to lining up host families, each team helped its players find local part-time jobs, stocking shelves at the local CVS pharmacy, maybe, or washing dishes at a restaurant, or sweeping and mowing at an old folks' home. Half of this year's A's players would work for the Chatham Athletic Association itself, maintaining the ball field and helping at seven weeks of youth baseball clinics. Almost all of the jobs were soft. They demanded little of the players and ran eight to noon, leaving plenty of time for weightlifting and the beach before evening games. Employers understood that they needed to be flexible. They liked the idea of having future big leaguers in the family, too.

The housing and jobs set the Cape apart from other summer leagues, the best of which hadn't developed the same high-level infrastructure for such things and the worst of which left players to fend for themselves. And the A's set a standard for how smoothly the arrangement could work. Chatham turned the logistics of matching players and host families into an intricate puzzle with moving pieces. The team's housing coordinator usually put at least two boys at each house, so that no player felt alone. She matched, as best she could, the personalities of the house parents and players. A couple of years before, when Laurie Galop was in charge, a master grid on a huge sheet of construction paper dominated her family's living room during the first weeks of June. As the players checked in, she moved around their names and associated paper icons—the players with and without cars; their positions (she kept pitchers apart, to avoid jealousies, a labor-intensive courtesy that subsequent housing coordinators didn't extend); allergies; proximity to day jobs. The right match could make a big difference over a summer.

A waiting list of families usually gave Thoms all the flexibility he needed. This year, though, for some reason—Thoms thought it might be a negative reaction to the drinking and girl chasing in *Summer Catch*—a couple of long-time families had dropped off the list, and others had asked for only one kid instead of their normal two. Just a few days away from the season opener, not all of the players had housing. Thoms—almost unthinkable for the Chatham A's—was running an ad in the local paper that week.

After the first practice most of the seven players made their way back to Thoms's house. This early in the season, before the crush of summer traffic, it was an easy five-minute drive from the field to the woodsy cul-de-sac on Chatham's west side. On the cement court in the back yard, Blake Hanan, who'd been an excellent point guard on his high school basketball team, shot hoops with Adam Yates. Ginor flipped hamburgers and hot dogs on the grill. Pauly and Hindman stretched out in the living room, watching the preview of the Lewis-Tyson fight on a big-screen TV. Charlie Thoms poked his head in, and the two Princeton pitchers followed him out to the garage to get their uniforms. Passing through the kitchen, they saw a computer printout of the team's updated roster taped to the fridge. Thoms

CHATHAM ○ 13

tracked the players' arrivals on the printout, jotting dates next to the names. Earlier in the day he'd caught Blake Hanan changing his height and weight on the sheet from 5′8″ and 155 lbs. to 5′9″ and 165 lbs. He'd said to Ginor, "Blake's a pistol. He's lugging around a huge jug of protein powder. He wants to be six foot three and he thinks eating that stuff will help."

Hanan, dripping with sweat, wandered into the garage. Pauly and Hindman were choosing their gear. Thoms held up a box of stockings and said, "Some of the players still want stirrups." Most major league and college players followed the newer fashion of solid elastic socks, pulling their pant legs down to the ankles. "I'll take 'em," said Pauly. He pantomimed the kick in his pitching windup. "I like them better for my 'leg thing.'" Thoms tossed him a pair, and Pauly stuffed them into his new duffel. Hanan grabbed one of the Louisvilles out of a box and held it in his hands. He was a long way from Siena. He said, "This is going to be awesome here."

THE NEXT MORNING Schiffner sat in a dim, windowless banquet room at the Marriott Courtyard Hotel in Hyannis, fulfilling one of the few unpleasant duties the Cape Cod League asked of him. Hyannis was choked with traffic even in the shoulder seasons before and after the summer. Schiffner had given himself extra time hopping onto Route 6, the mid-Cape highway, for a fifteen-mile drive that could take forty minutes or more. The time allowed him to think through the short speech he needed to give, something he looked forward to even less than the traffic.

He sat with Charlie Thoms, A's treasurer Paul Galop, and other volunteer officers of the Chatham Athletic Association at a round, linen-clothed table spread with china plates and crystal water glasses. Out of uniform—without a hat, without the Oakleys hiding his tired eyes, with his full dark mustache—Schiffner looked a little like Peter Sellers's Inspector Clouseau. The effect didn't suggest comic as much as it did "regular Joe." His hair had thinned almost completely on top, and he looked beefy in a golf shirt.

Here, at the annual kick-off luncheon, each of the league's ten coaches previewed the upcoming season and, more important, chatted up representatives from Coca-Cola, Fleet Bank, Keyspan Energy, the U.S. Army, and other league sponsors. Schiffner called it a "dog and pony show," understood the value of it only in theory, and resented the time it took away from bringing his team together. Still, the A's leadership always made a good showing at these occasional meetings. For the strongest organization in the league, it would have looked arrogant not to. Beyond that, the group believed and preached that the Chatham A's did things right, and being at the annual kick-off luncheon in force was the right thing to do.

Bob Stead, the league's commissioner, congratulated league president Judy Scarafile on her appointment to the board of directors of the Yawkey Trust in Boston. He thanked one of the sponsors, Dinegift.com, for coordinating the food for that day's luncheon, which had been donated by a dozen different area restaurants. He addressed the volunteers and the head coaches, five of whom were new to the league. "The Cape Cod Baseball League," he said, "is a sacred national monument that all of you in this room hold in trust."

Paul Galop stepped away from the A's table and gave the chairman's report for the league's hall-of-fame committee. He announced the twelve inductees for 2002, which included the former Cape players Ron Darling, Jason Varitek, Paul Mitchell, and Buck Showalter. The official induction ceremony would be held in November, at Chatham's fancy seaside resort, the Chatham Bars Inn.

The Cape managers spoke only briefly. Jeff Trundy, in his fourth year coaching for Falmouth, said, "The season seems like it's over in minutes, and you're suddenly saying good-bye to kids you've just become close to, some of whom you'll never see again but will always follow." Many of the coaches apologized in advance, fretting about the probability of starting their seasons short-handed, because their recruits from Rice, Notre Dame, Stanford, and other powerhouse programs appeared to be headed for the College World Series in Omaha. Yarmouth-Dennis's coach, Scott Pickler, echoed that concern, and Schiffner, annoyed by the excuse making, whispered to Thoms, "It's the friggin' same thing for every team. I'm tempted to get up there and say, 'Well, all my guys are here. I guess that means we're gonna suck this year.'"

Schiffner, though, as the league's elder statesman, stayed cool. Stead introduced him as "John Schiffner of the Chatham A's, who needs no introduction." Schiffner walked stiffly to the lectern, sweating, then generously gave credit to the tireless volunteers of the league and special thanks to those in Chatham. He wished the five new managers luck. He said he believed he had the greatest job in the world. His eyes teared as he said it.

MORE PLAYERS ROLLED IN. At the team's second practice, Schiffner got his first look at Chris Iannetta, a freshman catcher from the University of North Carolina and the closest thing to a local boy on this year's team. Iannetta had grown up in Providence, Rhode Island, two hours west. Thickly built, with a square jaw and broad shoulders, he looked like a catcher born of a brick mason, which is exactly what he was. He drilled a batting-practice pitch into the front rim of the batting cage, and Schiffner yelled, "Cage killer!" from the dugout. Iannetta drove the next pitch solidly to deep center field, and Schiffner said, quietly, "Nice comeback."

Colt Morton, a catcher from North Carolina State, pulled his shiny black Ford F-150 into the parking lot next to the field while Iannetta took his swings. Tall, tanned, with a mop of sandy hair and the fresh-faced good looks of a young cowboy, Morton answered Schiffner's questions politely, with a hint of a drawl, "Yes, sir." "No, sir." Southern boy. He had driven from North Carolina with his mom. Before he took his turn in the batting cage, he dropped to one knee, held his helmet in his hand, bowed his head, and said a prayer. Southern Baptist.

Schiffner wandered around the field, looked busy, appeared not to be watching his players closely. But he noticed nuances right away. Outfielder Steve LeFaivre ran to track down a long fly ball, and his head bounced with each step. He laboriously positioned himself

under the ball to catch with both hands, a slow, old-fashioned tech-
nique. First baseman, Jeremy Cleveland, seemed to have a lazy foot
that almost dragged along the ground as he ran. He started his
swings with his feet close together, forcing a long stride susceptible
to off-speed pitches.

Simon Williams, a center-fielder from Maine, looked fast—he
glided over the ground—and had a muscular, lithe build. "That's a
major league body," Schiffner said, passing Fincher. But Schiffner
had mixed impressions of Williams, who batted from the right side
out of a low, unorthodox crouch. Only a handful of major league
players had ever employed such a drastic stance, and all of them, including the batting champion Rod Carew, slapped the ball or slashed
low line drives. Williams attacked pitches with a powerful uppercut
swing. The crouch introduced some mechanical problems that
would become more acute as Williams faced faster and better pitching. "We'll change that," Schiffner said, almost under his breath,
from behind the batting cage. And then Williams hit two balls over
the left-field fence and Schiffner added, "I don't think we had a
right-handed batter who hit two balls out in left all last year."

More worrisome to Schiffner, Williams treated his throwing arm
tenderly. The Maine coach had said that Williams was coming off an
injury. Schiffner had seen him wince while lobbing the ball in from
the outfield. He'd watched him sitting alone in the dugout after the
other players had taken off, an ice bag taped to his shoulder and a
grim expression on his face. "Simon doesn't look like a player coming
back from an injury to me," Schiffner said to Fincher. "He looks like
an injured player."

Schiffner gave his second speech of the day at the end of practice.
"I know you guys are young ballplayers and you're on Cape Cod for
the summer. We're not going to tell you not to have a good time.
Look, I've been here, I've been to the places you guys are gonna go
to, I've done the things you're going to do. Don't even ask me about
the old twenty-five-cent beer nights at the Improper Bostonian. I've
probably dated some of the mothers of the girls you're going to try to

go out with—if any of those girls says I'm the father, just ignore the comment. Absolutely not true."

The players glanced at each other, smirking, not sure whether they should laugh out loud.

"We want you to have fun, but you have to use your heads. We don't want to get a call from the Chatham Police and have to call your coaches back at school and explain why so-and-so did whatever. Some cops in this town will cut you some slack, and others won't like you, just because you're in the Cape Cod Baseball League. So be smart. Don't embarrass yourselves, your families, or your schools. You'll be hearing this little talk again.

"You guys are here to have fun, to play baseball, and improve. Our goal is to make the play-offs. Some of last year's guys, when they get here, will tell you how much fun it is to play in front of five thousand people at the end of the summer. That's what it's all about. You'll never forget it.

"We aren't going to tell you how to go about your business. We're here to make suggestions, to offer help if something isn't working and you ask for it. Some coaches in this league don't do things that way. They're here to prove something. They want you to do it their way. But you guys are some of the best baseball players in the country and you come from winning programs. You do it the North Carolina way, the Maine way, the way that has worked for you. That's how we do things in Chatham, and we've been pretty successful doing them that way."

THE DAYS WERE lengthening, extending the setting sunlight past eight o'clock. Salt marshes greened up. Cranberry bushes and black locust trees blossomed. Some of the players had their first fun in town. Scott Thoms, Charlie's nineteen-year-old son, squeezed five or six A's into the Yukon to go four-wheeling on North Beach. They curved north along winding roads through scrubby pitch-pine woods and past trim, well-tended houses. The steep rooflines, silvery wood shingles, and small-paned windows gave the houses an old charm, even though

they dotted a newer residential part of town. Thomas Pauly had noticed the houses here as soon as he'd arrived. They were different than
in Florida. They seemed like New England to him, or at least the New
England he'd seen in the movies. They made the place feel exotic.
Flowers—pale purple wisteria, white peonies, pink wild roses—colored the hedgerows and split-rail fencelines. The truck full of players
turned left on Route 28 where the dark blue water of Pleasant Bay
suddenly opened in front of them, and pointed toward Orleans.

Pleasant Bay, an intricate, fingery inner harbor, spread around islands and fed marshes, estuaries, and saltwater ponds. For centuries
the bay had been shielded by an eleven-mile-long arm of sand
known on most maps as Nauset but referred to by locals as North
Beach. The writer Henry Beston called the fringe of sand "the out-
ermost of outer shores," noting that the Cape Cod peninsula juts farther out to sea than any other part of the Eastern Seaboard.
Chatham's location at the elbow of the Cape made its shorefront especially vulnerable. North Beach protected much of Chatham's sixty
miles of shoreline from the full-on brunt of waves and weather from
Nantucket Sound to the south and from the serious weather that
rolled in from the bold Atlantic Ocean to the north and east.

For much of Chatham's early history, North Beach sheltered fishing, whaling, and ship-building trades. Beginning in the late 1800s, it
guarded an economy that was shifting to summer residents and
tourism. Storm winds, tides, and surf, though, continually redrew the
sand. Occasionally water broke through the bar, creating or closing
inlets into Pleasant Bay. These scars healed over with subsequent
tides and yet more shifting sand. In 1987 pounding surf from a winter nor'easter opened a cut in the bar opposite Chatham's old brick
lighthouse and Coast Guard station. The slice, only eighteen feet
across and a foot deep at the beginning, grew wider and deeper with
each passing day. In two weeks the cut had extended to five hundred
feet; by spring the break was three-quarters of a mile long and no
longer looked like a cut. It looked like ocean, and North Beach had
effectively become two beaches, North and South.

Once exposed, the sand beneath Chatham's well-appointed eastern shoreline washed out under the relentless power of moving water. Waves undermined, then demolished, parking lots at two town landings. Lighthouse Beach, which once stretched five hundred feet back from the water, washed away completely over four years, all the way back to the cliff at the Overlook. Expensive shorefront homes listed, then slid into the water—nine alone between Holway Street and Andrew Harding's Lane. In October of 1991 the "perfect" unnamed hurricane made famous by Sebastian Junger's book battered the barrier beaches and the inner shoreline with eighty-mile-an-hour winds and ten-foot waves. After it was over, a hundred houses onshore had been damaged and fourteen cottages on North Beach had been sent sailing. The break had widened to two miles. In the aftermath, sand collected and curled back to the mainland from the southern end of the break, and South Beach was no longer an island, but a peninsula connected to shore by a natural land bridge. In the following decade, sand continued to pile up, restoring much of the beach that had washed away below the Chatham light. But the break itself stayed wide open to the Atlantic.

Scott Thoms turned onto the sand at Nauset, where North Beach joined the mainland in Orleans. Traveling south he kept the truck to the outside of the bar, the ocean side, but the A's had a clear view over the sand to the wealthy summer homes and shingled estates that stretched along the Chatham shore of Pleasant Bay. The players eyed the cottages and rambling, turn-of-the-century grand hotel of the Chatham Bars Inn, where suites went for as much as sixteen hundred bucks a night during the high season. Beyond the Inn, the sun dipped close to the horizon, backlighting fishing boats on their moorings and sailboats skimming along on the stiff breeze. Lacy whitecaps trimmed the dark blue water of the bay. The players drove along on the thinnest of edges. They were boys, out four-wheeling, on moving sand that seemed solid and forever. The slanting, golden light put a shine on everything. At that moment, before the summer proved otherwise, they all belonged here, in this place, in this league.

TWO

D'Antona Arrives

JAMIE D'ANTONA HAD BARELY CROSSED into Chatham when he learned just how little slack the Chatham Police Department would cut a Cape Cod League baseball player. He had driven down Route 137 through Harwich, overshot the turn on Old Queen Anne Road, realized his mistake, and was racing back up 137 in his black Mercury Sable. He had already missed the first few practices and was close to running late as it was for the one that afternoon. The radar gun nailed him at sixty-three in a forty. The cruiser pulled him over on the straightaway near the Middle Road cut-off. D'Antona explained that he was a member of the Chatham A's and was hurrying to his first practice. The cop handed him a ticket with a $200 fine.

The ticket pissed D'Antona off. He'd racked up twelve hundred dollars of debt at school and was counting on his summer job on the Cape to knock it down. He'd been using a checkbook for the first time in his life, but hadn't yet gotten the hang of recording his checks as he wrote them. His parents had set up the account with overdraft protection, as a way of easing Jamie into the adult world, but he still lost track. He liked paying for his buddies' meals at the Japanese steakhouse near the Wake Forest campus. He'd bought stuff for the apartment—posters and a black light for his room, a grill. He didn't want to ask for money from home during the summer. Both parents had recently taken medical leaves from their teaching jobs, and D'Antona didn't want to add more stress to their lives. He wanted to make things right on his own. And now, less than two minutes in Chatham, he was another couple hundred in the hole.

He had just enough time to grab his uniform at Charlie Thoms's, get over to his host family's house, toss his bags into a small bedroom just off the kitchen, throw his workout clothes on, and get down to the field.

The players' parking lot, tucked in among leafy shade trees, extended back from a chain-link fence lining the left-field side of the diamond. D'Antona pulled the Mercury into the lot and saw the players stretching on the other side of the fence. He grabbed his gear out of the back, shoved a dip of Skoal inside his lower lip, and hustled out to join them.

He'd traveled a lot thanks to baseball. He'd played with all-star and select teams in Germany, Alaska, up and down the East Coast. He'd gotten used to adapting to new environments, new teammates. But this was something different. Chatham was only four hours from home, and half of this year's Chatham A's, it seemed, came from the Atlantic Coast Conference. D'Antona had sought those players out during the ACC tournament that spring. He'd walked around with them during the down time, clowning on those he'd done well against and getting ragged by those who had done well against him. At a Cape Cod ball field a thousand miles away, he greeted the guys from Carolina and State like old friends, grinned when he saw his Wake Forest teammate Steve LeFaivre. Even David Bush, a graduated Wake player, was here. D'Antona saw him talking with the coaches down by the third-base dugout and waved.

Bush had already spent two summers in Chatham and was headed for the pros. He had been a dominant two-time all-star pitcher in the Cape League. He'd come north for a few days to work out and see some old buddies on the A's while he negotiated a contract with the Toronto Blue Jays. (More to the point, he'd come to spend time with his girlfriend, one of the A's student trainers. The two had been dating since the previous summer. A year and a half in the future, Bush would propose to her inside that very dugout, and she'd say yes, and

Bush would call Schiffner from there on his cell phone to give him the news.) D'Antona was climbing at a pace set by Bush, and he carried the same high profile and expectations. Bush had thrived under the pressure. After an outstanding junior season in college, he had turned down a fourth-round selection from Tampa Bay in 2001 and followed it with a brilliant senior year. The Blue Jays had taken him in the second round of the 2002 draft. They were working out a signing bonus that would reach close to half a million dollars.

As a freshman at Wake Forest D'Antona had batted clean-up, hitting .364 with seventeen home runs and seventy-seven runs batted in. ACC coaches had voted him the conference rookie of the year. *Collegiate Baseball* had named him the NCAA freshman player of the year. He'd added a superb sophomore season in which he'd hit twenty home runs and driven in eighty-three in fifty-seven games. He'd helped lead Wake Forest to a national top-ten ranking before Tim Stauffer and the Richmond Spiders upset the Deacons in the Regionals. D'Antona came to Chatham with a brand-name label and a history of playing on winning teams. Scouts rated him one of the top pro prospects among the 230 players coming to the Cape that summer. He tried to keep all of it out of his mind.

D'Antona and Bush shared a free spirit as well as talent. D'Antona had been suspended for four games that spring for breaking a team rule. (There was mention of something about alcohol in D'Antona's hotel room following Wake Forest's big win at Clemson, but his coaches and teammates had closed ranks and refused to discuss the incident. "Let's just say it was a stupid thing to do," D'Antona told a student reporter afterward. Something subtle in the team's chemistry had changed during the suspension. The team lost its momentum and never recovered it. Weeks later, D'Antona sounded contrite. He said he'd never let the team down again.) He still rolled his eyes when he made errors, still joked around and talked trash on the field. He didn't apologize. He said things like "Our team is really loose. We're basically the assholes of the ACC. But you can't talk shit unless you can back it up. Fortunately we know we pretty much can." Along with Dave Bush and a few other teammates, D'Antona had dyed his hair yellow that spring, just for fun. It hung now in tight curls below his dark baseball cap, looking something like a bleached Afro, jarring on a white kid from Connecticut. A bright shell necklace glowed against his tanned skin. Everything about him seemed loud, large, uncontained.

George Greer, D'Antona's college coach, had seen a lot of athletes at Wake Forest. He wasn't bothered by D'Antona's seemingly careless attitude. Greer imagined D'Antona fitting in not with typical baseball guys but with a locker room full of boisterous, trash-talking black football players—their talk a part of who they were and how they dealt with pressure.

D'Antona spit out some Skoal juice, took his place in one of the lines, and threw lightly, loosening his arm. It felt good to be moving again after his long drive. He couldn't remember when he'd gone three days without touching a baseball. After just a few tosses his throws snapped with authority—he had a smooth, powerful arm, a major league arm. After a few more throws he was ready to have fun again. He mimicked a pitching windup, tried to flutter a knuckleball with absolutely no spin on it.

Schiffner wandered over and stood next to Assistant Coach Matt Fincher and they watched the players warm up. "Well, Schiff," said Fincher, in a Southern drawl, "Dee-Antona has arrived." Schiffner had never met the player before, but Jamie D'Antona was impossible to miss. Schiffner widened his eyes in mock surprise and said, "Hoo, boy," in a tone that meant *interesting* and, simultaneously, *This could be trouble*.

PLAYERS WASHED INTO Chatham in waves. Daniel Moore from North Carolina. Fraser Dizard from the University of Southern California. Zane Carlson from Baylor. Chad Orvella from North Carolina State. The names could have become a blur, but Schiffner had lived with them in his mind for months. He greeted the returning 2001 players with hearty handshakes, welcomed the newcomers, and wondered, as he always did, if he could pick out the future million-aires with his first impressions.

The air grew softer, more humid. From behind the trees in back of left field, from the Monomoy Theater's shady outdoor rehearsal area, choruses from *South Pacific* floated out over Veterans Field. The distraction bothered Schiffner, and he muttered under his breath. The incongruity, though, seemed natural in a place like Chatham. In what other league could the sounds of summer theater and baseball mix?

A day or two earlier the field had seemed thin, almost empty. Now it was filled with color and motion. Schiffner counted his players. Only five or six had not yet reported. Suddenly it felt like summer. He looked out and said it was like somebody had just watered the grass.

A field full of players, however, did not make a team, and Schiffner knew the difference. He'd worried about it for several weeks as his carefully tailored plan for 2002 had begun to unravel.

Schiffner had put his roster together nine months before, back in August and September of 2001. Competing against the other Cape League coaches for the same thin top of the talent pool, Schiffner couldn't afford to wait until spring to pick all his players for the coming season. In the fall, on white lined paper, the team had looked loaded. Schiffner had created an almost ideal balance among left-handed and right-handed batters, power, speed, older and younger players, flexibility, and a deep pitching staff. Looking at his list, Schiffner couldn't see any weaknesses. But assembling any roster that far ahead of time involved risk. Every year, recruited players went down with injuries during their school seasons, or performed worse than expected, or flunked a class or two and had to stay in school over the summer. And no one could guess which players they'd be. Schiffner had no control over the injuries, of course, but then, who did? That risk was the same no matter when he put his team together. Schiffner believed in building a dream roster far ahead of time, then dealing with the fallout of attrition as needed.

He translated the uncertainty into the insurance of extra names on his backup page.

Putting together his team for the 2002 season, Schiffner had gambled more than usual. He had penciled in nine juniors on his roster—an unusually high number in this league and, given the mechanics of the major league draft, an extraordinarily risky approach. The amateur draft took more than a thousand players every year during the first week of June, a week or so before the Cape League season began. In essence, the draft worked like thirty separate film companies putting options on individual screenplays—the team that selected a player won the exclusive right to negotiate with him for a period of time to work out the terms of a contract. Teams paid no retainers for that right, no money at all until a contract was signed. Once signed, the player became the property of that major league club and was assigned to a minor league team to start the intensive process of grooming and development. A typical major league player might have spent three or four years climbing the ladder of the minors—low A, high A, AA, AAA—before making it to the Big Show. If a club and a drafted player couldn't come to terms, at the outset, the player could reenter the next year's draft.

Major league teams could start selecting college players after their junior year. Almost invariably, all of college baseball's best juniors were drafted. Though some of those players headed to the Cape while they negotiated, most signed professional contracts within weeks, if not days, of being tapped. As a result, coaches on the Cape typically stocked their league with freshmen and, especially, sophomores—the best nineteen- and twenty-year-old players in the country.

The junior-heavy approach was an experiment for Schiffner, and he understood the risk. But he liked the idea of having older, more mature guys in the mix of players, and six of the nine juniors on his sheet had played for him in 2001 as sophomores; they'd led the A's to within one game of winning the league championship. They were known quantities, and Schiffner liked what they added to a team, even if there might be some more highly rated prospects out there in the sophomore class. Schiffner had taken a good read on his juniors. At the season's end a number of scouts had, off the record, told Schiffner how high they guessed the juniors might go in the next year's draft—a crucial indicator of the money and commitment the major league teams were willing to put behind their selections. The signing bonuses paid out by the big-league clubs dropped dramatically as the draft progressed. A first-round pick looked at real money—two or three million dollars just to sign. Just ten rounds later the average bonus dwindled to $70,000, and forty more rounds played out below that.

Half of his juniors, Schiffner was sure, would be bypassed in the 2002 draft. They were the safe bets. A couple others would probably get drafted in early rounds and turn pro—Schiffner accepted those as long shots with big pay-offs if he was able to keep them. His gamble hinged mostly on three players in the middle that he hoped to bring back to Chatham for a second year: center-fielder Adam Greenberg, catcher Luke Carlin, and infielder Mike McCoy were all likely draft picks. At different points toward the end of the previous summer, Schiffner had sat down with each of them and talked over their prospects. He believed Greenberg and Carlin would go "somewhere around fifteen," a gray area of the draft where the signing money might entice, but where many juniors opted to stay in school, betting they'd be worth more after another year of college ball. Schiffner saw McCoy going later, closer to the thirtieth round. He sensed that any of these players would sign if drafted higher than projected. He bet they'd come back to Chatham if drafted lower.

Schiffner's balanced roster relied on the three players for speed and strong defense "up the middle" of the field, a hallmark of winning teams. Of the three, Schiffner felt least certain of holding on to Greenberg, an aggressive speedster from the University of North Carolina. Despite his small size, he was a special player.

"If Greenie is the only guy we lose," Schiffner had told Fincher on the phone back in September, "I still like our chances."

The first of forty-four games would be in a week. Schiffner knew he held two strong cards in his hand, sophomores the draft couldn't touch. His ace was Tim Stauffer. Jamie D'Antona was the wild card.

THE SPRING HAD hit Schiffner's pitching staff hard. He'd lost three arms to injuries and one to academic problems. One other player—shortstop Donny Murphy of Long Beach State—had simply and inexplicably failed to show up at school back in the fall. But the team's delicate balance was still in play when the two-day amateur draft began on June 4. One hundred forty-eight former Cape Cod Baseball League players would be selected—the highest number in the league's history. Fourteen of them had played for last year's Chatham A's. Shortstop Drew Meyer, in the first round, received $1.8 million from the Texas Rangers. One of the fifth-round choices was none other than Donny Murphy, the mystery no-show, who had apparently enrolled at the last minute at a small junior college in California, telling neither Schiffner nor his coach at Long Beach State. (Schiffner consoled himself with the knowledge that he'd picked a good one.)

The Chicago Cubs chose center-fielder Adam Greenberg in the ninth round, and Schiffner lost his first bet.

Luke Carlin's tenth-round selection by the Tigers was more complicated. Heading into the draft, Schiffner had learned from scouts that Carlin might indeed go that early. So Schiffner had made a calculated risk, grabbing Colt Morton from North Carolina State. But Carlin balked at Detroit's initial offer and told Schiffner he would play at Chatham while he and the Tigers haggled. Schiffner suddenly had a few problems: He'd made three commitments at a position with room for two. He had two players—Carlin and McCoy, the latter taken in the thirty-fourth round by the Cardinals, lower than Schiffner had pegged him—who might or might not sign, and might or might not tie up roster spots while deciding. He had three pitchers rehabbing injured arms, and one of those, Scott Hindman, could go to the Angels at any time.

Variations of the drama played in ten towns across Cape Cod. The league, sensitive to this postdraft scrambling, gave coaches extra time to submit final rosters. Schiffner's deadline was June 23, more than a week after the season's first game. But every passing day narrowed his chances of finding high-level replacements. He kept his cell phone handy. Missing a call-back from a college coach could mean losing one of the few blue-chip players left.

ON THE TWELFTH of June, two days before opening day, Schiffner lost his second bet. Junior Mike McCoy called Charlie Thoms and said he would probably sign with the Cardinals. Thoms, who was just getting ready to drive to Providence and pick McCoy up, broke the news to Schiffner on his cell phone.

The Cardinals had offered McCoy a small signing bonus and money to complete college. Major League Baseball had created such two-part packages at the urging of the NCAA, out of concern that so many college athletes were turning pro before graduating. A decade ago, major league owners began pooling scholarship money to reimburse drafted players for remaining college expenses. The arrangement was a win for the NCAA, which benefited from the good press. But it was a windfall for the club owners. The scholarship was reflected in the overall value of the bonus, yet most players never took advantage of the free tuition. Consequently, the major league clubs had saved millions in true bonus dollars since the program began. They had set a cap of seven years on the time after signing that the money could be used for tuition, but they made it difficult for the players to get the necessary spare time on campus. Teams highly encouraged—virtually required—young players to play in fall or winter baseball instructional leagues. Spring training started in February, and the playing season stretched from April to September. Many players soon married and started families. Who'd make time to swing two or three remaining semesters? The players spoke about bonuses as "money plus school," distinguishing what was real and what was probably nothing, as in, "How much of it was money and how much school?"

McCoy's signing dominated the conversation between Schiffner and his two assistant coaches that June night at Schiffner's house in East Harwich, where he lived full-time in the summer but only weekends during the school year. The rest of the school week he lived apart from his wife, Martha, in a small suburban-looking ranch in Danielson, Connecticut, a tired mill town a few minutes north of the high school. Schiffner had held on to the house he'd shared with his first wife because it was close to the best-paying, most secure job he could find, and because Martha had a comfortable contemporary house and an established house-cleaning job near Chatham. He kept the Connecticut house neat, though he'd more or less set it up as a bachelor pad. A big-screen TV ruled the living space. In the kitchen a plastic garbage bag for recycling beer cans hung next to a large wastebasket. He complained a little about lonely nights. November, when he had his new roster completed and little to do for the Chatham A's, stretched interminably. But the arrangement gave him more undistracted time than any other Cape League manager had, as far as he knew. He considered it a competitive advantage.

For his two coaches, dinner at Schiffner's place in East Harwich was a nightly summer ritual, a chance to rehash the games, talk baseball, have a drink. A place to go. Schiffner liked saving his assistants a little food money at the same time. He couldn't pay them much.

Martha ordered takeout Chinese food for the men. After dinner, the coaches sat in the living room and assessed the team. Bobby Myers, a thirty-year-old pitching coach from Azusa Pacific University, joined Fincher and Schiffner. This was Myers's first season on the Cape. He'd arrived a few days earlier, leaving a wife and young daughter behind in California while he came to Chatham to build his résumé. Around the league—Schiffner was one of the few exceptions—it was the same thing: Young, ambitious coaches with dreams of bigger jobs were drawn to the Cape League hoping the prestige and exposure would reward the long hours and low pay and time away from home. Schiffner had lent Myers his Jeep Wrangler for the summer, so he'd have a way to get around.

Schiffner nursed a martini while they talked about McCoy. He had a soft spot for martinis. They helped when he was feeling cranky. These first weeks of June always put a strain on him. He was still commuting more than four hours each day between Chatham and Connecticut. He had to read final papers and turn in final grades after the coming weekend. He was running on short sleep while Fincher and Myers handled the early-afternoon practices.

Schiffner was cranky about Mike McCoy's coach at the University of San Diego. Earlier that day, the coach had told Schiffner he would try to change McCoy's mind about signing—a self-interested act, Schiffner thought, one of the bigger sins in his book. The coach simply wanted McCoy on his team again as a senior. Schiffner, revising his earlier assessment, said to Fincher and Myers, "I don't think McCoy is going to get a better offer. I think he's smart to jump at it."

Schiffner had made some calls that day to locate another middle infielder but had come up empty. Now he was considering his other versatile players to fill the hole.

Schiffner was cranky about Thomas Pauly and Scott Hindman too. He told Fincher and Myers that he thought the two "Princeton brothers" were already hurting the team. They'd been a distraction during parts of the early practices, refusing to take drills seriously and acting dumber than they could possibly be. Pauly couldn't get the pitching signs straight. During one drill he'd spun the wrong way on a pick-off move to second—a basic mistake you might see in junior high—then laughed and said, "Sorry. I didn't throw any picks to second this year." Pauly had seemed both earnest and immature, acting at times like a foreign athlete in a brand-new sport. Schiffner had good instincts about young men, but he couldn't figure Pauly out. He was used to baseball players—simple guys who didn't play mind-games. He had seen plenty of guys masquerading with bravado, and he'd heard a lot of manufactured excuses and complaints from players trying to deflect insecurity, but Schiffner didn't know what to make of a supposedly brilliant kid who seemed so clueless.

Hindman, by contrast, seemed to have all the answers. Myers had watched Hindman's front foot land too heavily during his delivery in the bullpen, and suggested a slight change. "I slipped," said Hindman, making an excuse and signaling that he needed no help from Myers.

On a college team, Myers might have lit into Hindman, laid down the law. Or he might have bided his time, patiently nurturing a player for a longer-term pay-off. But this was a summer league, where power shifted from coaches toward players. Myers had little leverage, and little patience for someone with his own agenda. "I didn't say another word to him," Myers told the other coaches. "I just let him throw crap for twenty-five more pitches." Schiffner had asked Hindman to start the third game of the season, but Hindman had declined, saying his arm wasn't quite ready. "I have no use for Hindman," Myers said. "But I'll give Pauly a chance. At least he says, 'Show me that, tell me how to do it.' I can work with someone who asks for help."

Schiffner was cranky about the way Simon Williams babied his arm. "I'm afraid he's going to come to me and say he can't play after all," Schiffner said. "And I trusted the Maine coach when he told me I'd be getting someone who was ready to play."

Schiffner was also cranky about outfielder Steve LeFaivre's defense. LeFaivre ran from heel to heel, a jarring motion that complicates running and watching the ball at the same time. He seemed to compensate by loping at three-quarter speed, or by slowing up and fielding balls on the bounce instead of sprinting and reaching them on the fly. His two-handed catches added to Schiffner's doubts. In fact, Schiffner was worried about his team's defense in general.

Jamie D'Antona in particular baffled him. D'Antona rifled the ball and made athletic, spectacular plays with seeming ease, but routine ground balls ate him alive. He sat back on balls; he pulled up on others skimming low along the grass. In the language of the game, D'Antona let the ball play him. "Every time he drops his glove to field a ball this summer," Schiffner said, "it's going to cost him $50,000 in the draft."

George Greer, D'Antona's coach at Wake Forest, had told Schiffner that D'Antona fielded beautifully when he just saw the ball and reacted. "It's when he has time to think that he gets in trouble." Schiffner had promised Greer he'd play D'Antona at third base all summer. He let the longer-term benefit of the relationship with Greer outweigh the short-term cost to Chatham's defense.

Player by player, the coaches went through the roster. They'd seen some good signs, too. Fraser Dizard and Zane Carlson, returning pitchers, had thrown without pain—they looked healthy. The University of Richmond had finally lost in the Super Regionals, so Tim Stauffer would be in town before the season really got going.

Schiffner suggested batting lineups and pitching rotations. He typically let his assistants work directly with the players, let them run the practices, put them in charge of teaching the few signs and plays the team would be using. He trusted their judgment on the field, and here in the living room. "What about Hanan in the two-slot?" Schiffner asked.

"You can't have an out in the two-slot," said Myers. "Hanan's a good guy, but he's an out."

"You think so?" Schiffner asked Fincher.

"Yup," said Fincher.

"Okay, let's move him to the bottom," said Schiffner.

Finally, the coaches sensed there might be something special about this team, despite the problems. That came out as they tried to settle the heart of the batting order, those important hitters who bat third, fourth, fifth, and sixth. Generally those players hit for both power and high average, compensating for more limited hitters ahead of and behind them. During the early practices, D'Antona, Colt Morton, LeFaivre, Jeremy Cleveland, Simon Williams, and Chris Iannetta all hammered the ball. Schiffner couldn't remember when he'd seen so many balls flying out of Veterans Field. D'Antona and Morton had hit homers as far as any right-handed batters he'd coached. The terms players used for home runs changed with the

generations. The current vocabulary included *jack*, *bomb*, and *dong*.
D'Antona and Morton hit *mega-jacks*.

The three coaches tossed around several possible batting orders
before Fincher drawled, "Okay, we have a problem. We have more
good hitters than we have room for." They finally settled on an open-
ing-day lineup that, on paper, leaving aside pitching and defense and
speed and injuries, looked as strong as any Schiffner had ever put together.

Chad Orvella	shortstop	North Carolina State
Steve LeFaivre	left field	Wake Forest
Jeremy Cleveland	first base	North Carolina
Jamie D'Antona	third base	Wake Forest
Ryan Johnson	right field	Wake Forest
Colt Morton	catcher	North Carolina State
Chris Iannetta	designated hitter	North Carolina
Simon Williams	center field	Maine
Blake Hanan	second base	Siena

THE TEAM'S ANNUAL welcome lunch filled an ornate, oak-paneled
wing of the main building of the Chatham Bars Inn. In the Harbor
View Room, the 2002 Chatham A's sat at round tables in golf shirts,
khaki pants, and button-down Oxfords, with their hair moussed.
Mike MacDonald and Simon Williams, the teammates from Maine,
had driven that day to the Cape Cod Mall in Hyannis and bought
Williams a nice shirt and a pair of pants for the event. Two tables
over from the Maine guys, Jamie D'Antona wore a bright, flower-
print Hawaiian shirt. He'd started a little dark goatee to go with his
dyed, bright yellow hair.

Outside, beyond the floor-to-ceiling windows, sunlight leaked
through thin overcast. D'Antona's eyes swept out to sea: over the
blue-and-white ticking of the Inn's beach cabanas, beyond the blue
water of the inner harbor, past the white sandy strip of North Beach,
out to the deeper blue-gray of the Atlantic. Most guests here simply

relaxed in the presence of such a view, but D'Antona looked out at the water and thought of bluefish and striped bass. He had a couple of his rods in the car. He'd fished more than anybody else on the team, and he loved it almost as much as he loved hitting a baseball.

He'd spent part of nearly every year in the Florida Keys, fishing all day from a boat with his father while his mom and sister lounged back at the time-share. After supper he'd walk back to the water and fish off the dock into the darkness. He had the same focus with a fishing rod that he did with a bat in the batting cage, and his perseverance had been rewarded dozens of times over. He'd caught bonefish, tarpon, hammerhead shark, amberjack, barracuda, dolphin, and a yellowfin tuna that had set a Florida state record. For his tenth birthday his parents had given him a day on the water with Bouncer Smith, a legendary guide out of Miami, and D'Antona had ended up winning a South Florida fishing tournament. Following his freshman year at Wake Forest he'd chosen to play in the Alaska summer league, not for the baseball but for the salmon fishing.

But fishing was fun, as hitting was fun—it wasn't a chore to put in a lot of time at either one. And fishing was pure: D'Antona didn't have to lift weights or run or practice defense as part of the package. Those parts of baseball really were work, and D'Antona got by on the minimum requirements.

He was aware of how his new teammates perceived him. He knew they expected a lot from him, knew that his press clippings and credentials set him apart. He hated that part. He wanted nothing better than to be one of the guys. The bleached hair, the goatee, the loud Hawaiian shirt—those were all D'Antona refusing to take life so seriously. If they also hid the extra pressure he felt, well, that was a good thing, too. Most of the players here, though, took the game seriously. Nobody talked about the goal of the major leagues, but it was understood. In this league, players respected seriousness. If D'Antona thought his clowning made him seem more like one of the guys, he had misjudged the kind of guys who came to the Cape Cod League.

Apart from the Schubert emanating from hidden speakers, the buffet seemed a nod to the college boys—grilled burgers, barbecued chicken, hot dogs, potato salad. The dessert, though, a fine crème brûlée, seemed a nod to the inn. At D'Antona's table, none of the players knew the custard's name, but all of them thought it was awesome. Everson and Hanan went back for thirds—about twenty-eight dollars' worth of crème brûlée if they'd had to order retail off the Chatham Bars menu.

Charlie Thoms stood up to deliver the riot act he read to the team before each season. He gave the speech partly out of his duty as general manager, and partly to take the bad-guy role away from Schiffner.

He stood nervously, smoothed his mustache, and got the players' attention. He asked someone to turn off the music. He held up a card showing a bold numeral, "27."

"What's this?" he said. "No, it's *not* R.J.'s helmet size." (Ryan Johnson's head was so big that he'd needed to bring his own size-eight helmet from Wake Forest.) "Twenty-seven is the number of years of Cape Cod League experience represented on this year's coaching staff. These guys know how this league works. They'll be in constant touch with your coaches back at school. They'll treat you properly. Listen to what they say."

He held up a card with "85" on it.

"No, this is *not* the number of times Hanan has shown the same card trick so far. It's the number of volunteers in the A's organization. Every one of them has helped make this summer possible for you. All the food, the arrangements we make for you, the way you're treated here—all that stuff doesn't just happen automatically."

He held up "125."

"This is *not* the number of credits Michael Moon still needs to graduate." (Moon had stayed eligible, barely, at Southern California, but would need to pass a class while he played on the Cape to remain so.) "It's the number of kids at every game who will come to watch you. Toward the end of the summer that number will be much higher. Every one of those kids will be looking at you guys and wishing he could be doing what you're doing. They won't care if you went oh-for-whatever or walked in the tying run. To them you're heroes. We want to make sure you remember that, and that you live up to the image they have of you."

He held up "1."

"That's *one* flag, *one* national anthem, *one* minute, maybe a minute and a half. We'd like to ask you to not pick your butts or spit or talk with your buddies for that one minute. Every year someone comes up to me and complains about that kind of behavior. I've always said, 'We've fought wars for the right for them to do whatever they want during the national anthem.' But last year a full-dress Marine who had done two tours in Vietnam came up to me and asked the same thing, and I realized I'd been giving a pretty lame answer."

He held up "8."

"This isn't the number of girls that Jeremy Cleveland told his cast was from a Super Bowl injury. It's the average number of girlfriends every year who call and say they can't live without you, and can't they come and spend the summer with you? Well, it's *not* okay to have them come and live with your house parents. You'd better make other arrangements."

He held up "$1,050."

"That's the amount of money that six of Eric Everson's friends are paying each week for a dinky two-bedroom rental over in Harwich. If you don't know it, people are willing to spend a lot of money to be on the Cape in the summer. You should know how fortunate you are to be living in the places you do. Don't take it for granted."

He held up other numbers, asking the players to be prompt with their fifty-dollar-a-week rent checks; asking them to use their cell phones and calling cards rather than sticking house parents with unpaid phone bills; reminding them to be responsible in their day jobs; to take advantage of the surroundings and enjoy the Cape. He also warned them about the Chatham Police Department. He glanced at D'Antona and held back a smirk. "One of you has already discovered that they *will not* give you a break. If you need a ride at night, for whatever reason, call Paul or me and we'll come drive you home. Don't be stupid. Remember why you're here."

The boys had seen that day's *Cape Cod Times,* which had devoted two full pages to the opening of the Cape Cod League baseball season, dwarfing the coverage of Pedro Martínez's second straight loss for the Red Sox. The team-by-team preview hadn't predicted finishes, but it had been entitled "Catchin' Some A's." The reporter, Paul Godfrey, had opened with "Any forecast of the East Division has to begin with the Chatham A's. . . "

Schiffner sat at the banquet and worried. For two days he'd tried to get hold of a replacement outfielder named Ryan Hubbard, who was on the road somewhere between Wake Forest and California. That afternoon Schiffner had finally tracked Hubbard down at his girlfriend's in Austin, Texas. Hubbard had agreed to turn around and head back east to play for the summer. "That's classic Chatham A's," Schiffner quipped at his table. He loved telling stories like that. He'd stop worrying when Hubbard arrived.

That night Mike McCoy signed a professional baseball contract with the St. Louis Cardinals. He got fifteen thousand to sign, and twenty for school.

THE FIRST SPRINKLES fell on Opening Day just after two o'clock in the afternoon. Temperatures had fallen into the fifties and were dropping still. On Nantucket Sound, seas were building from three to six feet, with winds ten to twenty knots. The marine forecast called for visibility diminishing to less than a mile in rain and fog.

Penny Ruddock, Thomas Pauly's house mother, watched as the Weather Channel tracked the storm northward along the coast over Long Island. Pauly's housemate, left-hander Daniel Moore, was scheduled to pitch that night at seven o'clock, under the candles at Veterans Field. All over Chatham, house parents and volunteers kept their weather eyes out. The storm was following a familiar northeasterly pattern in New England, spinning low pressure back at the coast after picking up moisture at sea. New England's famous bliz-zards and hurricanes were usually the result of nor'easters, though rarely did those storms hit this late in the spring. By now, the north winds had usually given way to the fair southwesterlies of summer.

The players arrived for early batting practice at three-thirty in cold, spitting rain. Using a hard maple bat, D'Antona put on a show. He launched ten or twelve balls into the trees in left, frustrating the batboy, Andy Troy, who had to retrieve them. Chris Iannetta and Simon Williams hit balls out of the park. Colt Morton crushed a cou-ple almost as high and deep as D'Antona had. Schiffner had always favored pitching over power, and had a history of stocking his lineup with left-handed hitters. At Veterans Field in Chatham a southeast-erly on-shore breeze constantly blew out toward right, where the fence measured just 314 feet down the line, a relatively easy shot for left-handed hitters who managed to pull the ball up into the wind-stream. "I wouldn't be surprised," he said, "if Wareham or Orleans added an extra left-handed pitcher or two this year just to beat us." During batting practice, though, as he watched one right-handed batter after another drive balls into the trees in left, Schiffner said, "They're going to see us this year and say, 'God damn him! He's done it again!'" Schiffner did a better job than most coaches at hiding his ego; it came out when he felt gleeful and talked about himself in the third person.

At four-thirty, with the sky turning black, the full team gathered down the left-field line and stretched. The players wore the A's white-with-blue-pinstripe pants and their bright blue team jackets. By tradition, the day's starting pitcher got to choose what game jer-sey the team would wear, and Daniel Moore had picked the solid blue tops.

Schiffner taped the lineup sheet on the dugout wall. Players didn't need the sheet of paper to tell them their place on the team, but the distillation into black and white made it public. On sports teams, a sheet of paper taped to a wall announced whether a player was mak-ing the cut. It's how generations of managers had communicated the names of those who had made the varsity, made the travel team, made the twenty-five-man roster of a big league team. Daily lineup sheets were less dramatic, but still, they showed the players where everybody stood with the manager. Who'd he consider the weakest in the order—the eight- and nine-hitters? Who could carry the weight of batting clean-up?

The players were used to the ritual of lineup postings, and most took their time checking the sheet out, casually sauntering by, feigning indifference. D'Antona gave it a quick glance after taking his swings during batting practice. Clean-up. The usual. Thomas Pauly found his name along with those of the other relief pitchers at the bottom of the sheet in the category "available pitchers." Schiffner listed his extras in alphabetical order. There were no clues there. More than a couple of players—whose status was not yet clear—hid their nervousness as they glanced. Daily lineup sheets became routine only after a team had settled into a routine lineup. The first sheets of the summer were always nerve-wracking for somebody.

Music from the field's loudspeakers crackled and buzzed. "That's beautiful," said Schiffner. "You'd think they would have checked that before now. Christ." The spitting rain turned into a light drizzle. He looked up. "I hate these days. Either pour or let the sun shine, just do one or the other."

The Harwich players pulled their cars into the lot while Chatham was hitting. The team was carrying eight temporary pitchers, its roster depleted by missing players from Nebraska, Rice, and Clemson, schools still alive in the College World Series. "Do I feel sorry for them?" said Schiffner. "I do not." He had already grown familiar with the names of most of the players in the league. He'd either passed them over, or lost out on them, or let them go to the teams that had established pipelines with those particular schools. Schiffner honored relationships in whatever form they appeared.

Little in the way of ceremony marked the start of the new season. The drizzle turned steadier. A tiny crowd, maybe a couple of hundred strong including those in their cars up on the rise beyond the outfield, had braved the raw weather. Paul Galop announced the starting lineups over the PA system. At home plate, two teenage singers, Danielle Durkee and Stephanie Hynds, turned heads with their looks and sweet rendition of "The Star-Spangled Banner." The sound system distorted their tight harmonies. Galop mercifully turned it off in mid-song.

The 2002 season opened with a flared, off-field single by Harwich's first batter. He stole second and went to third when a low pitch skipped past A's catcher Colt Morton. The runner scored on a solid single to right, and it was 1–0 before, it seemed, the game had even gotten going.

The real rain poured down in the bottom of the third with two away and a driving wind out of the east. Fans shivered beneath blankets and ponchos, water streaming off their hats and pooling on top of the aluminum bleachers. The plate umpire threw up his arms, and Fincher and a few players scrambled to get tarps down over the mound and the dirt area around home plate, already turning to slop.

On Cape Cod the ocean called the weather. Rain seldomly washed out games in Chatham, but the fans had become accustomed to delays. Notoriously, Chatham fog interrupted and even canceled games at Veterans Field. Out at sea, the Gulf Stream carried eighty-degree water up from the Caribbean, gradually warming Chatham's beaches and the waters on the south side of the Cape. Winds out of the southeast and east typically pick up warm water vapor over the Gulf Stream. The vapor condensed as it passed over the cooler in-shore water, turning to fog. The thickest fog on the Cape blanketed the south shore along Nantucket Sound. Fog covered Chatham—the southeast tip of the Cape, the point of land closest to the Gulf Stream—more frequently than any other town on the Eastern Seaboard.

Fortunately, fog tended to evaporate quickly passing over the warmed land. But some evenings the fog thickened imperceptibly over Veterans Field, gradually registering as a dull haze that glowed eerily under the lights. Some nights it rolled in fast and blew out just as quickly. Some nights it hugged the ground. Then fielders floated on the milky whiteness, as if dancing on dry ice, visible only from the waist up under brilliantly starry skies.

In Schiffner's early days coaching here, back when he was an assistant with Eddie Lyons, the plate umpires called the players in out of the fog, and asked each team for an outfielder and a fungo hitter. After watching the outfielders try to catch fly balls, the umpire made the call about whether or not the game could continue. "It was pretty funny," Schiffner said. "If an outfielder's team was winning, you'd see him trying like hell to find the ball and somehow get to it and hold on to it. If his team was losing, a guy would look just absolutely clueless. He'd look up into the fog and shrug his shoulders and not move an inch. *Nope. Can't see it.*" Umpires eventually came to rely on their own judgment.

On opening day, 2002, fifteen minutes after looking out into a hard rain, the home-plate umpire stepped out of the A's dugout and turned toward the press box. He waved his hand and called the game, and the official start of the season was officially unofficial.

Overnight the storm's center slid off the coast toward Georges Bank, the famous fishing grounds east of Cape Cod. The rain slackened, then ended by noon, five hours before the scheduled start of the A's game at Yarmouth-Dennis. The soaking weather had turned Y-D's field into a swamp, though, threatening to disappoint the home team, which had brought in members of the New York City Fire Department and their families for a special pregame ceremony. At 2:45 the A's players huddled in the cold, damp parking lot next to Veterans Field and waited for the word from Schiffner.

The players clustered in two groups. The small-school guys hung together—Pauly and Hindman, Blake Hanan, the temporary pitcher from Bryant College in Rhode Island, Everson from Gonzaga, the teammates from Maine, the bullpen catcher who dressed in full uniform but was on the payroll, not the roster. Jamie D'Antona stood with the other ACC players, a black wool hat pulled over his baseball cap. He'd left Connecticut to get away from this kind of cold. He blew on his hands, swung his arms to keep the blood moving. The winter hat pulled low over his baseball cap felt warm. D'Antona couldn't have cared less about how it looked. On him, the dorky combination looked almost trendy, like something from the 'hood.

Just before three o'clock Tim Stauffer arrived.

He stepped out of his car wearing an untucked shirt and beach sandals. He appeared an unlikely stud. He had thick, dark eyebrows and jug-handle ears, a fleshy round face, surprisingly pale skin for the number of hours he'd logged outdoors. He recognized Blake Hanan from back home and strode over and shook hands.

Thomas Pauly saw them talking. He thought Hanan had run into a buddy from home, someone trying to do the beach thing and not quite getting it right. Then someone said it was Stauffer, and Pauly thought, *No shit.*

Normally, teammates in a league like this waited for the new arrivals to make the rounds and initiate introductions—it was cooler to hang back, to not appear too eager. But now, the players showed a measure of respect they hadn't shown even to D'Antona. One by one they came up to Stauffer and introduced themselves.

At three o'clock Schiffner gave the word. Umpires at Y-D had decided the field was unplayable. The game would be rescheduled for the A's' second off day. Last night's game had already been slotted for the first off day—the A's were now looking at sixteen straight days of baseball. "If we'd started at five o'clock last night we would have gotten the first game in," said Hanan.

"This is Chatham," said Fincher, underscoring the importance of tradition in this town, of ritual. "In Chatham games start at seven."

The rain had finished, but puddles spread over the dirt of the infield. Players helped Fincher take the tarps up. D'Antona and a few others grabbed bats and walked out to the batting cage behind the left-field fence for extra drills, hitting soft-toss and off the tees. Blake Hanan slogged out to the outfield to work on judging and catching pop flies. During last night's game, he'd dived for a short fly ball in shallow center, and the ball had popped out of his glove. Two runners had scored. His teammates had joked with him about it, but the bobble bothered him. Hanan knew he didn't have much margin for error in this league. Right now he cared most about proving he was "above the line"—that he belonged on the same field with these players, even if he wasn't going to stand out, even if he wasn't a starter. He believed in his defense, believed he already had the quickness and instincts to play defense in the pros. He still felt uncomfortable at second base, though, the new position Schiffner had assigned him. The angles seemed off. He was slower reading the ball off the bat.

Pauly pitched in the bullpen with Bobby Myers looking on, getting in ten minutes of hard throwing. In the parking lot Simon Williams lingered with Schiffner and the trainer, Daisy Kovach. Schiffner had expected Williams to beg off last night's game and had been impressed when Williams said he was ready to go. Williams had even hit a key two-out double in the game. Schiffner had registered the hit, even though the rainout kept it from entering the books. But Williams had felt something twinge in his shoulder during one of his at-bats. Schiffner asked him how the arm felt. Williams pursed his lips. He had an open, innocent-looking face, with pale blue eyes and red hair, and the whitest skin on the team. He smiled politely and said, stoically, "Crappy." Schiffner asked the trainer to get a referral from Williams's doctor in Maine so they could get an MRI done in Hyannis. At minimum, Williams would miss two weeks.

Luke Carlin, the last of Schiffner's juniors still in play, would arrive the next day. Schiffner sensed he was coming to the Cape only for show, to add pressure to the negotiations with Detroit. Carlin and the Tigers were fast closing in on a bonus of $50,000 (plus school). Schiffner knew he'd lost that bet, too. His gamble had failed, and his final roster was due in eight days. He was playing his cards, now, as they came to him.

ON THE THIRD try the sun finally shone on the start of the 2002 season, then the sky darkened. Before the game against Falmouth, sitting in the home dugout with his nylon jacket buttoned all the way up, the pitching coach, Bobby Myers, said, "I've seen more rain in three days here than in the past six months at Azusa Pacific." A weak low-pressure system had trailed the nor'easter into the region, and nothing seemed settled.

During batting practice, a siren wailed up beyond center field, from a cruiser pulling out of the Chatham Police Department. In the press box, Paul Galop quipped, "D'Antona's ride is here."

The weather decided to hold. The season would finally start.

In the first inning, with two runners on base, Jamie D'Antona came to bat for the first time, officially, in the Cape Cod Baseball League. He worked the count to three balls and one strike. He had more to prove than most everybody else on this field, and more to lose. Over the decades the curse of superior talent had ruined countless prospects, players held to a different standard, a different definition of failure.

The Falmouth pitcher threw a fastball over the outside of the plate, and D'Antona uncoiled. He crushed the ball high and deep to right-center field. The ball carried in the damp air all the way to the top of the grass embankment way past the outfield fence. In the dugout the players went crazy. They laughed, clapped, stood up and whistled. *"That's* retard strength," said infielder Michael Moon. They rushed out and greeted D'Antona as he crossed home plate and trotted back to the dugout.

D'Antona slowed to a walk along the line of teammates, high-fiving them and smiling. The sweet feeling of smashing a hard leather baseball with a hard wooden bat lingered in his hands. He reached Schiffner last in line.

"Welcome to the Cod," said Schiffner.

THREE

Cold Water

Nᴵᴄᴋ's Dᴇʟɪ ᴛᴏᴏᴋ ᴜᴘ ᴛʜᴇ ꜰɪʀsᴛ floor of a weather-beaten, four-square house a few minutes' walk from the ball field. Chatham's two most recent league championship trophies crowned the glass deli case. Framed photographs of the A's crowded the walls. Ballplayers wandered in every day—two, three, six at a time—for lunch after knocking off work, or to wolf down a steak-and-cheese before batting practice, or just to say hi to Billy and Mimi Nickerson, who owned the place. Most teams in the league had regular friendly hangouts, but none as convenient as Nick's.

The day after D'Antona's homer against Falmouth, the two assistant coaches, Matt Fincher and Bobby Myers, sat at a sunny table at Nick's in front of the picture window. On the deep window ledge next to them, in an elaborate beach scene Mimi had created, a sun-tanned Barbie doll reclined in a chaise longue, wearing shades and sipping a tropical drink. It was good kitsch for a summer town, the only touch in the place that wasn't baseball. At the other tables in the small dining room, Chatham A's sat eating grinders and watching ESPN's baseball highlights on the TV in the corner.

Fincher and Myers talked about the rain. It had come in again last evening. Showers had ended the game against Falmouth after six innings in a 4–4 tie. That made two rainouts and a rain-shortened tie in the team's first three games. The A's should have won. A leaky defense had hurt. Several low pitches had squirted by catcher Chris

Iannetta with runners on base. Michael Moon, playing center field in place of the injured Simon Williams, had simply never seen a routine fly. He had stared up blankly into the lights as teammates yelled directions to him. The ball had dropped close behind him for a triple, and two runs had scored. D'Antona had kicked around one ground ball at third and let another bounce past him into the shortstop hole, forcing Chad Orvella to try a desperation throw while his momentum carried him away from first base. The coaches had lingered in the dugout after the players had finished their sandwiches and gone home. "What the hell was that with Iannetta waving at the ball?" Schiffner asked, looking out at the drizzle.

Myers worried more about D'Antona's play at third base. "Let's get him over to first, where he belongs," Myers said.

"Can't do," Schiffner replied. "I promised George Greer we wouldn't. And he's not all bad—he comes in on the ball like friggin' Graig Nettles. He has an absolute hose for an arm. Let's see if we can get him to come out early and just work on moving left and right." Nettles had played third for the Yankees. He'd been the best in the game at a difficult play: charging a slow-rolling ball, grabbing it with his bare hand and, bent over and off-balance, firing it accurately to first. Infielders drilled for the skill every day, yet the necessary strength, coordination, and confidence for it seemed innate. D'Antona had it.

"Well, if we keep D'Antona at third let's get a shortstop who can go into the hole and make that play," Myers told Schiffner. "I say we use the last roster pick for a shortstop."

"Orvella's our guy," Schiffner replied. "We've got the people we're going to work with. We're not running a minor league program here."

Schiffner often said to his players, "Not too high, not too low." Emotion, he knew, shaped the game. Adrenaline could pump up college players for an important conference weekend. Off days and nonconference games gave breathing space or time to regroup after a devastating loss. But major league teams played 162 games a season—a long time to stay fired up, a fatally long time for any player down on himself. Finding the even keel, Schiffner knew, was a key part of the voyage from college ball to professional, high-pressure, day-in-day-out baseball. This was a sport that rewarded consistency and the long haul.

Schiffner carried the same level mood to his coaching. The coaches traded off times of bucking up each other, as needed. Often Schiffner needed the bucking up. Last night, it had been his turn to be positive.

At Nick's, with the players within easy earshot, Fincher and Myers kept their worries to themselves. They complained about the lousy weather.

THE PLAYERS DROVE in caravan to their first away game. The trip to Wareham might have been disorienting to D'Antona, Stauffer, and the other first-year players, if they had been ones to focus on their surroundings. They'd gotten a taste of Cape Cod from the salty water of Chatham, where marshland and fishing boats still painted at least part of the landscape. It was natural to assume the rest of the Cape still looked that way.

The narrow spit of sand that is Cape Cod curled forty miles into the Atlantic from Massachusetts's southeastern coast. The players cut through it on a flat, four-lane highway. Scrubby pine and oak trees hemmed the players into a long, green, sandy tunnel, blocking views of the water just a few miles off both sides. The hints of Cape Cod came only through the names on the exit signs, *Brewster, Barnstable, Hyannis, Sandwich, Woods Hole.*

Across the Cape Cod Canal, on the off-Cape side of the Sagamore Bridge, the players poked along a suburban strip that had little to do with the Cape or with anywhere in particular. The bland surroundings didn't bother them. Fast food mixed in among the convenience stores and tired motels. Many of the players had looked forward to the Wareham trip for that reason alone. Chatham, incredible to the players, had no Taco Bell, no KFC, no McDonald's. The players drove with a narrow focus and their windows down, radios rattling WCOD, rock for the Cape and Islands.

Fincher and Myers drove together. Schiffner's recent commuting schedule had given the two assistants a lot of time together. Schiffner, though, had been good; he was turning in his grades early back in Connecticut. He had worked ahead and cleaned out his classroom, put all his paperwork in order. He'd gotten permission to be out sick the last two days of school, as he did every year. Teaching for nearly a quarter century at Plainfield High School had earned him some favors. He planned to meet up with his team at suppertime in Wareham and then plant himself in Chatham for the summer.

Fincher was starting his sixth summer in Chatham, long enough to know the A's had trouble winning in Wareham. He'd spent many a late night at Schiffner's nursing Cokes—preferring them to the harder stuff enjoyed by the others—hashing over why things so often had gone wrong in Wareham. Since 1988 Wareham had won thirty-nine of its fifty-five games against Chatham. It was the only team in the league over that period with more wins and more titles than the A's. In the previous year's championship, Wareham had beaten Chatham by a single run, in the bottom of the ninth inning on a squibbed hit that barely got past the pitcher's mound. Schiffner had questioned, again, fate and the fairness of the umpiring in Wareham. For Fincher and Schiffner the loss still rankled.

Fincher's relationship with Chatham transcended coaching. He was a beloved figure at the field—there from morning to night, overseeing the maintenance, coaching third base, working with the players. Players loved his enthusiasm, his piercing whistle, his dry humor. During the rest of the year, he lived alone with two cats in Spartanburg, South Carolina, in a barely furnished two-bedroom condo. Charlie Thoms had visited him once and couldn't get over how spare Fincher's life seemed. In one bedroom Thoms had seen only a couple of cat dishes. The fridge held nothing other than Coke and milk for cereal. T-shirts, neatly pressed and hung, filled Fincher's closet, next to an ironing board. No art, no homey touches, furniture that looked rented.

Forty years old, with the looks of an ex-Marine sergeant gone soft, Fincher coached at the University of South Carolina at Spartanburg, a tiny Division II school that put scant resources into baseball. As few as twenty-five or thirty fans might show up at home games. He'd come to his job the hard way, climbing up through small, no-name programs at Eastern Illinois University, Georgia College and State University, and Andrew College in Georgia. He'd coached summer teams in New York State, Missouri, and Alaska before landing in Chatham. Chatham, to Fincher, was the big time—the chance to work with the best players he would likely ever coach. He'd once thought of summer ball as a stepping stone to better coaching jobs, but he'd become so close to John and Martha Schiffner over the years that he couldn't imagine being anywhere else now. He looked forward all year to the ritual of heading north: the drive up to his sister's in Virginia; his annual visit with an old friend in New Jersey; finding Schiffner in Connecticut and playing nine holes at the Willimantic Country Club; driving on up to Chatham and whipping the field into shape. The friendship had become more important than the baseball.

"We got a *shot* today with me driving," he said to Myers. "With Schiff driving to Wareham we got *no* shot." Like a lot of baseball men, Fincher was superstitious.

Beyond the shopping plazas and fast-food joints, the grassy banks and blue water of the tidal Agawam River colored the north side of the highway and brought Cape Cod startlingly back into view. The caravan slowed across the bridge over The Narrows just below Wareham's village center. Off to the left, players saw sailboats moored in the harbor and a small forest of masts rising above the slips of a local boatyard. The caravan passed maple and cherry trees shading the lawns of old Colonial houses along Main Street. A minute or two later the A's piled out into the parking lot in back of the old brick high school. The long white afternoon turned mellow. Shadows stretched across the green-and-gray home ground of the Wareham Gatemen. In a cluttered concession stand, volunteers sold hats and programs and aerial-view postcards of the field. Across the upper edge of the postcards snaked the wild-looking Broad Marsh River as it widened into Buzzards Bay just a few hundred feet from the field. Once you were here, a more Cape Cod setting for baseball was hard to imagine.

No SCOUTS SAT in the private fenced-in deck alongside the elevated press box behind home plate. They had learned that hitters needed time to switch from the metal bats of college to the wooden bats on the Cape. And all of the players needed time to get comfortable in the humidity, and with the high caliber of the pitching, and with the routines of new teams and day jobs and host families and games every day. In many ways the Cape League was about overcoming adversity, and thus it was great preparation. Scouts on the Cape glimpsed how players dealt with failure, how they might perform under similar difficult conditions in the pros. Still, the scouts gave players some time to get their sea legs. The first week or two could be pretty rough.

Fraser Dizard, Chatham's left-handed sophomore from U.S.C., tested his arm for the first time since tearing a ligament in his elbow back in March. Dizard had seemed quieter to Schiffner this year, not as cocky as the Dizard who had turned down good signing money out of high school. When Dizard was four years old he'd caught his left index finger in the wheels of an exercise bicycle—the tip, severed at the first knuckle, flew across the room. He'd worn a protective mitt for a year and a half, and had still become a left-handed thrower. In time the grotesque stub of a finger gave Dizard's fastball a wicked sink.

He had arrived in Chatham the previous summer after playing in the College World Series, and immediately rubbed Schiffner wrong. Dizard, a freshman then, felt he deserved to be one of Chatham's starters. He sulked after Schiffner told him he'd need to earn the honor. Schiffner read arrogance, which went along with Dizard's aloofness and sunglasses and dark-haired good looks, his motorcycle riding, the check his parents had sent out for him to buy a used SUV for the summer. But Dizard had worked and earned a starting spot. Now a college sophomore, Dizard had found his pro prospects thrown into doubt by an injury. Injuries humbled players in a hurry.

Schiffner had promised the U.S.C. coach, Mike Gillespie, that he'd ease Dizard into the summer. He'd limit Dizard's pitches, then gradually increase them.

Dizard, in his first start, looked confident on the Wareham mound. He stood squarely on the rubber, raised his hands up slowly in front of his face as he rocked into his motion. His arm came around smoothly, efficiently—one of the prettiest deliveries on the A's staff. But as the evening cooled, his pitches didn't look so pretty crossing the plate. He threw balls in the dirt, couldn't get his curve ball over. He repeatedly lifted his cap off with his pitching hand and swiped the sweat on his forehead with his undersleeve. In the first inning each at-bat seemed like a battle, then again in the second. Still, he gave up no runs, struck out four, and showed a good changeup and that tough sinking movement in his fastball, even if it bounced in the dirt. He hit his forty-pitch limit in just two innings. His arm felt sore as he pulled on his jacket in the dugout, his first test of the summer over. But it was a good sore. That was the main thing.

Scott Hindman, the reluctant pitcher from Princeton, replaced Dizard on the mound. He was testing a more seriously injured elbow. He stood taller than Dizard, was broader in the shoulders and the hips, but looked tentative by comparison, as if he was unsure of his place out there on the rubber. He stared ahead blankly, with none of the self-assurance he usually showed off the field. He fired a handful of impressive low strikes that looked almost unhittable, but he walked the first man he faced, and hit the next. He threw wildly for three innings, from the edge of danger, and never found a rhythm. The last batter he faced looped a sinking line drive to center field. Ryan Hubbard from Wake Forest, on the Cape for less than twenty-four hours as a replacement for the drafted Adam Greenberg, misread the drive, started late, dove and missed the ball, straining a hamstring and reinjuring a back muscle. The only run Hindman gave up scored on the play.

Injuries were a part of every Cape Cod League season, but Schiffner couldn't remember another team that had so many injuries so early on. Hubbard would likely be out of commission for weeks, not days—that was Schiffner's new worry. For Hubbard, a junior who had been bypassed in this year's draft, the loss struck deeper. More rode on this season for him than for Schiffner. A series of niggling injuries had kept him from starring at Wake Forest. His last-minute chance to play on the Cape had given him a reprieve, the best shot he had left at impressing scouts. And now even that was in danger of disappearing. The threat of a career-ending injury hung over every player on the Cape. All of them knew it. None of them, though, could afford to pull back, to play as if they were guarding against it.

Scott Hindman threw seventy-five pitches in a game for the first time since his senior year in high school. Afterward, watching two other pitchers finish the game, his arm felt dead.

The A's won 5–2, despite the shaky pitching, despite eleven Chatham strikeouts, despite another error by Jamie D'Antona. For whatever reason—early-season jitters, the wet week just ended, all those adjustments the players hadn't yet figured out—the ragged play looked far from the smoothest amateur talent on the planet.

Schiffner climbed into his GMC Jimmy with his wife, Martha, at ten-thirty for the drive to Chatham. A bright half-moon sailed high above Buzzards Bay. He was on the cell phone before they'd even left the parking lot. He had another injured outfielder to replace.

On his backup sheet Schiffner had circled "Ben Himes, Texas A&M." Schiffner reached Himes's agent, Rob Martin, who called Himes's mother, then Himes. The outfielder had just started playing in the Valley League of Pennsylvania. When Martin called, Himes was asleep on the living-room floor of a tiny house crowded with four other college baseball players, and was coming off an injury of his own. The Cincinnati Reds had drafted Himes in a late round but wanted to see him to play that summer so they could gauge his recovery before making an offer, as the Angels did with Hindman. Himes's agent knew that the Cape League could boost his client's value.

Himes's mother got onto the Internet and bought her son a plane ticket to Providence for $226 (which the A's would reimburse). Schiffner met him at the airport the next day at one-thirty in the afternoon. By three-thirty the newest member of the 2002 Chatham A's stood in the outfield at Veterans Field, stretching for early batting practice before the game against Hyannis.

"You don't need to be a great coach to win in this league," Schiffner liked to say. "You need to be a great recruiter."

THIRTEEN HUNDRED FANS got their first look at Tim Stauffer that night in Chatham against the Hyannis Mets. The A's, rained out in their first two tries, had tied a game and won a game, and now had their best pitcher on the mound. Stauffer wore his uniform in the old style, hat pulled low over his crewcut, pant legs tucked into his socks just below the knees. An observer could tell at a glance—from the uniform, the big ears, the thick eyebrows—that Stauffer didn't come from some posh suburb in Florida or southern California, the sunny places that seem to spawn most college ballplayers these days. He was a clean-cut northern boy from a middle-class Catholic family. He didn't even look like an athlete. But looks were deceptive. In his ragged workout clothes, unshaven and sweaty, he showed some of the steel beneath the surface. Stauffer could run a sub-seven-second sixty-yard dash—splendid speed for a pitcher, where running counted for nothing—and he could dunk a basketball with ease. He had unusually long arms, disproportionately long legs, and big hands—all advantages, as it happens, for someone who throws baseballs. Over the past spring and summer Stauffer had won twenty-three games and lost only four. The losses had all been close, low-scoring games. His consistency was extraordinary; he hadn't had a single bad inning in more than a year. That spring he'd struck out 140 batters and walked only thirty-four. He'd posted the lowest earned run average among college starting pitchers. He'd allowed just over a run and a half per game, four runs lower than the average across Division I. Schiffner had tracked Stauffer's spring with growing excitement. He worried only about the high number of innings that Stauffer was racking up. In Schiffner's darker moods, thinking of young arms and injuries (and maybe his own team's fortunes), he looked at the mounting inning totals and called Stauffer's handling by his coaches at Richmond "criminal."

Although Tim Stauffer had beaten Wake Forest and lost a brilliantly pitched game to Nebraska that spring, most of his success had come at the expense of relatively weak teams in the Atlantic Ten Conference. He had proved he was a good pitcher, but a question remained as he faced the Hyannis Mets in his first start on the Cape: How would he fare against the best college hitters in the nation?

Buzz Bowers, a semiretired scout for the Boston Red Sox, had driven over from East Orleans to see the young pitcher. Bowers sat in the stands behind home plate and clocked Stauffer's fastballs on a radar gun at ninety-one and ninety-two miles per hour. The gun confirmed what was hard to calculate with the naked eye: Stauffer had major league speed, even if he appeared to be just tossing the ball. Bowers watched him with interest. He usually downplayed these early games, expecting Cape League pitchers to be rusty their first times out, from having rested so long since their last outings. But Stauffer showed no rust at all.

He struck out eight of the first twelve batters he faced. He played with the corners of the plate, masterfully varying the locations of his fastball, hard curve ball, and change-up. Over the first five innings, he didn't allow a single ball out of the infield. He froze one batter with a sharp curve ball—the batter tensed with the ball hurtling at him, then watched it dart across the plate for a called third strike. In the dugout, Fincher said, "The guy's a freakin' surgeon." Stauffer didn't retire the Hyannis batters, he blew them away. The A's high-fived each other on the bench, yelled "Sit!" as another Hyannis batter struck out and walked back to the dugout. They hooted and laughed time and again—as if trying to hit Stauffer were a joke. Schiffner barked at them for making fun, but he was feeling pretty good, too. As the scouts would say, Stauffer was a complete package. Anyone watching could tell.

He ended his night striking out eleven batters and giving up just three hits, and he still wasn't happy when he peeled off his uniform top to ice his right shoulder. He forced a weak smile as his teammates congratulated him. He'd walked three batters—inexcusable for him—and he'd thrown 102 pitches over seven innings, a total he felt should have been closer to ninety. He was pitching from a higher plane than others were used to.

Taking Stauffer's place on the mound to start the eighth inning, Thomas Pauly warmed up for his first appearance in the Cape Cod Baseball League. If anything, the crowd had grown larger since the first inning, and Pauly felt butterflies. In the dugout, Schiffner walked past the trainer and said, loud enough for the others to hear, "Daisy, do we have any toilet paper in the bag?" He expected Pauly to shit the bed, and he wasn't afraid to joke out loud about it. The comment was out of character from a coach who had a reputation of being loyal to his players to a fault. And it came with an edge. Pauly's goofy attitude irritated Schiffner.

The carelessness Schiffner saw was a mask, Pauly's way of saving face in a league that still intimidated him. Pauly couldn't shake the feeling that he was different from other players here, guys who acted as if they'd been groomed for this appointment from the moment they'd started playing the game—as if that summer was simply their turn to be in the Cape Cod League.

Pauly had initially shied away from the big-program guys, preferring to hang with players who seemed closer to his level. Over his first ten days in Chatham, though, he'd spent some time with his housemate, Daniel Moore, and Moore seemed like a regular guy. He pitched at the University of North Carolina and had been an all-star on the Cape the previous year. Pauly was spending a lot of time with the guys in the bullpen, too, and found them easier to get to know than his more complicated classmates at Princeton. Refreshingly, the players here reminded him of his friends back home in Florida— they thought mostly about baseball and having fun. Even Stauffer seemed like a normal guy. He'd come over to Pauly's house once or twice to play a Tiger Woods video game against Moore. He didn't put on airs. Around adults Stauffer talked in safe, predictable clichés, came off as serious and reserved. He was even private around his parents, who often wondered what he was thinking. But Pauly had already seen Stauffer's sense of humor and how he took his team-mates' ribbing in easy stride. They told him what fancy cars he should buy them once he turned pro and became a zillionaire. They ragged him when he overslept once and showed up late at the field, called him "Big leaguer!" Stauffer laughed with them, shook his head. Pauly was getting comfortable around the A's. What he was un-sure of was himself.

Pauly had the durable, resilient arm of a starting pitcher—and a fresher arm than most twenty-year-old pitchers, who by then had thrown thousands of hard pitches in their young lives. But Princeton coach Scott Bradley chose to have that resilient arm make a differ-ence in as many conference games as possible; he used Pauly as Princeton's closing relief pitcher. Bradley brought him in to nail down the final innings of two or three games each week. With the A's, Pauly would get his innings on a less-predictable schedule. He could tell already that he wasn't high on Schiffner's go-to list.

Pauly pitched with a stripped-down rock-back-and-throw motion. Nervous, he walked the first man he faced. He tugged at the waist-band of his pants, pulled at his shirt, as if the Cape Cod League uni-form didn't quite fit. One of the calls was borderline, and he had to talk himself down on the mound, not let the call stay with him, dis-tract him. He noticed the crowd, full of color and life, and felt a rush of adrenaline. He took a deep breath. Then he settled down and threw hard strikes, almost all fastballs, and struck out a batter. With two outs he gave up a little spinning pop-up down the third-base line. D'Antona reacted slowly, backpedaled, then circled clumsily back toward the foul line, and watched the ball drop safely a foot in front of him, a run scoring on the misplay. D'Antona grabbed the ball angrily with his bare hand, squeezed it hard, then tossed it back to Pauly. Pauly said, "Don't worry about it," and threw a strikeout to end the inning.

In the bottom of the inning, A's outfielder Steve LeFaivre hit a high home run to right field. A few batters later with two runners on and two men out, Colt Morton marched slowly to the plate. Morton looked like a young Carlton Fisk, the Hall of Fame catcher who walked deliberately, feet slightly splayed, with all the grace and purpose of a gladiator. Morton stood six foot six and had every inch of Fisk's poise and golden-boy looks. Morton had struggled to make contact in these first games, though. He'd struck out six times, including twice earlier that night.

He'd changed his bat, hoping to change his luck. He'd picked out a brand-new ash bat made by the local Barnstable Bat Co. He swung it, and the crack of the impact sounded qualitatively different than any yet that summer. Morton's ball took off and kept climbing, eventually disappearing in the trees high beyond the scoreboard in left field. Not just a bomb—a *mega-bomb*. In the dugout Schiffner widened his eyes and said, "Oh . . . my . . . God."

The runs, coming while Pauly was the pitcher of record, gave Pauly—not Stauffer—a win in his first Cape Cod League game.

After the final out, both managers huddled their teams around them on opposite sides of the outfield, as was the custom in the league. Down the left-field line Schiffner spoke gently to his players. He told them to tone down the hilarity in the dugout and to "lock in" earlier in the game. "I'm not pissed," he said. "I just want you to know this isn't a beer league. This is the Cape Cod League." He and Finch and Myers walked away. Charlie Thoms was already in the dugout, dropping off ten large pizzas donated by a downtown restaurant. A horde of little kids crowded against the fence next to the dugout, ready for the okay to run onto the field and approach the players for autographs—not for collections or for trading, but simply to get close to greatness. Teenage girls in halter-tops and tight shirts clustered by a gate, too, down by the bullpen, waiting. The players drew in close among themselves, as was the A's' custom. They reached in and put their hands together up high. They murmured and giggled and whispered for a moment. Then chanted, in unison, "One, two, three, *bombs!*"

Afterwards, as Pauly and Hindman signed autographs out on the field, a pretty, petite woman approached them. Players were routinely approached by women after games—the baseball uniforms created allure, gave the players a clue, maybe, of how women must feel when they were treated as objects. A lot of the girls in Chatham were young. Most were there for just the summer, with no strings. But Pauly recognized this one.

"I've seen you before," he said to her. "In a weight room. Florida?"

"No," she said.

"Oh—I've seen you from school!"

"Yes."

"Field hockey, right?"

"No. Lacrosse."

Her name was Ingrid Goldberg. Her family had a vacation place in Chatham. The two exchanged phone numbers. The summer was looking brighter.

THE COLD WATER hit in Bourne. After three games, four Chatham players were hitting better than .300. But suddenly the A's batters appeared tentative. They fell behind counts, watched as called third strikes flew past. Two Bourne pitchers shut them out on just three hits. The next night at home against Harwich, a slender right-hander named Brad Ziegler toyed with the Chatham lineup.

A couple of innings into that game, with Harwich batting, the strains of *South Pacific* rose again from the trees beyond left field, at odds with the tension building on the baseball field. In the dugout Schiffner said, "Christ, it sounds like the gates of heaven here in Chatham." Out on the field, D'Antona looked over to the dugout and quipped, "What's this, the Chatham Men's Chorus?"

"Don't be afraid to concentrate out there, Jamie!" yelled Schiffner.

An inning later, with two outs and runners on second and third, D'Antona fielded an easy ground ball, then hesitated. He tried to tag the runner coming toward him from second, but the runner slowed. D'Antona started after him, changed his mind, hurried a wild throw that sailed past first base into foul ground, and handed Harwich the lead.

In the bottom of the ninth, with his team trailing 1–0, D'Antona came up with two runners on base and a chance to be a hero. Since the home run in his first at-bat of the season, he had hit safely once in fifteen times up. He had struck out six times.

D'Antona had suffered through slumps before—all batters had. He had responded in the usual way: He took extra batting practice, worked harder, tried to "focus down." He tried to recapture that beautiful, instinctive swing that had made him an all-star in the past. He mashed the ball in batting practice. Nothing reassured him more than the feeling of a solid impact on the sweet spot of a wooden bat, that magical spot six inches or so from the end of the barrel that yielded the longest, most powerful hits.

But batting-practice pitching was one thing, and the stuff D'Antona faced in these games was another. The league's relentless good pitching humbled hitters. In any college conference, a team might face one or two excellent pitchers during a series, after which the quality fell off to competent, or less. Batters typically saw top pitchers only once or twice a weekend, when conference games were played. Against the third and fourth starters, and against the middle relievers, good hitters teed off, building (or rebuilding) confidence, and fattening statistics. Midweek, against weaker teams and younger, less polished pitchers, batters sharpened their swings as if taking batting practice. The Cape Cod League didn't distinguish between weekend and midweek games, though, and provided almost no off days to recover. Day in and day out, batters faced not only a number one pitcher, but one of the country's toughest number one pitchers. The caliber of the competition worked both ways, of course. Pitchers on the Cape couldn't coast through the bottom of an opposing team's lineup the way they could during the college season. Every hitter in a Cape League lineup was dangerous, the best or one of the best on his team back home. But baseball's relentless law of averages favored pitchers, and good pitching almost always beat good hitting.

When D'Antona was hitting well, when his sweet, unconscious swing stroked home runs to right-center and doubles to left no matter who he was facing, he sensed pitches arriving more slowly than they actually were. When he was slumping, he had the opposite illusion. He was surprised by how quickly the pitches came in on him. D'Antona wasn't yet thinking he couldn't hit in this league. He was frustrated by his slow start, and had gotten quieter over the past couple of days, but he still felt confident. He worried, though, that the pitches hadn't slowed down for him yet.

And that was only part of it. Possibly more important was the wooden bat the league required D'Antona to use.

At Wake Forest D'Antona used a thirty-three inch, thirty-ounce bat called a "TPX Gen 1X" made by Louisville Slugger and Alcoa. The bat's space-age alloy included aluminum, zinc, copper, zirconium, magnesium, and traces of titanium. The materials and hollow-cylinder design created a light bat with a thin handle and fat barrel. With such a bat in his hands, the speed of D'Antona's swing was frightening. He could sit back and wait on a pitch until it was almost on top of him before he pulled the trigger and whipped the bat through the strike zone. Wood was a different animal.

Hickory and ash had furnished most of the bats in baseball's early days. Hickory, a strong, durable, flexible wood, was the traditional

choice for hammer and ax handles. It was also heavy. Ash, in particular northern white ash (*Fraxinus americana*), the driest standing
hardwood, had similar properties but was much lighter. It had been
used for running gear in horse-drawn carriages, for the spokes in
wheels, canoe paddles, snowshoes, chair spindles, and anything else
that needed to be strong but light and flexible. (Maple, a harder,
stiffer, heavier wood, was used for the hubs of wagon wheels,
butcher blocks, and, later, airplane propellers. It had rarely been
used for handles.) Ash had emerged as the material of choice for batters at every level of baseball: It gave the ultimate combination of
strength and lightness.

Despite the lighter wood, batters of the old dead-ball era swung
heavy, long bats. Rabbit Maranville, a light-hitting shortstop, used a
Spalding bat that weighed fifty ounces. Babe Ruth wielded a forty-
seven-ouncer when he swatted sixty home runs in 1927. Lou Gehrig,
Jimmie Foxx, and other sluggers typically swung bats that weighed
forty ounces or more. By the time Roger Maris broke the Babe's
home-run record in 1961, though, hitters better understood the importance of bat speed, and the heavy weights of the earlier era were
sinking into history. Maris's bat weighed thirty-three ounces. The
thin-handled, gently-tapered, thirty-two- or thirty-three-ounce bat
favored by hitters such as Ted Williams and Henry Aaron became
standard. In today's major league bat racks, you wouldn't find a bat
longer than thirty-five inches or heavier than thirty-six ounces.
Though, increasingly, you'd find maple. As athletes became bigger
and stronger—particularly in the past decade—some switched to the
harder, heavier wood. D'Antona, on the Cape, was one of them. He
swung a maple "Sam Bat" made in Ottawa, the bat recently made
fashionable by the major league home-run king, Barry Bonds. D'Antona had brought the bat with him from Wake Forest. Some of his
teammates in Chatham had treated it like an exotic species; they'd
gripped it, checked its balance, taken a cut or two with it.

The problem with wood, any wood, is durability. Major league hitters routinely break two hundred bats in a single season. An ash bat

that doesn't break will start deteriorating after a few hundred batted balls. That replacement cost (twenty-five or thirty dollars per bat), easily absorbed by the cash-rich professional teams, forced amateur leagues to consider alternatives. In 1970 Hillerich & Bradsby, a big maker of wood bats, collaborated with Alcoa on its first generation of a new kind of bat, one made of aluminum.

The original idea—to produce a long-lasting alternative to wood—may have been encouraged by thrift, but aluminum bat makers soon beat wood's performance. Not constrained by the even density and length-to-weight ratios inherent in solid wood, engineers toyed with the balances. Within a decade, lightweight, thin-walled aluminum had completely replaced wood at every youth and amateur level. A thirty-four-inch, twenty-nine ounce bat made by Easton sold millions in the 1980s—its handle was so thin that players felt like they were swinging a golf club. A $100 bat might last a full college season before becoming too dented for play. And even then, some of the players liked the slight dishing that gradually flattened the bat's sweet spot. It made hitting a round ball squarely a little easier.

By the mid-1990s the high-performance technology had gotten pricey. At the college level, bats made of magnesium and titanium, superlight and superexpensive, lasted only a few games. But boy, could they hit. During the 1995 College World Series, ultralight aluminum bats stroked forty-eight home runs in fourteen games. Some scores looked like football, not baseball. In 1998 the overall batting average of Division I colleges had climbed to .306. The average team scored more than seven runs per game. Researchers estimated the speed of the ball coming off those supercharged bats at better than 180 feet per second—too fast for infielders to dare position themselves at their normal depths. Pitchers got hurt. The bats had changed the game.

In the years that D'Antona had been in college, the NCAA had restricted bat performance. One crucial change was the "minus three" limit—the length of certified metal bats could be no greater than three inches more than their weight in ounces. And committees were studying other ways to bring the college game's offense back toward historic norms.

Professional baseball, protecting the integrity of the game and its almost-sacred records of human achievement, had gone against the grain, had held firm against the high-tech veer that golf and tennis couldn't resist. Professional baseball continued to use wooden bats.

In 1985, as metal bats were changing amateur baseball everywhere, one of the NCAA summer leagues—the Cape Cod Baseball League—made a bold decision. It became the first NCAA-sanctioned wooden-bat league in the country. The league had long fed the pros. The decision established the league as *the* preeminent summer showcase for college players. Wooden bats let scouts on the Cape gauge a player's potential without calculations or adjustments in the record. The bats also added a dollop of nostalgia, a sense of old-fashioned simplicity, even as they helped scouts implacably sort out players.

In the years following the move to wooden bats, college players endured something akin to boot camp in the Cape Cod League. They struggled with the newness of the old-fashioned bats together—a collective trial—and got a season or two of experience before starting out, on their own, in the minors. Struggle was one of the rites of passage in the fraternity of wooden bats. Failure at this higher level was a necessary part of the learning curve.

D'ANTONA GRIPPED HIS wooden bat and looked out at the Harwich pitcher. Through his supple leather batting gloves the maple handle felt thick, solid. It was only a matter of time before he found his swing again and broke out.

He jumped on the first pitch. His swift uppercut connected with the ball just a trifle low. At Wake Forest, off an aluminum bat, the ball would have flown four hundred feet to the fence in center field. But Chatham wasn't Wake Forest. The outfielder drifted back several steps, then another—the ball carried well. He easily caught it, and the game was over.

The A's hopped up out of the dugout and lined up to shake hands with the winners, a college ritual, not done in the majors. Before he joined the end of the line D'Antona stood by himself off to the side of the Chatham dugout. He unstrapped his shin guard and slammed it to the ground, then slammed his two batting gloves down, then his helmet.

He drove back alone to the Galops' house. He had an uncommon knack for living in the moment, for letting both good and bad performances roll off him. He rarely carried a bad at-bat with him into his next, rarely dwelled on poor performance. He clowned around on the field and in the dugout, no matter how he was playing. While his less-than-serious approach bothered Schiffner and the other A's coaches, fans watching him at Wake Forest routinely told him he was a pleasure to watch—a kid who savored the game, who didn't take it so dead-seriously.

"You can't dwell on this crap, because it will kill you," D'Antona said, in a less-stressed time. "I've met college players who are really bitter. As soon as they make an out, even if they're hitting .380, they get pissed. I feel like saying, 'You know, you're not supposed to get a hit every friggin' single time. It's not high school anymore.' We all hit over .500 or .600 in high school. College is a little different. You hit .400 and you're a god. If you take every at-bat as your last at-bat, you're just going to hurt yourself. This game is supposed to be *fun*."

At the Galops', D'Antona grabbed a trash can from the kitchen and walked into the small bathroom next to his room. His house-mom, Laurie Galop arrived a few minutes later and found him there, leaning over, taking a barber's razor to his bleached hair. *I suck, I suck, I suck,* he said over and over, as his yellow curls fell into the can.

SCHIFFNER KNEW HIS players needed time to get their heads around this new level. He still believed he had as potent a lineup as any in the league, and that it would just take time for his hitters to settle down. Schiffner let them find their own way. But to players used to dominating the game, the wake-up call on the Cape sounded loud and lonely as a foghorn.

Chatham beat Brewster the next evening, 5–3, with a gentle on-shore breeze blowing out to right field. The A's put up four runs in the first inning, their first runs in eighteen innings. D'Antona, with his subdued hair and minus the goatee, struck out once and grounded into two double plays in three at bats.

Against Orleans the next night, D'Antona went hitless again. The A's were shut out on just four hits. More players now muttered under their breath after striking out, swearing at themselves. Afterwards, Schiffner tried to reassure his young players. "I'm not here to give an inspiring football-type speech," he said. "I'm not going to ride any asses. The fact is you guys are here for a reason. You've been recommended by your coaches, by scouts. You're All-Americans, all-stars in your conferences. You all know how to hit and play the game. What you need to do is relax and go up there and play the game like you know how. I'm not telling you not to give a shit. At some point you'd better give a shit—this is a showcase league. But you need to relax, be confident . . . I'm not worried about any one of you. I have a good feeling about this team. It *will* come."

A FEW HOURS after the annual "Meet the A's" lunch at the Chatham VFW, the hitting coach, Jon Palmieri, arrived at Charlie Thoms's to pick up his uniform. Palmieri's employer, Georgia Tech, had finally been knocked out of the College World Series. Palmieri had been an all-star here in Chatham. He'd torn up the record book at Wake Forest and had gone on to play a couple of years in the pros. He had the kind of knowledge that could make a difference.

The Chatham team batting average had slipped to .197. Thoms greeted Palmieri and said, "Do you realize you're coming onto a team that, not counting one inning against Brewster, has scored exactly one run in the past thirty-six innings?"

"I'm looking better already," Palmieri answered, grinning.

Colt Morton passed them in the kitchen and got introduced. He was hitting just .150, three hits in his first twenty times up. D'Antona's slump was even deeper, .083, two for twenty-four. They had struck out twenty-one times between them. Morton said to Palmieri, "We've been waiting for you . . . "

Stauffer pitched brilliantly again that warm, humid night at Harwich, allowing no runners past second base and striking out twelve in seven innings. Eric Everson pitched two scoreless innings to finish, but as even he admitted, it was hard to look good following Stauffer.

Schiffner had dropped D'Antona from cleanup to seventh in the batting order, to shelter him from the pressure. D'Antona, for his part, had tried a time-honored method of busting out of his slump. He'd been flirting with a couple of girls he'd met, and his teammates ragged him about it, urging him to go for it with one or the other, D—— or C——. At a party the night before, Jamie had gone for it with C——, and she'd said yes, and the whole team knew about it.

He had two walks in the game and hit the ball hard twice, one of them a bullet to left-center for a standing double. Down the right-field line, the bullpen guys went crazy. "Slump BUSTER!" they yelled. D'Antona crushed a long foul ball as well, and though it was just a towering strike, he was glad to hear the sharp crack coming off his bat during something other than batting practice. The players breathed out. The A's scored six runs and won easily. After the team huddle in the outfield the players pulled in close again. They seemed loose, relieved, psyched. And happy for D'Antona. They crowded in and put their hands together up high: "One, two, three . . . D-C!"

The easy moment didn't last. In Falmouth the next evening, with the sweet smell of honeysuckle thickening the air, the A's faced Thomas Martin, a left-handed starter who represented a different kind of Cape League relationship: He and Tim Stauffer had roomed together at Richmond. Teammates from school often competed against each other in the summer, especially in the handful of leagues that drew their players from the top programs. Nine players from Wake Forest currently played on the Cape, including four in

Chatham, the maximum number from one school that the NCAA allowed. Most enjoyed playing against each other—the personal rivalries added spice, set up bragging rights, gave chances to catch up and trade stories. Martin threw Chatham back into its runless funk. The A's scratched out just four hits and lost 5–0. D'Antona struck out twice, once with the bases loaded against reliever David Aardsma from Rice. Aardsma's fastball would be clocked later that summer at ninety-seven, the fastest gun on the Cape. D'Antona walked back to the dugout after his futile at-bat. "That was fun," he said. "That guy throws friggin' *cheese*."

The A's had received some good news earlier in the day from Hyannis. The MRI of Simon Williams's left shoulder showed no tear or permanent damage. "Just an impingement," explained the trainer, Daisy Kovach, who'd driven to Hyannis with Williams. She'd hoped to learn something from the doctor's analysis—part of her education, part of the value of spending her summer in the Cape League. But the doctor's report was perfunctory, lasting just a few minutes. She passed the recommended treatment on to Schiffner: physical therapy and a couple of weeks' rest.

Ryan Hubbard's hamstring and back, however, remained tender. Schiffner had talked with him alone before the game. The league's final roster deadline loomed. Schiffner wanted to do right by Hubbard and by Wake Forest's coach, George Greer, but couldn't hold a roster spot all summer for an injured player. He'd told Hubbard to talk with Greer and get back to him. He wanted Greer in on the decision. The courtesy showed that Schiffner understood what it took to succeed over the long term in this league. He had a reputation for not running players out of town, but more than one injured Chatham player had agreed to leave after talking things over with his coach back home. In ways like this Schiffner preserved important relationships. Still, the roster he'd crafted almost a year ago was in shambles.

A CROWD OF FIFTEEN HUNDRED fans spilled out of the bleachers and down both sides of the field in Chatham for the game against

Wareham on the first truly warm evening of the summer. The burn of hot dogs and burgers on the grill wafted from the food tent behind the third-base bleachers. A pack of kids romped on the fancy tree-lined playground in back of the fans down the right-field foul line. The growing number of lawn chairs and picnic blankets on the grassy bank beyond the outfield hinted at the even bigger crowds that would surround Veterans Field later in the season. Nobody seemed worried about the team's poor start. Summer had finally arrived. This was a beautiful ball field on Cape Cod on a delightfully warm June night.

The A's stayed cold. Held without a hit for the first six innings, Chatham tied the game in the seventh at 2–2. In the bottom of the eighth, newcomer Ben Himes squared to bunt a fastball. It rode in on him. He pulled away, but the ball smashed against his left hand and ricocheted off his face. He dropped to the ground and lay for several seconds before stirring. Simon Williams, still resting his sore shoulder, took Himes's place in the batter's box. He let a couple of close pitches go by for balls and trotted to first. The A's' dugout ignited. Stauffer and Pauly turned their hats backward to keep the rally alive. But Jeremy Cleveland and then Colt Morton struck out with the bases loaded, killing the threat. Colt walked slowly, erectly, back to the bench. "Dad GUMMIT!" he said. He slammed his helmet down inside the dugout. "Dad gummit…"

Blake Hanan struck out to end the game. The A's limped off the field. D'Antona had felt his hamstring pull while running out a slow ground ball his first time up. Michael Moon, himself favoring a sore hamstring, had replaced him at third. With Himes down, the team was fresh out of spare outfielders and infielders, both. Catcher Chris Iannetta had finished at first, first baseman Jeremy Cleveland third, a hobbling Moon center field. As the game had ended, pitcher Adam Yates was on deck, having never batted in this century. The fans packed up and the kids gathered at the gates for autographs. In the press box, Paul Galop cranked Gloria Gaynor over the P.A. system, "I Will Survive!"

The special postgame meal at Nick's was subdued. D'Antona, still in uniform, insisted on helping Mimi with the last-second things in the kitchen. He'd instantly liked Mimi and Billy, considered them family, and had made himself at home behind the counter. He especially liked Mimi, barely five feet tall with a head full of kinky black hair, with Puerto Rico and Spain in her blood. She talked with a fast New York accent and went out of her way to make the players feel special. She called them "dear," gave them hugs, asked about their families, wished she had sons of her own. D'Antona had started to pitch in during their busy times, for no pay. Mimi had gone to some trouble making salad and big pans of lasagna for the postgame meal. The boys ate quickly, though, and left early. Himes's left index finger had broken in two places. Ryan Hubbard was going home. Schiffner, Fincher, and Myers sat at a table long after the players left, contemplating their options.

"I'm officially worried about this team," said Schiffner.

He had two days to submit his roster to the league. He worked the phone late that night, again, and confirmed a replacement outfielder from Grossmont College in California, and another from Duke, who'd been playing nearby in Bourne and Brewster as a temporary. At one o'clock in the morning Schiffner left a message on George Greer's office phone at Wake Forest. "We've got three hamstrings, a broken finger, and four guys on suicide watch," he said. "Wish us luck."

THE DAY AFTER losing to Wareham, on a hazy, heavy afternoon in Cotuit, with thunder clouds building in the west, the A's hit a low-water mark. Cotuit won its twelfth straight game of the season, the best start in league history, with a no-hitter against the A's.

Chatham's pitchers faltered for the first time, giving up nine runs on seventeen hits.

Pitcher Mike MacDonald sat apart from his teammates at the far end of the dugout following his early exit, icing his elbow, seething. He was angry at himself, angry at not making the adjustments he needed to get his curveball under control. George Biron, a part-time area scout for the Anaheim Angels, saw past the off day and liked the looseness of MacDonald's arm. He'd clocked fastballs consistently at eighty-seven to eighty-nine, and the ball had jumped, looked lively. "I like the way he throws," Biron said to the other scout sitting below the cinder-block press box behind home plate. "He's a competitor." MacDonald's mood might have lifted had he heard the comment, but he was brooding about his team, too. He heard guys coming back to the dugout after striking out, blaming the umpire. He heard Blake Hanan say, "Man, every one of these guys can swing the stick," and Jeremy Cleveland, "What are these guys eating?"

MacDonald didn't like it. "Cotuit is sticking a bat up this team's ass," he said. "Maybe that's a good thing—it might get our heads out of it." He wasn't one to look elsewhere for blame.

D'Antona's average stood at .121, four hits in thirty-three at-bats. He had been pressing, making a classic mistake of someone who was slumping: He was trying too hard to make up ground too fast, trying to smash the ball instead of trusting his swing and letting that innate talent take care of the results. Behind his back, some of his team-mates called him overrated.

After the loss, Schiffner gathered his players down the right-field line. He told the team it was on the verge of a long, hot, ugly summer. Slow starts were one thing. But the A's had lost six of their last eight games. The team batting average had dropped to .178. With the exception of one inning, they'd just gone eighteen innings *without a single hit*. "I've said I'm not worried about this team," Schiffner began. "I've said we've faced great pitching, that it takes a while to adjust here. I've been saying a lot of things. But you're embarrassing me, you're embarrassing yourselves, and it's time each one of you started to take account. You better think hard about why you're here, and start playing like you belong in this league."

He finished quickly. He usually took his time after these games, hanging with Fincher and the other coaches, chatting with fans, straightening up the dugout. But he grabbed a bag of helmets and left, passing Martha without a word, and walked alone to his car.

FOUR

Legitimate Juice

MAJOR LEAGUE SCOUTS FLOCKED TO Cape Cod with the warming weather. The migration would build over the next month as clubs sent their regional supervisors and national cross-checkers to confirm, contradict, and enhance the assessments of the lower-level scouts who alighted first. Jamie D'Antona appeared not to notice. But every player knew the scouts had come.

The younger scouts stood behind the home-plate backstops in tasseled loafers—slick, tanned, trim, in polo shirts and wraparound sunglasses, cell phones on their hips. They looked busy and important, like Hollywood agents.

The older ones lounged in the bleachers or in lawn chairs. With folded arms and heads tilted back, they quietly assayed the field from beneath their baseball caps. They seemed casual, and if you didn't know better you might suppose they had nothing more urgent to do than take in ball games all summer. Yet the scouts held players' dreams in their hands.

The scouts' power made the Cape Cod League special, and it was for them that the players showed off. Winning was nice—no competitive athlete enjoys losing, and every athlete who'd made it to the Cape was competitive. But players came here, first, to be seen, to impress. Schiffner and most of the other league coaches managed accordingly. College and high school managers typically decided game strategy by the book, playing percentages. They asked batters to sacrifice, to move runners over, lowering their own averages in the process. They pulled tiring pitchers at the first hint of trouble, ordered intentional walks. Schiffner worked by the book only in the late innings of close games. Otherwise he let his big horses run. ("Nobody comes to these games to watch me manage," he said.) His teams played an aggressive, go-for-broke brand of baseball. Baserunners stretched doubles into triples. Catchers snapped off risky throws, just to show their arms. D'Antona brought the mind-set into the batter's box, though not at Schiffner's urging: He swung for the fence every time up. He figured that no team wanted a kid who'd hit for power in college and then tapped singles on the Cape. So far, though, he'd had trouble even making contact. Still, only a handful of scouts had been on hand for D'Antona's poor performance. That would change as the summer grew hotter and more intense.

PULLING HIS MERCURY into South Cape Seafood a few minutes before 7:00 A.M., D'Antona felt the twinge of a pulled hamstring and the seed of a dull ache growing in his lower back. "This is *way* too early in the morning," he groaned to pitcher Aaron Trolia, next to him in the car.

D'Antona had hoped to land a fishing-related job on the Cape. The jobs, though, had been handed out on a first come, first served basis. The Maine players, Williams and MacDonald, got the only fishy work, delivering fresh and frozen catch for South Cape Seafood. The two players had realized after just one morning, though, that throwing around fifty-pound totes of cod and swordfish wouldn't help their baseball any. MacDonald's body—slender, sinewy—looked fragile, especially next to the built-up ballplayers on the team. Williams's shoulder was killing him, even without the heavy lifting. An A's volunteer had made a call to the local CVS, and the store manager had agreed to take on the Maine players for the summer, even though she really didn't have the work.

D'Antona had grabbed one of the vacated South Cape Seafood jobs, and he couldn't have been happier. He liked being around fish, dead or alive, and he enjoyed physical work. He had asked for extra hours, even, to pay off the speeding ticket and the overdrafts. South Cape's owner had extended D'Antona's hours from 7:00 A.M. to 1:00 P.M., a shift that pushed out to 1:30 or 2:00 on most days. D'Antona was putting in an extra day each week, too.

In a small, cluttered office, South Cape's owner, Mark Bulman, had toiled for a couple of hours already, preparing for the day. He nodded to the boys and continued registering the overnight orders that played back from a phone answering machine. Trolia lingered in the office. D'Antona sauntered over to the retail case in the next room. A burly Brazilian fish cutter named Al was laying out the day's specials.

"Ha!" D'Antona boomed. For days the two had kept up a running argument about who'd advance in the World Cup soccer tournament. "I *told* you it would be Germany and Brazil in the final! Ha! I knew it!"

"Yeah. You're a smart college boy," Al said in a thick accent.

D'Antona looked different out of uniform. He dressed like a jock—oversized red T-shirt, long mesh shorts, sneakers—but he wore small round glasses in place of the contact lenses he used on the field. The glasses gave him a boyish, bookish air. Unlike a lot of the players, he didn't wear a baseball cap off the field. He talked fast, with a slight lisp.

"So how'd you guys do last night?" asked Al.

"We lost," D'Antona chirped. He paused awkwardly, not sure if he should say anything more. He turned to join Trolia in Bulman's office. D'Antona made only brief eye contact with people. He had a habit of looking away even before finishing a sentence, his eyes opening wide, giving the impression that he was talking only to himself. "They stuck it up our ass," he said distractedly.

Bulman read part of the day's orders to the two ballplayers: "Moby Dick's in Wellfleet: thirty pounds cod; one bushel steamers; five pounds lobster meat; thirty pound-and-a-quarter lobsters; three sides salmon; twelve pounds razor clams. J.T.'s in Brewster: two gallons shrimp; one gallon oysters; fifteen gallons clams; fifty pounds cod; five pounds sole; ten pounds salmon—"

D'Antona grabbed the order sheet and headed back to the storage rooms. Trolia lagged behind. The two pulled on orange bib rain-pants, heavy waterproof boots, elbow-length rubber gloves. The wet cement floors of the back rooms glistened under the fluorescent light, smelled of fish and bleach. A radio droned "Imus in the Morning" from a high shelf. Chilled air seeped through the rubber strips hanging across the door to the walk-in freezer. Ice-filled plastic tubs, called fish totes, stood loaded with cod, flounder, tuna, swordfish, sole; small mesh bags of littlenecks and cherrystones, fifty-pound bags of scallops. D'Antona got to it. He wheeled a hand-pulled fork-lift and shifted pallets around to get at the day's orders. He shoveled some shaved ice into a fish tote and followed it with a bag of steam-ers, a plastic bag full of cooked lobster meat, large damp fillets of cod. He latched on to the tote with a grappling hook and slid the fish across two rooms to a stainless-steel sorting table. Trolia methodi-cally pulled live pound-and-a-quarter lobsters from a tank and dropped them into plastic bags. D'Antona kept up a banter of com-plaint—about the cold, the ungodly early hour, his pulled ham-string—but he kept moving. Salmon. Razor clams. Shrimp. More ice. His presence filled the space. He should have been careful about the way he lifted, should have used his legs instead of his back, but he whipped the totes around as if they weighed nothing. Trolia, by comparison, acted half asleep.

Occasionally, other South Cape workers wheeled in more fish from the loading dock, the day's catch from what was left of the local Chatham fleet. The hard, scruffy workers had started out consider-ing D'Antona a pretty boy—a *baseball* player. But his strength was obvious. And they couldn't fault his attitude. Bulman said he was the hardest-working player he'd ever hired.

D'Antona worked more hours than any other Chatham ballplayer. After his South Cape job he usually dropped off Trolia and drove straight to Nick's to pitch in at the grill.

D'Antona and Trolia had the orders batched and the truck loaded by 9:30. Mark Bulman asked as they finished. "How's the leg?"

"Tight as a mother," said D'Antona.

"Okay. I'll get Victor to run to the restaurants today," said Bulman. "No point in pushing that leg. Why don't you take two or three days off from driving? You and Aaron can go through room-by-room here. Hose everything down and buff the floors."

"Fine by me," said D'Antona looking away, reaching for the hose. "I'm not bitter."

A HALF DOZEN scouts showed up early for the five o'clock game in Brewster. The afternoon start allowed them to watch for a couple of hours, then shoot over to Harwich or Orleans for a couple of hours more under the lights. In the Eastern Division of the Cape Cod League, five teams played home games within a six-mile radius. Except for the handful of big showcase tournaments, no other place in the country served up seventy or eighty real prospects so conveniently for a scout.

The pregame batting and infield practices gave scouts many chances to witness things they might not see in any one game—a shortstop might go three or four games without ranging far to his backhand side and throwing from deep in the shortstop hole. An outfielder might wait a week between long throws with a runner on the line. During practice a scout could watch a kid move, sense his mechanics, his body, see him execute something over and over again. The players never forgot the scouts were there. Schiffner drilled the point home in his speeches: Scouts came here not just to watch players perform, he told his players, but to get a sense of character—to see how seriously a kid took infield drills, how he conducted himself in the dugout, how, during games, he reacted to bad umpiring calls or to striking out or blowing a save. Small bits of subjective data joined an accumulating file on each player, and every positive bit helped.

The Brewster Whitecaps played their games on the low-tech field of Cape Cod Tech High School. The field lacked the charm, downtown setting, and lights of Chatham. A steep grassy hill sloped along the first-base side of the playing field. Fans approached the field from above, walking from the parking lot toward a bare plateau with a press box and bleachers that were perched, incongruously from that perspective, above a sharp drop-off.

Wind raked the field. Wind always blew here—the only question was whether high or low. When the wind was low, as it was that day, it snapped the American flag near the press box, whistled over the top of the plateau, and swirled across the diamond toward left field. The wind jerked fly balls, suddenly shifted them, gave outfielders fits.

Wind sculpted Cape Cod summers, here and elsewhere. The prevailing sea breezes were southwesterly only in a general sense: The actual wind directions depended on local idiosyncrasies of land and water. On the west-facing beaches of Buzzards Bay, local and prevailing patterns piled up together from the southwest, creating strong, gusty winds. Farther out on the Cape, at Brewster, on the Cape Cod Bay side—the inside of the curved arm—a northeast wind counteracted the southwest breeze, calming the air over Brewster's beaches. A few miles inland, though, above the high school field where the Whitecaps played, windstreams collided, swirled, accelerated.

Fans arriving early at the Brewster field settled down on the hillside in the lee of the wind, some on blankets. A thick stand of hardwoods, its leafy canopy rustling loudly, spread behind the chain-link outfield fence, screening the houses of a recent subdivision. More chain link enclosed community tennis courts beyond right field. The setting had the feel of a rec league, a place for care-free summer ball, a long way from the pros.

The scouts betrayed the idyll. Chatting among themselves at the foot of the slope behind the backstop, they looked bored. This was just another evening among thousands—a temporary assignment before moving back to a home territory, maybe, or evaluating a rival club's minor league system from top to bottom. Three Brewster batters rotated in and out of the batting cage, cracking balls sharply into the outfield, and a few scouts scratched notes onto index cards, notes that might later translate into rearranged names on their teams' prospect lists.

The completed scouting reports would eventually contain personal observations, hard statistics, and numerical grades of a player's "tools." Scouts rated position players in five fundamental categories: field, hit, run, throw, and hit with power. Of the five, the last three tools were considered "natural"—a player could be taught to turn a double play or hit a ball to the opposite field, but no coach could teach a slow kid to run fast, or coax a weak arm into becoming strong, or compel a hitter to hit a baseball a very long way. A player either had those abilities or he didn't, and anyone who had at least two of them was a prospect, no matter how he performed during games. A player's size alone could make or break him. In recent years, as athletes in the major leagues had become bigger and stronger, the conventional scouting wisdom had unofficially established six feet as a minimum for serious prospects. Eighteen of the twenty-three players in the A's' dugout stood six feet or better.

John Schiffner had been around long enough to accept those black truths. He had mentioned to Fincher one night that every player on this year's team had a shot at being drafted—with the exception of Blake Hanan, who stood five foot eight. To anyone who had watched Hanan play back in upstate New York, the comment would have said volumes about the brutal competition of professional baseball. Every good college in the land had a Hanan: a virtuosic player whose spark lit up the field but whose short stature, or slow foot speed, barred him from going on. As the sieve got finer, shrinking differences in inches and fractions of seconds separated out the cream.

No other profession had as wide a recruitment base and as narrow an entry point. Hanan had already emerged from three million kids playing in organized Little Leagues. By the year 2000 he was one of 115,000 boys who had survived competitive play all the way through senior year in high school. He'd become one of the two out of fifty who had gone on from high school to play baseball at an NCAA college. A year into the future, after his junior spring, he hoped to be among the 800 college players who'd be drafted to play professionally. (He'd have one more shot after that, at the end of his senior year.) In the minors, if he made it that far, he'd join 5,000 players, including hundreds from Latin America and the Caribbean, competing for the ultimate prize: one of just 750 spots on major league rosters.

Hanan didn't worry himself with the ultimate long shot. Since junior high, he'd looked only at the level just above him and had seen that he was still good enough to play there. He'd proved it again and again. He wasn't just any college player, he was a *Cape Cod League* player, one of the chosen. One of every three major league players who had played in college had played Cape ball. *Against all odds...* Hanan had played against lesser players who had been drafted. He knew he could play with them, at the single-A level, even double-A. Didn't people compare the caliber of the Cape League to double-A? *Against all odds...* If he worked hard and turned heads here on the Cape, played solid defense, did all the little things right, helped his team win, he didn't see why he couldn't move all the way up, a level at a time.

In the game at Bourne early in the season, Hanan had shown what kind of player he had been on every team he'd played for. He lined a crisp single to left, one of the team's three hits that day. He moved a runner over with a deft sacrifice bunt. Late in the game he hustled backing up an overthrow at first and threw out the Bourne runner trying to stretch his luck to second. He bounced around, took charge. Even playing second base—he had always played short-stop—his body moved smartly.

To casual fans Hanan looked quick. Over the winter, after several months of working with a private running coach, Hanan had run the sixty-yard dash in 6.65 seconds, a very good time. But the iliotibial band on the outside of his left knee had tightened, and—though he didn't know it yet—he'd partially torn the lateral meniscus in the same knee. The injuries hadn't stopped him from playing, but he'd lost a couple of steps off his top speed back at Siena, where he'd stolen forty-three bases over the past two seasons. In the unforgiving climate of the Cape Cod Baseball League, Schiffner knew what a few tenths of a second meant over the ninety feet between home and first base. The rules and distances in the game of baseball had been so delicately arranged that a nearly ideal balance existed between offense and defense. The perfectly proportioned diamond, with fences at the limit of human excellence, with the sixty feet, six inches between pitcher and batter creating the same fair contest generation after generation, was one of the subconscious attractions of the game. The high number of close, "bang-bang" plays at first base was but one example of the balance. A guy who could get down the line in 4 seconds flat would outproduce someone making it in 4.3 by one hit in twenty at-bats—that single hit distinguishing a mediocre .250 hitter from a star .300 one. Among major league regulars, the difference between hitting .275 and .300 was one hit every two weeks. The cumulative effect of running speed over the course of a long season was huge. In many organizations it was the most highly regarded tool.

Schiffner didn't know about Hanan's hurting knee. Privately he called Hanan "the slowest small guy" he'd seen on the Cape, and had come to believe that Hanan was probably overmatched in this league. A standout game, like the one against Bourne, would happen occasionally to any player, simply because statistics guaranteed one every twenty or thirty games.

The hard reality was this: Scouts didn't look at just the next level up. They measured players not against peers, but against the average major leaguer. They earned their salaries by projecting potential three and four years out; they scouted prospects, not players. They placed a higher value on bodies that would likely grow even bigger and stronger, whose raw talents would only improve with instruction and practice. With overachievers like Blake Hanan, scouts couldn't project any improvement. Hanan had an average major league arm; that was a tool. Without speed, he was a one-tool player. Few scouts would bet on a one-tool college player who—they already knew—

would get caught in the strainer at single- or double-A. Even if that one tool were excellent. As one of the Florida Marlins scouts said, there was no worse feeling than to see a minor leaguer with skills but few tools struggle to keep up with the increasing speed of the game.

BEFORE THE GAME in Brewster Jamie D'Antona showed why he was a genuine multitool prospect. The batting practice, like batting practices everywhere, had a comforting, natural rhythm. Batters dropped in and out of the cage and perfunctorily angled bunts down each baseline, then sprayed line drives into the gaps. Flyballs drifted to the warning track, and occasionally disappeared beyond the out-field fence. Hitters worked on flaws, put themselves in game situations, adjusted their swings for specific purposes—subtleties lost in the clockwork drills. It was easy for them to do their work against batting-practice pitchers, typically coaches or ex-players throwing fat pitches at three-quarter speed right over the middle of the plate. Batting practice washed over early-arriving fans like the soft noise of gentle surf. D'Antona shattered the rhythm, made people look up from conversations. His hits rang out, reverberated through long arcs of air. He hit baseballs up into the windstream, piercing the leafy canopy halfway up the trees beyond left field, long towering drives to center and right-center. He hit homers on three, four, five consecutive swings. Even casual observers could sense a different order of fury in the contact he made.

Only one other player on the A's, catcher Colt Morton, hit with the same explosiveness. Morton had grown up in Florida, a state patched with more baseball fields per square mile than any other. He'd played at a small Christian high school, away from the main action. Yet he'd been drafted in his senior year by the Tampa Bay Devil Rays and recruited by powerhouse college programs, eventually settling on North Carolina State. He had great height and long arms that eas-ily extended against the slow pitches of batting practice. In the terms of physics, he had a long lever, and his swing generated extraordinary energy. Morton didn't cock his bat by moving his hands back. He kept his hands quiet as he moved into his swing and so he had to start his swing early in order to generate power. In the terms of scouting reports, he had "plus-power" but a "long swing," a weakness that would amplify against better, faster pitching. He had trouble recognizing and hitting off-speed pitches, especially curve balls. In his first two years at N.C. State Morton had hit a respectable twenty-five home runs, but had just a .260 average and had struck out 122 times. His problems making contact had intensified here on the Cape. He was missing pitches by such wide margins that Schiffner had quipped, "Colt will hit a breaking ball only if it happens to find his bat."

It was natural for a player like Blake Hanan to watch Morton struggle and wonder how *The Scouting Report* had pegged Morton as the number seventy-one college prospect in the baseball draft class of 2003. (Thanks to the Internet, prospects could track their stock through a variety of sources. *Baseball America*, for one, published updates of the highest-ranking draft-eligible players, beginning with high school seniors. Once a year it rated the top handful of prospects in the country by age, starting with twelve-year-olds.) But Colt Morton had a major league body and two other major league tools in addition to power: excellent defensive skills and a rifle of a throwing arm. He could be taught to hit a curveball. Blake Hanan could spend years lifting weights and practicing his heart out, and he'd never hit balls into the trees behind the left-field fence in Brewster. Morton followed D'Antona in batting practice and did just that, over and over, with seeming ease.

IN THE TOP of the second inning, with the stiff breeze still blowing out to left and clouds thickening in the east, Colt Morton led off against Brewster's right-hander Bobby Sawicki. Morton had been tired after his morning's work at the youth clinic in Chatham and had grabbed a couple of hours of sleep before the game. He looked confident at the plate, relaxed and strong. Sawicki tried to throw a fastball by him, and Morton turned on it and lined a bullet to left field for a single. D'Antona followed and quickly fell behind in the count, one ball and two strikes. The scouts in back of home plate checked their radar guns, jotted notes. D'Antona stepped out of the box. He had tightly bandaged his hamstring. He wore a plastic shin guard on his left leg, protecting an ugly blue-black welt against another foul ball. He ignored the distractions, inched his hands up from the bottom of the handle to add a little control. He wasn't swinging for a home run with the count against him. Sawicki had averaged better than a strikeout per inning at Southwest Texas State. D'Antona fouled off a nasty slider, then another, then fought off a tough inside fastball. He grew more confident with each pitch. He'd drawn a walk and had two hits at Yarmouth-Dennis the day before, including his first home run since the one that opened the season. The past few games he had dreaded batting—a weird, disorienting feeling for him. But suddenly, he couldn't wait to hit again. Sawicki left a fastball out over the plate, and D'Antona stroked it up the middle for a single.

In the third inning, with the A's leading 3–0, Colt Morton hammered a hanging curveball high and deep to left field. Normally a ball hit that high was called a major league fly ball—the swing just under the ball by a fraction of an inch, most of the power put into the ball's upward flight. But Morton's ball kept going, and going, and finally fluttered down through the tops of the tall trees way beyond the left-field fence. Its flight was unbelievable. Fans behind home plate gasped at the unnatural trajectory; even the scouts smiled, involuntarily shook their heads. Watching from the on-deck circle, D'Antona knew the ball was gone in an instant. He laughed about it later in the dugout. "I wasn't watching the ball," he said to the teammates around him. "I was watching *him*." He pantomimed Morton's long swing, pretended to stand for a moment admiring the blast, then slowly walked toward first, still watching. "I hit that a *fucking* long way," he said, and everybody laughed. (A second later, infielder Michael Moon ribbed D'Antona. "Oh, now that you're hitting you've decided to start talking again?" And again everybody laughed.)

D'Antona's joking seemed to restore the natural balance to the dugout.

Just after crossing the plate Morton took off his helmet, dropped to one knee, and bowed his head. The prayer delayed his gathering teammates' congratulations. He'd made the same prayer after scoring a run in a game at home against Wareham. Some of the Gatemen had taken offense. They thought Morton was showing them up, and jeered him from the dugout. In the stands here, an older man mused, "There's a lot of 'me' in that religion." A younger woman said she thought he was cute. But the A's hardly noticed. The players all liked and respected Morton, who didn't preach or judge. He showed his faith in subtle ways—scratching the form of a cross in the dirt behind home plate before each inning, penning a small cross next to his autograph. He and a couple of teammates went to a local Baptist church on Sunday mornings. But Morton was easy being himself in a subculture where conformity was prized. He was a Christian, and he liked to drive fast and listen to loud music. At home in Florida he cruised wildly on a jet ski, water-skied aggressively. And he played the game hard. He guarded the area around the catcher's box with ferocity. He was equally protective of his mother, a young-looking blonde with a deep tan and the body of a dancer-turned-professional-trainer. She had spent a couple of days in Chatham after driving up from North Carolina with her son, and Morton said to his teammates, "If any of you says one word about my mother, I'll deck you."

D'Antona stood in and crushed a Sawicki fastball into the trees, almost exactly following Morton's trajectory. D'Antona had hit the ball even harder. Schiffner jumped up out of the dugout and shouted, "This is more like it!"

In the top of the fifth inning, with a 6–0 lead and the clouds darkening the sky, a pitch crunched into Morton's ribs. He tossed the bat casually toward the dugout and trotted, erectly, to first. D'Antona took two pitches for balls, watching them all the way into the catcher's mitt. He looked menacing, something more than confident. You could almost sense the electricity of a hitter who was hot. It was a great thing to feel. And D'Antona felt it. He lashed at the next one, launching a monstrous drive over left field for another home run, his third in six at-bats.

The scouts noticed. They saw not only D'Antona's power, obvious even without the helping wind, but his opposite-field power. He was so strong he didn't need a swing's full arc to hit a baseball 400 feet. They saw a bat that cocked and waited and waited and waited then flashed through the strike zone. They wrote "good bat speed" and "above average bat speed" and "plus bat speed" on their report cards. This critical skill, difficult to teach, separated out the prospects advancing against higher and higher levels of pitching. Bat speed was the v in the kinetic energy equation: ke = $\frac{1}{2}$ mv^2. The mass of the bat mattered, but its velocity was exponentially more important.

"Hitting with power" was a strong enough tool to merit its own category. It was a tool crucial for corner infielders and corner outfielders especially—positions where speed and defense mattered less. D'Antona had what the scouts called "plus power," or "plus-plus power"—better, already, than the average major leaguer. Some scouts who needed more language to distinguish power like D'Antona's called it "light-tower power."

The scouts paid attention, also, to the fact that D'Antona's power showed with a wooden bat. A lot of strong college hitters fizzled fast in the minors, mysteriously losing their power.

Moving from metal bats to wood bats, the physics of collisions worked in the other direction. Struck at most points along its length, a wooden baseball bat flexes and vibrates like a guitar string, creating waves far too fast for the eye to see. Anyone who has ever hit with a wooden bat, though, has felt the stinging hands that result. But one spot on the bat's barrel, near the bat's "center of percussion," is a "node." That so-called sweet spot transfers maximum force to the incoming ball but no vibrations to the handle. In the thousandth of a second that the ball and bat touch, the sweet spot almost completely flattens the ball, and the ball's subsequent decompression, like a spring releasing, sends it flying back the other way. A baseball hitting the sweet spot is like a heavy rubber ball hitting the fulcrum of a see-saw. Only at that point does the rubber ball bounce back. If it hits on either side of the fulcrum the energy dissipates, causing the seesaw to vibrate, deadening the bounce. That's why, with a wooden bat, only balls struck on the sweet spot result in long hits or home runs.

But a hollow aluminum bat transfers energy to a pitched ball more efficiently over a greater area of its surface than does wood—result-ing in less vibration, fewer stinging hands, and many more solidly hit balls. A so-so hitter, fooled by a sharply breaking slider, won't luck into a double hit off the handle of a wooden bat. If he connects a fraction of a second late he won't muscle a home run to the opposite field.

Perhaps even more important, while wood bats compress little on impact, the surface of an aluminum bat folds and then straightens during a collision, in effect catapulting the ball back into play. This "trampoline effect" supplies the extra power of today's metal bats—and of today's college power hitters. Engineers estimate the "achiev-able hit distance" with a metal bat at, amazingly, 160 feet farther than with wood. In other words, a 400-foot home run in college ends up a 300-foot out in the minors. D'Antona's second home run of the day carried more than 430 feet, off a wooden bat.

Tim Stauffer, meanwhile, was shutting down the Brewster hit-ters. He gave the scouts behind home plate everything they'd come to see. They lifted their radar guns in lockstep on each pitch and cap-tured Stauffer's fastball at ninety-two miles an hour, four or five miles above the major league average. Local boys shyly peered over the scouts' shoulders, glimpsing the radar results, major league baseball so close that they could almost touch it.

In the second inning, two scratch hits landed runners on first and second with no outs. Suddenly Stauffer's fastball hit ninety-three and ninety-four. A couple of the scouts glanced at each other—a good trait, a pitcher who reached back for more when needed. Stauffer froze one batter on a hard inside curve for a third strike. He got out of the inning without another hit leaving the infield. His fastball ran down and in to right-handed hitters. It had the barely teachable quality of movement, the sign of a live arm. He added the advantage of deception: Stauffer threw loose and easy, from an old-fashioned windup that started by bringing both hands over his head. (The modern trend favored a shorter, fewer-moving-parts motion.) He kept his head absolutely still throughout his windup, a tip-off that a pitcher was "staying within himself," not flinging the ball with maximum effort even as the radar guns lit up.

In the old days, scouts would have described Stauffer's pitches in words. *Throws smoke with a sinking tail. Can really bring it. Sneaky quick.* Some room still remained for commentary in today's scouting reports, but the profession had become increasingly bureaucratic. The idea of grading potential dated back more than seventy years to Branch Rickey, a baseball innovator best known for hiring the major league's first black ballplayer, but who also was the first to quantify and systemize the recruitment of talent. But if Rickey added science and order to the traditional gut instincts of the scouting establishment, a more recent trend toward statistically evaluating prospects threatened to do away with the establishment altogether. Small-market teams such as the Oakland Athletics proved they could succeed by using sophisticated computer modeling, which shed new light on what most influenced the currency of the game—the creation of runs. Surprisingly, according to the computer models, it wasn't batting averages or runs batted in, but less-valued skills like drawing walks and working pitchers into deep counts. Also according to sabermetrics (the name given to the new science) a player's past statistical performance—not his physical tools—was the single best indicator of future performance. Projecting a player's future by merely observing him was far too risky and far too often wrong. Oakland wouldn't flag players as "bad-body" players or as too slow—as long as they kept hitting the ball and getting on base. A lot of brainy, statistics-savvy people had infiltrated front offices in the last few years. Armed with formulas and data they could get over the Internet, some of them believed that scouting in person was no longer even necessary.

Still, in a stubborn, tradition-bound sport, the wide majority of clubs still looked for the time-honored traits in their prospects. The modern scouting reports, though, standardized for computers, forced their creators to speak the same language across an organization, like academics bound to a university's grading system. Indeed, since 1974, in order to cut costs major league clubs had pooled resources, forming a centralized scouting bureau that generated reports for all major league teams. The rationales included efficiency and leveling the disparity between rich and poor clubs. Before 1974, rich teams spent more money on scouting and held a continual advantage in identifying the sport's best prospects. The bureau's uniform reports created a minimum standard, a breadth of information, available to all teams. (The richer teams still funded their own in-depth scouting and hung on to at least a thin edge.) Two hundred fifty full-time scouts had lost their jobs in the process.

The new Major League Scouting Bureau weakened a style of scouting that was already fading. Nine years earlier, in 1965, Major League Baseball had landed the first blow to the traditional scouts, holding its first amateur draft to try to reverse or slow down the signing bonuses that had risen so high in the freewheeling free-market system long in place. In the short run, bonuses did fall, but the true impact on scouting was more subtle and far-reaching. Before the draft, a scout's dual mission had been to find and sign ballplayers. Worn shoe leather, secrecy, and salesmanship marked the successful scouts. They competed. They held their cards close, and spent a long time courting players and their families to coax signatures. With the draft in place, the odds grew long that a scout's team would get to pick a player the scout had cultivated. The scout's new mission, increasingly, involved advising teams but not making any decisions. Old-era scouts had to sell organizations to the players. In the draft era, scouts had to sell the player to the organization—and hope that by draft day the scouting director and general manager were persuaded to put that player high on the club's wish list.

Scouts didn't receive a commission on players drafted. (Salaries for area scouts started around thirty grand.) Their success had a lot to do with luck. Gone were the days of discovering an unknown talent. A good scout today might see some small, important thing that had eluded all other eyes watching the prospect. But he was judged on how many of his reports proved to be accurate. Ultimately, a successful scout still guessed right only a small percentage of the time. Fewer than one in ten drafted prospects became regular players in the majors.

In Brewster, scouts from the Yankees, Red Sox, Indians, and Angels sat alongside one from the Major League Scouting Bureau. George Biron of the Angels used a combination of numbers and letters to rate Tim Stauffer. Biron, in his forties, with tanned, playboy good looks and wraparound sunglasses, was scouting for his fourth organization in twenty-five years. He liked seeing size in a prospect. Biron stood exactly six feet tall. He could check the accuracy of a listed height by looking a player directly in the eye.

He used Anaheim's A-H grading system. "A" stood for the rare player who was virtually a lock to make the majors. "G" and "H" were the long shots, or "organizational players," who filled out minor league rosters. Every minor league team needed a minimum number of players to operate. With minuscule signing bonuses and small monthly salaries, the second-tier minor leaguers cost the big-league clubs little to carry. Those players would have to shine especially brightly, over several seasons, to enjoy the attention and nurturing granted the front-line prospects.

Biron also graded tools on the bureau's standard forty-eighty scale, with forty the minimum grade for a major league prospect, sixty the major league average, and eighty Hall of Fame big league talent. Anything above sixty was considered "plus," and Biron had Stauffer down for three "plus" pitches: a ninety-one to ninety-three fastball with movement, a plus "twelve-to-six" curveball (it broke straight downward, like clock hands at six o'clock), and a plus changeup. He had Stauffer down at seventy for an overall score—a definite first-rounder. Biron liked the twelve-mile-per-hour differential between Stauffer's fastball and breaking pitches. He gave Stauffer a top grade for control and command. He jotted "backs off players" in a comment section of his index card. To be successful, major league pitchers had to dare to pitch over the inside part of the plate, not stay on the outside corner, where mistakes were more forgiving. Inside pitches—which could be met with the full arc and energy of a batter's swing—skirted dangerously close to a hitter's strength. Stauffer threw inside fearlessly.

He seemed to be pitching according to a different standard. In the third inning he walked Anthony Gwynn, the son of Hall of Famer Tony Gwynn. The younger Gwynn had spoiled four pitches in a row after working the count to three balls and two strikes. Stauffer fooled him on the next pitch, a fastball that stood Gwynn up as it crossed near the inside corner of the plate. The umpire called it a ball, but it impressed the scouts. Stauffer showed no emotion, went right on with his work. He rarely changed expression at an umpire's call or a teammate's error. But you could almost hear him talking to himself, reminding himself, pushing himself as he flirted with and fell short of perfection. In the fourth inning he got ahead in the count no balls and two strikes, then grunted angrily after putting his third pitch too close to the middle part of the plate. The batter barely fouled it off, but Stauffer clenched his jaw. He'd made a mistake that perhaps only he understood, with a pitch that would have pleased most college pitchers.

In the fifth, with an 8–0 lead, his fastball registered in the low nineties, touching ninety-four. He worked methodically, efficiently, the only uncertainty being the black clouds that threatened to wash his performance from the books.

IN THE SIXTH the game became official—the minimum number of innings had been played—and Colt Morton smashed a double into the right-center field gap. He was hot, too. D'Antona stroked a single to left field, his fourth hit of the game. Two innings later Morton delivered his own fourth hit, a bomb to left-center for another home run. D'Antona followed with a long drive that fell just short of the center-field fence in the deepest quadrant of the ball field. Between them the two sluggers had eight hits and four home runs, scored eight runs, and drove in seven. It might as well have been batting practice.

The dark clouds lightened, thinned. The wind quieted. The rain never came. Stauffer finished his work after six innings. He'd given up only three hits and no runs. Chatham won 12–2.

The scouts dutifully concluded their grading. George Biron packed his cards away and drove back to the Marriott Courtyard in Hyannis. At the hotel later that night he'd file his reports with the main office in Anaheim, via laptop computer. He had just a couple of more days on the Cape. Other, higher-level Angel scouts would arrive in his wake. Biron hadn't used numbers to describe what excited him about Jamie D'Antona. Biron saw a rare, violent quality in D'Antona's bat, one that couldn't be taught. He called it "legitimate juice."

The players lingered after the game, in the moment. Two local reporters interviewed Morton and D'Antona. A pack of kids fanned out among the A's with balls and ballpoint pens. Stauffer finished icing his shoulder and ran his laps along the outfield fence with the day's other pitchers. They had waited many games for this victory. It had all finally come together.

D'Antona lingered longer than the others. As the last players and fans trudged up the bank to the parking lot, D'Antona grabbed a seat on the dugout bench, faced the field alone, and stripped off his uniform pants. He gingerly unrolled the bandage that had wrapped his left hamstring. He'd played flawless defense at third. He'd raised his batting average 120 points in the past two days. He had taken the league lead in home runs and slugging percentage, and was about to be named the Cape Cod Baseball League player of the week. *Now THAT was fun*, he thought.

He had entered what athletes call "the zone," a feeling of intense focus and clarity that came on suddenly and unpredictably. D'Antona rode the feeling, not cocky or smug, but buoyed. He had no way of knowing how long he'd stay hot—hitters could stay in the zone for a game, or a string of games, or a month. And then they could lose it just as quickly and mysteriously. D'Antona knew only that for two weeks pitches had been bursting in on him quicker than in real time. Now, finally, they'd begun to slow down.

FIVE

One, Two, Three, Disgusting!

O N THE TWENTY-NINTH OF JUNE the A's record stood at
.500—six wins, six losses, and a tie. They were only a game out
of first place in the crowded standings of the Cape League's Eastern
Division. Chatham, suddenly, seemed like a different team than the
one Cotuit had embarrassed a few days earlier. John Schiffner told
his players he was proud of the character they'd shown, proud that
they hadn't rolled over after the no-hitter.

The victory against Brewster had been Schiffner's 208th in the
Cape Cod League, putting him fifth among Cape League coaches in
career wins. Besides seeing his former players make the majors,
those wins meant more to him than almost any other achievement in
his professional life—more than the high school coaching awards,
more than his teaching, more than the success he'd had as a player.

His high school teams had also won a lot of games and given him
something of a name in Connecticut. He could have said that teaching and coaching high school baseball were his day jobs, his career,
and they made a worthy life. The American Baseball Coaches Association had recently crowned Schiffner High School Coach of the
Year in the Northeast.

But his heart beat with the Cape Cod League. He had come into
the league as a player in 1974, "back near the beginning," he'd say,
less than a decade after the NCAA had gotten involved. In the best
of his three summers playing third base in Harwich, Schiffner had

hit .240 and was named an alternate to the all-star team. He had a flat, line-drive swing, a strong arm, and a good glove, and he'd subsequently been drafted by the Pittsburgh Pirates. But Cape ball—especially his first season when he'd waltzed into the league from Providence College and hit a buck seventy-four—had handed him a rude reality check. "That was when I knew I'd probably need a plan B," he said. He was what baseball people called "a 'tweener." He was too slow to play second or shortstop at the highest level, but didn't hit with enough power to make it at first or third. He washed out of the pros after a year and a half. He'd scouted for the Montreal Expos for a time after that—scouted here on the Cape, in fact. He'd jumped at a better-paying, secure teaching job at a high school in eastern Connecticut, 120 miles west of Chatham. He'd been there ever since.

In 1978, Eddie Lyons, who won 331 games over fourteen seasons as a coach in the Cape Cod League, took on Schiffner as an assistant and understudy in Chatham. Schiffner emulated the older man's style and approach, shared with him a dislike of umpires and bureaucracy. He looked up to Lyons as a legend and a father. In January of 2001, at a major-league-star-filled ceremony at the Chatham Bars Inn, Schiffner had presented Lyons as one of twelve inaugural members of the league's hall of fame. The moment was the culmination of Lyons's career. "This is my Cooperstown," he said. Both men had wept.

Schiffner was still relatively young. He planned to remain with the A's. There was a real chance that he would pass Lyons and the others ahead of him and become the winningest coach ever in the league. Schiffner appreciated the mystique and history of the Cape Cod League, though, not just the wins. He savored the idea of joining that legendary company. And his success vindicated him, gave his life's story a positive spin. It indirectly proved he had what it would have taken to be a Division I college coach, something he had desperately wanted, though not desperately enough to risk a well-paid teaching job in order to get it. He had, likewise, turned down chances to coach and scout in professional baseball. He had passed on the early offers, he said, because his first wife refused to share a life that involved his spending so much time away from home. But he'd turned down the last one—a full-time, unusually lucrative $50,000-a-year position scouting the Pacific Northwest and British Columbia—because he didn't think Martha would be happy so far from her family on the Cape. The calls had tapered off over time, and eventually had stopped altogether. Security came with hidden costs.

Schiffner worked year-round for the A's for a stipend of $5,000. He respected the dedication of the volunteers who ran the bigger show and raised the money. He respected the fairness of an organization that paid him an extra three grand toward his mortgage each summer, because that's what they would have chipped in for a summer rental had he not had his own house. He enjoyed the status around town that his coaching brought him. He liked having locals come up and buy him a drink at the 400 East Club, liked being treated like a big wheel at Pate's Restaurant and Chatham Hardware. In the movie *Summer Catch*, the actor Brian Dennehy played *him*, John Schiffner. Unlike the other Cape coaches, who used the league as a springboard for promotion, Schiffner didn't come for the short term; nor did he disappear into another life after the season. He lived in Chatham all summer and on weekends year-round. His wife, Martha, a local girl, called Schiffner "the mayor of Chatham." He kept his powerboat, the *Summer Catch*, moored in Stage Harbor.

Coaching in the Cape Cod Baseball League placed Schiffner on a national stage. His work here touched history, touched celebrity, touched the big time. College coaches around the country wooed him. Major league scouts talked to him off the record. Major league players left tickets in John Schiffner's name at Fenway Park in Boston. Being a somebody was hard enough to achieve in any realm—theater, politics, academics, business. Schiffner's stature in the Cape Cod league made him a somebody.

He didn't feel the pressure to win that many of the other Cape League coaches felt. He wasn't building his résumé. He had passed the stage where a losing season would blow his chance of being asked back the following summer. He'd been through that fire.

His appointment in 1993 had been one of those internally ugly affairs that rarely make it to the public eye. Doubters within the Chatham Athletic Association had criticized his application for the head job. Some on the committee didn't think a high school coach could have the contacts or authority to succeed. He wasn't a college coach, and the Cape was a big-time college league. Over the previous few years he'd put his hat in for ten other openings around the league, and had been rejected for the same reason. But he'd impressed a lot of the A's' volunteers during his years as assistant coach, and in the end the A's took a shot on him.

In his first full season as head coach Schiffner's A's lost twelve one-run games. He finished fourth out of five teams in the division. He survived a no-confidence vote, but only barely. Charlie Thoms had stood up and defended the roster Schiffner had first put together, before Team USA had lured away three of Schiffner's recruits. Schiffner could identify talent. An injury had swiped another of his expected starters. Time proved Thoms right: Eight players from that year's original roster made it to the majors, including Jacques Jones, Geoff Jenkins, and Mike Lowell. ("If my '94 team had shown up," said Schiffner years later, "it might have been the best Cape team ever assembled.") Schiffner won the Eastern Division title in '95. He won the Cape League championship the following year. His job security was never in question after that. In 1999 his team won thirty games and he was named the Cape Cod League coach of the year. Of all the awards and plaques and trophies he'd earned over the years in various levels of organized baseball, the clock he received for that honor was the only one he displayed in his home.

Winning mattered to Schiffner, and he knew it also mattered to the volunteers of the Chatham Athletic Association. But beyond that, Schiffner understood that his main job was to nurture players. He seldom taught approaches that conflicted with what a kid's coach taught back at school. He respected the primary relationship between a player and his college coach. He didn't always put his best team on the field; he gave all his players a chance to show what they could do. He never sat any kid on the bench for more than two games running. He promised to give all of his pitchers work, but none so much that it wore out an arm. He managed games "major league" style, essentially rolling the ball out on the field and letting his players play. His players were grateful that Schiffner "got it." They liked playing for him.

He said that Cape League championships were won on paper, on the strength of recruiting. "In this league, the best team on the field usually ends up having the most success," he modestly said.

Schiffner, though, wasn't the only good recruiter in the league. Yet every year his team seemed to take one of the four play-off spots. If Schiffner had a genius for something beyond identifying and attracting talent, it was for motivating talent within the constraints of the Cape Cod League. He didn't have the leverage of a school or pro coach, nor could he offer the same incentives.

Players arrived in Chatham drained from a long, intense season chasing a conference or even national championship. They came with mandates to show off, but little incentive to win as a team. Most of them came knowing that the summer was their only break from a year of relentless hard work. Schiffner coached players twenty years old, barely supervised, in a place where beaches and bikinis and the summer-resort nightlife tugged more strongly than any summer league trophy could.

Schiffner understood the subtle lines between fun and seriousness. He'd been a college ballplayer on Cape Cod. He knew how failure could work on a kid. Knew about homesickness, about fatigue. He also knew that college baseball players could smell bullshit a mile away at low tide. He never made winning all-important. But he steadily reminded his players that their success reflected on their schools. That scouts looked at the whole league early in the summer, then narrowed their focus to the top teams. He told them their goal was to make the play-offs, because that's when the games turned special. He promised them they'd never forget playing in front of those play-off crowds. He impressed upon them that they weren't merely Cape Cod Baseball League players, they were *Chatham A's*. He could get away with corny stuff like that because he had the credibility. He'd been in the league so long, and he believed it, and he knew to hit the notes lightly.

Schiffner should have been feeling good on the quick drive over to the high school field where Yarmouth-Dennis played its home games. The bare, unadorned field wasn't much to look at, but Schiffner liked playing at all the yards where games started at five, not seven. ("They give me some semblance of a life," he'd say, in one of his cranky moods.) The hot weather was coming. That morning, out beyond the tip of South Island, Schiffner had even landed his first good striper of the season, a thirty-incher.

But the sheet of lined paper he carried in his briefcase troubled him. Schiffner had penciled in thirty-six different names so far for his twenty-three-man roster. The team he sent out on the field at Yarmouth-Dennis looked far different from the one he'd imagined and reimagined. He'd stocked his lineup with All-American, all-conference, and all-league players. It had all the parts of a winning team. But it wasn't a planned menu. It was potluck, a thrown-together feast. It didn't all fit. It had been impossible to replace players and then replace replacements and not lose something in the balance. The team he brought to Yarmouth-Dennis lacked a true center-fielder (the position requiring speed and especially good defense), lacked a true lead-off hitter, lacked an infielder whose range made everybody around him look better.

A day after beating Brewster by ten runs, Chatham got just two hits against Yarmouth-Dennis and lost 6–1. The zone that D'Antona and Colt Morton had found vanished as mysteriously as it had appeared. They had just one hit between them. D'Antona reverted to form in the field, making a couple of spectacular athletic plays but pulling up early on a low-skimming ground ball for an error and later bobbling one of his trademark bare-handers. The game lasted only an hour and fifty minutes. Afterwards, the team huddled down the right-field line. Schiffner said, "If someone can explain this game, can you please explain it to me?" He told his players he wasn't upset with them, that they'd made a couple of mistakes and had simply been beaten by a good pitcher.

Even Schiffner's best teams often started slowly. Every summer the Chatham A's seemed to bump along around .500 until the Fourth of July, then get hot. Matt Fincher had already told the first-year assistants, Bobby Myers and Jon Palmieri, "This team will struggle until the middle of the summer, then Schiff will give a little speech. Just when the guys on other teams are getting ready to call it a summer, this team will catch fire and cruise right into the play-offs. It happens every year. You just watch." The 2002 A's were playing to script.

Back home after the game at Yarmouth-Dennis, Schiffner baked the striped bass and grilled pork ribs on the deck. He complained with his coaches about the team's poor play. He openly wondered about the commitment of Tim Stauffer, whose reserve and preference for running by himself sent a warning signal. "I wouldn't be surprised if Stauffer packs it in early," said Schiffner. "He's proved he can pitch here. I wouldn't be surprised if he gives us a couple more starts, just so more scouts watch him, then heads home and relaxes a little. I wouldn't blame him. I'd be pissed, but I wouldn't blame him."

"Does D'Antona ever *not* back up on a ground ball?" drawled Fincher.

"He's horrible," said Myers. "In Mat-Su last year, in Alaska, I told my guys, 'Just put the ball in D'Antona's hands.'"

"He's hurting himself," said Schiffner. "I don't understand a kid whose goal is to make the major leagues, who's working extra hours at a fish job instead of putting in the time to make himself stronger and better while he's here. He isn't even working out. When does he have time?"

D'Antona was more complex than many of the other players in Schiffner's experience. Schiffner had instantly liked him. The kid was friendly, outgoing, positive. He had boyish enthusiasm for every-thing—"My job is the *best*!" he'd say; "Seeing moose on road trips in Alaska was the *best*!" "You and Martha have a pug? Sweet! Me, too! His name's *Otis*." But he was also immature enough to avoid working on skills he wasn't already good at. He had no interest in lifting at Willy's Gym up in Orleans, where the other A's went. "I'd rather put a hundred bucks into new fishing gear," he said. D'Antona wanted to have fun playing while he still could—he'd start working at it when the game became his job. Schiffner had expected a leader. Instead he got someone who sang out loud with the music in between in-nings, who dealt with failure by joking around. Schiffner had been a fiery player in his day. He couldn't understand the ones who laughed off their mistakes.

THE NEXT NIGHT, in Chatham, in the second inning of a rematch against Yarmouth-Dennis, catcher Chris Iannetta fired a low throw to second base on a stolen base attempt. The simple, routine play un-folded as a matter of course, one of baseball's many rehearsed se-quences that seem tightly choreographed—except no one showed up to catch the ball. Second baseman Michael Moon inexplicably failed to run over to the base, and the throw skipped through to center field. Y-D scored its first run. It was Moon's second such mistake in two days. The lack of concentration infuriated Schiffner, especially with Michael Moon, a likable kid with loads of talent who played in-tensely some days and at other times seemed to be going through the motions. Moon was "pure California" in Paul Galop's words. At the moment, he had dyed his hair blond and was wearing a chinstrap beard, and he looked like a leprechaun. At second base he impro-vised, sometimes bizarrely—flipping the ball backhand to first, spin-ning 360 degrees before throwing. "Have you even seen anybody so *un*-fundamentally sound?" asked Matt Fincher once.

At the end of the inning, Schiffner stomped to the middle of the dugout steps and intercepted Moon and shortstop Chad Orvella. For the first time that season, and in full view of the team, he lost his temper. "I don't care who it was!" he screamed. "One of you *fucking needs to get there!*" Moon started to offer an explanation, and Schiffner cut him off. "I don't want to fucking hear it! Just *get there.* Work it out. Don't let it happen again!" He stomped back to his spot down at the home-plate end of the dugout. His tirade was aimed at Moon, even though he'd included both players in it. It was a small sign of grace and tact even in anger. He'd delivered the message without singling out a player in front of his teammates. He'd left that sliver of room for saving face.

Thomas Pauly entered the game in the fourth inning. The crowds at Veterans Field had swollen with the summer heat; more than two thousand fans watched him throw his warm-up pitches. The morning fog had long since burned off. Above the trees in left, the last warm colors of day drained from the western sky. The bright lights, already on for an inning, extended the illusion of golden twilight.

Pauly had done okay in his first four appearances, at least had put up decent numbers: six innings, two runs, six hits, eight strikeouts. He was holding his own against the best competition he'd ever seen. But he wasn't throwing with the confidence he had at Princeton. At Princeton, when he was in a groove and pitching well, his mind emptied on the mound. He locked in. Here he kept talking to himself. He felt as though he'd been getting away with something.

He gave up an infield hit to his first batter. The second batter, center-fielder Adam Bourassa of Wake Forest, dropped a bunt in front of him. Pauly grabbed the ball, but flicked it hurriedly and wildly past first. Good defensive pitchers occasionally made such errors, but Pauly's awkwardness on the play reinforced the impression that he didn't quite have the makeup of a front-line pitcher. He was angry at himself. But as Jeremy Cleveland returned the ball to him, Pauly hid his anger behind a broad grin, and in doing so he crossed a line.

Baseball players followed unwritten, mostly unexamined protocols for how to act after making mistakes. The opportunity for error hung on every pitch, every swing, every ground ball and pop-up, every throw—and there was no place to hide. The game didn't continue flowing and drawing away the spectators' attention. Teammates didn't cluster together, obscuring the offender. In baseball, a player who's struck out or made an error stands alone, out there under the bright lights, knowing that a hundred or a thousand or tens of thousands of eyes regarded him.

Every player at every level had to learn how to act during those excruciating few seconds before the next pitch swept it away. Ten-year-old kids sometimes cried or threw their gloves down. Young batters let third strikes go past them, knowing full well they were strikes, and swore at the umpire anyway, deflecting blame. As the players progressed up the pyramid, they made fewer mistakes. An error in a major league game startled. It interrupted the expectations, the subconsciously felt rhythm of the game. Professional players made most hard plays look so routine that the average fan stopped realizing how difficult a game baseball really is. (A non-baseball player, dropped into a game, would be shocked—even terrified—by how fast a hard leather ball hurtled along the ground at him, how impossible it felt to judge the trajectory of a spinning ball plummeting from a hundred feet in the air.) As players matured, most moved toward the professional model of stoicism in the face of mistakes—not nonchalance, but rather a get-back-to-work cool, an expression of Schiffner's "not too high, not too low" pro mentality. At advanced levels of the game, teammates, respecting the signs of self-acknowledgment or competitiveness, accepted variations on the model. An infielder who booted a ground ball might pound his fist in his glove once, or swipe at the dirt with his cleats, then quickly appear as if nothing had happened. A pitcher who had given up a home run might turn his head and spit. Scouts on the Cape looked for such signs of maturity. They granted a player a few seconds to react and exorcise the mistake. Then it was time to get back to the task at hand. Scouts, and teammates, didn't want errors to distract or erode the confidence of any player. Too much thinking diminished the intense focus that baseball players needed to play the game in the split seconds of the present.

Pauly was smart enough to know that serious players didn't grin after an error. That was exactly why he grinned. *This isn't that important to me. It doesn't matter if I fail here. I'm not serious about baseball like the rest of you.*

So he grinned, feeling all those eyes on him, and then he went back to pitching. He gave up a hard run–scoring single up the middle, then a solidly hit sacrifice fly to left field by a UCLA All-American freshman, Wes Whisler, and then, with two outs, Pauly threw a fastball over the meat of the plate to Stanford's Chris Carter. Carter drove it over the center-field fence. Inside Pauly's head a voice prattled on. *THAT was brilliant*, he thought. *Why am I even out here?*

The scouts behind the home plate backstop put their radar guns down and chatted. They'd picked up Pauly's fastball at ninety-two miles an hour, as fast as Tim Stauffer's, faster than that of any other pitcher that night. "But they're sittin' on it," said Jim Bretz from the Padres. "It looks like he has no confidence in his curve ball—he's relying too much on one pitch."

"The fastball looks dead to me," said the scout next to him. "No movement. When it's flat, ninety miles per hour is just like batting practice for major leaguers."

In the dugout, with Yarmouth-Dennis suddenly leading 6–0, pitcher Adam Yates stood on the top step and tried to get the guys going. "C'mon, c'mon! We can do it! Let's go!" Yates had been a standout high school quarterback in Tennessee. He'd passed up football offers to pitch for Ole Miss. But he missed his old sport. He missed the way football players got fired up and shouted and pounded each other on the back and left their sweat and blood out there on the field. He missed the raw emotion of a sport where *believing* you would win was sometimes enough to make it happen. Unlike Pauly, he lost himself in the game. He couldn't care less about the image he projected. He had never played on a losing team in his life, and he didn't plan to start that summer.

He was one of the few pitchers who watched the action from the dugout, preferring it to the laid-back chat and fooling around in the bullpen.

"Yeah, right," said Pauly, next to him. "We're down six-nothing."

Yates pushed back, said there was still time.

"Who gives a rat's ass about summer ball, anyway?" said Pauly.

Pauly said if he got two outs with nobody on base he was going to hit someone. Maybe he thought that sounded tough, competitive, what the big-time pitchers might do when they were actually angry about their own poor performance.

"*Why?*" asked Yates.

Pauly didn't answer. He didn't even shrug.

In his second inning Pauly gave up a single, did indeed hit a batter, threw a pitch in the dirt that was scored a passed ball against the catcher, and gave up his fourth run. The hit batter was a mistake, though. The ball had slipped and sailed in too tight, nicking the batter's uniform.

In his third inning, with two outs, no one on, and another run already in, Pauly backed second baseman Steve Sollmann off the plate with an inside pitch and then drilled him in the back with a fastball. Sollmann winced and arched his body. This one was on purpose. The pitch's intent was so blatant, and so out of place, that it stunned the fans. Baseball was a sport in which nothing was precisely predictable, yet its grooves were so well worn that any one of a thousand scenarios seemed predetermined once a play was set in motion. Down 8–0, struggling with control, with no obvious reason for retaliation, pitchers simply didn't drill light-hitting second basemen. Sollmann slammed his bat down and glared—incredulously—at Pauly, then slowly trotted to first, still staring.

Pauly walked the next batter, then gave up a three-run homer to right. His numbers in the Cape Cod League abruptly blew up. In three innings his earned-run average shot from three runs per game to eight. He had lost some of the respect of his teammates. And he had inflicted some deeper hurt upon himself in the process. In his mind, and in the minds of Schiffner and very likely of the scouts, Pauly's performance raised a serious, damning question. Had it been only a matter of time before he'd sunk to this, his true level?

On the mound, the voice in his head was loud. He hadn't expected to give up a home run, not after he'd shown how tough he was by hitting someone. *What are you DOING?* he asked himself. He tugged at his uniform pants, his shirt.

In the dugout, Adam Yates muttered, "Stupid. *Stupid.*"

At Harwich on the first of July, on yet another warm, clear evening, Brad Ziegler shut out the A's again, just as he had earlier in Chatham. The slender right-hander gave up only three hits and struck out eleven. He stretched his string of walkless innings to twenty-one and two thirds, a new league record.

The *Cape Cod Times* noted Ziegler's achievement. The paper covered the Cape Cod League as if the teams were in the majors—the paper carried standings, recaps, and line scores, human-interest features, a regular department, "On This Date in Cape Cod History." The players, though, barely paid attention to their place in local history. Baseball players rarely left the present—their skill came out in the moment, from acting instinctively, and the skill typically reflected the nature of the person. Ballplayers always knew their own statistics, and many had photographic recall of certain at-bats and crucial pitches that endured for years. But the records and history of the Cape Cod League seeped unnoticed around them, adding texture to the landscape like the rustle of marsh grass, like clouds floating across the bay. Newspaper reporters, volunteers, and long-time fans lugged along the institutional memory of the league, not the boys who created it.

One kind of history glowed brightly as an exception, a beacon drawing the Chatham players toward the future. They knew which Cape Leaguers before them had gone on to the majors. (Or most of them did. Thomas Pauly claimed not to know any, or even exactly which teams played in the American League and which in the National. His seeming lack of general baseball knowledge was one of the incomprehensible gaps that he played up, or maybe made up, and that so baffled the others.) A lot of the A's, watching SportsCenter at Charlie's or Nick's, would call out matter-of-factly: "He played for Chatham" or "He was a Cape player" whenever highlight clips showed even relatively little-known players such as Jeremy Giambi or Lou Merloni. Every night they saw somebody different. The night before the Harwich game, Adam Yates, Eric Everson, and Michael Moon sat at a table by the TV in the corner at Nick's. ESPN announced the 2002 major league all-star teams. Eight former Cape Cod League players made the squads, including Mike Lowell of the Marlins, who'd played in Chatham in '94. That was history the A's relished, history that gave hope.

The touch of celebrity lent its aura to even the most mundane aspects of Cape League life. It somehow seemed cool that Baltimore's Jerry Hairston had been "employee of the month" the summer he worked in the Bourne Stop & Shop supermarket; that the future Yankees manager Buck Showalter had flipped eggs at the counter of the old Hyannis News Store; that Frank "The Big Hurt" Thomas had mowed lawns for the town of Brewster the year he won the league home-run hitting contest against seven other future big leaguers, including Jeff Bagwell, Eric Wedge, Chuck Knoblauch, and Mo Vaughn. Thomas had played for the Orleans Cardinals that year. He'd disappointed the Orleans fans by leaving before the play-offs began, to get back to football practice at Auburn, where he'd played with a two-sport phenom named Bo Jackson. In '94, Darin Erstad left Falmouth early to get to Nebraska's football camp. He punted for the Cornhuskers that year, helping them to the national championship, then gone number one in the country in the '95 amateur baseball draft. Those stories were passed down. The players, little as they might pay heed, added their own layer to the league's history. They left their marks on and off the field.

To the current A's, Brad Ziegler had a more personal history. The returning players knew Ziegler from the previous year. He'd pitched in Chatham. Schiffner had hoped to bring him back from Southwest Missouri State for the 2002 season, but Ziegler hadn't turned pro as Schiffner had expected after being drafted, and Schiffner hadn't kept a spot open on his roster. Ziegler had scrambled and hooked on with the Harwich Mariners. The prior summer the *Cape Cod Times* had profiled Ziegler's religious faith and clean living. The reporter had asked Ziegler if he was the only player on the A's who didn't drink or smoke. "Oh, I don't know," Ziegler had answered, incautiously, without even thinking. "Probably."

The reporter had given the quote a sharper edge, implying that Ziegler thought that he alone on the A's was not a drunken idiot. Ziegler felt bad about the quote as soon as he read it. His teammates had been furious—at the accusation, and at his breaking the code of silence players honored about off-field behavior. They'd treated Ziegler roughly after that.

It might have seemed a small trigger to a such a strong reaction, but the players had grown aware of the power and reach of their public images—they weren't just celebrities in training, they were already public figures. Parents read papers. So did host families, employers, coaches, teammates. Character flaws or transgressions out there in public touched feelings of shame, violated privacy, felt like a betrayal. Negative press stirred deep, inarticulate emotion. The easiest reaction for a twenty-year-old baseball player was anger, directed at somebody.

Some of the A's still held a grudge. During Ziegler's first start against the A's in 2002, Zane Carlson had led the jeering from the bullpen. The relief pitchers had taunted Ziegler about his sobriety, his disloyalty, even the signature eye-black he wore on his cheeks to cut the sun's glare. The eye-black was an easy target—it looked out of place on a pitcher, especially at night when there was no sun to worry about. Ziegler had tried it one summer and had pitched beautifully. After that he wore the eye-black every time out, for luck. He'd silenced the A's hitters in Chatham and again in Harwich, silencing the jeers at the same time—by pitching righteously, as though God were indeed on his side.

Schiffner, Charlie Thoms, Paul Galop, and a maybe a few other hard-core fans might remember such details about Ziegler, but only if he made the majors would the stories spread and stick.

At the moment, Schiffner cared mostly about Chatham's history of turning a season around come the Fourth of July. In his postgame comments he told his players to hang on for just a few more days. At home, he said to Martha, "The phone doesn't even ring anymore. You lose a few games and suddenly nobody wants to talk to you."

The scouts were still coming out—they hadn't given up on this team. Not yet. Gutting it out till the Fourth seemed reachable, easier to imagine than struggling through a long summer. The A's had an off day and another game in front of them, but the Fourth loomed above them both as a clear, bright start, almost a new season. It couldn't come fast enough.

SIX

Fourth of July

T HE STAGE WAS GRANDLY SET for a revival. By dawn on July Fourth, rows of colorful folding lawn chairs, white plastic deck chairs, and blankets blocked the sidewalks and covered the lawns fronting Chatham's winding Main Street. American flags hung from store awnings and second-floor balconies. Sunlight filtered through the green leaves of oak trees, the last shimmering cool on a morning thick with heat and anticipation. It was the kind of day that lived in your mind's eye, all those earlier Fourths blurring together into this, so that the day unfolded as though it had already happened.

The ballplayers gathered at nine o'clock, an hour before the parade. They stood in the shade, and some hopped up and sat on the A's' float on Chatham's premier address, Shore Road, just up from the Chatham Bars Inn, across from a waterfront motel called The Hawthorne. The previous year a local boatyard had built a twenty-seven-foot-long baseball bat to dress up the float, calipered to the specs of a Barnstable Bat model M-110, covered with wood-grained contact paper—the whole nine yards. Tom Bednark had burned a big "Barnstable Bat" logo into it. Players had taken turns walking out ahead of the float inside a giant revolving plywood baseball. The plywood contraption had been a disaster. It wobbled and repeatedly strayed off-course. After the parade Charlie Thoms threw it out in back of the A's' equipment shed, down by the left-field corner of Veterans Field, and that's where it stayed. This year's float was simpler:

a flatbed trailer with a long double-sided bench running down its center, covered with a blue tarp that nearly matched the blue of the A's uniforms. The players sat in A's uniform tops and A's caps, legs dangling over the sides of the trailer, trying to stay cool, waiting for the caravan of floats to start rolling. Their flatbed sat fifty-first out of sixty-seven floats, a good half mile back from the start.

Thoms, the ever-present A's general manager, pedaled up on his bicycle. Sweat streamed down his face, drenching his dark blue A's shirt. He'd parked his truck far on the other side of Main Street. He dreaded the traffic after the parade. Every year, he and Schiffner downplayed this whole incredible event. They let the players think they'd be riding along in some hokey, small-town, two-bit parade— until the float turned a corner and they saw forty thousand people going nuts, cheering for them. The returning players talked it up— said it was *unbelievable*—and of course their descriptions sounded exaggerated, so D'Antona, Stauffer, Pauly, and the other newcomers didn't know exactly what to think.

Thoms stood in the shade of the dump truck that trailered the flatbed and killed some of the wait by telling stories of past parades. Like the time the parade committee forgot to reserve a flatbed, and Thoms drove all twenty-three players in and on his Ford F-350 pickup. Twenty guys hung off the back, two sat on the hood, three on the roof. Every time Thoms needed someone to move a leg to clear a view, he turned on the wipers. His truck had taken a beating, the hood dented, the roof caved in. He told the players about '98, when all the floats parked on the outfield grass at Veterans Field, and he'd been pulled away from his postparade barbecue to scare up a couple of loads of loam to fill in the deep ruts before the game that evening. Mike MacDougal and Kevin Mench, two of the players who jumped in to commandeer the loam from a closed-down sand and gravel yard, had made it to the majors. More recent stories spun around the miniature Chatham A's Styrofoam baseballs that players threw into the crowd. Two years ago a juggling unicyclist had called out for a ball from the players' float—and was pelted by a dozen of them. Last year one player had written his phone number on a ball and thrown it to a good-looking girl in the crowd—turned out to be his house-mate's girlfriend. The stories primed the new crop of players, gave them ideas.

A couple of the A's persuaded batboy Andy Troy to dip into this year's stash of balls. The three thousand balls, stuffed into a dozen trash bags, filled the back of the dump truck along with others hold-ing plastic Chatham A's drinking cups and water bottles. "We bring out anything that Paul's having trouble selling at the merchandise tent," Thoms told the players. "One year it was pens. That was a mis-take—I thought we were going to kill someone." Blake Hanan grabbed a few balls and scribbled his name, uniform number, and cell number on them. Scott Hindman wrote "Nukes!" on one, "Thomas Pauly" on another. A few with "Show us your tits!" passed around the float. The morning sun beat down. It glittered on the water out in Pleasant Bay, whitened the sandy strip of North Beach slicing down the middle of all that blue. A couple of players dashed into The Hawthorne, where Colt Morton's parents were staying, to take cold showers in the bathroom.

Finally the caravan lurched forward, then crept haltingly along Shore Road toward the turn onto the eastern end of Main Street. Jamie D'Antona stared at one of the summer homes and its sweep-ing, meticulous grounds. "I'd love to play whiffleball on that lawn," he said. "That would be *sweet!*"

"Hey, Stauffer!" someone at the back of the flatbed yelled. "You could *live* there!"

When the players turned the corner onto Main Street, they real-ized they weren't in Podunk anymore. Pauly and Hindman regarded the throng and whooped. D'Antona said, "Fuck." Folks were packed three-, four-, six-deep along both sides of the road. Lawn chairs crowded yards and driveways. Storekeepers stood in their doorways. Kids held out their hands, yelled up to the players. Moms and dads pleaded for just one ball, for the kid. The players laughed, looked stunned, tossed baseballs left and right. "Slow down!" yelled Andy

Troy. "You'll run out of balls before the end!" Styrofoam balls practically filled the massive bed of the dump truck—running out didn't seem possible, but Andy Troy had been in the parade before.

The sun bore down. In the steamy air, no shimmering cool remained, even in the shade. Spectators gulped water from sweating water bottles, fanned themselves with hats. The players didn't seem to notice. They threw Styrofoam baseballs as if they were quarterbacks checking off primary receivers until finding an open target. They scoped out the crowd for the hottest-looking, most scantily clothed young women. They passed a pickup full of sweating, shirtless men. Hindman grabbed a ball, wrote "Put your shirts on," and threw it into the truck. "Read it!" he yelled. One of the men read it and returned fire, and the A's unloaded on him with a flurry. Daniel Moore scanned for early drinkers and women in low-cut tops on second-floor balconies. He lobbed balls just out of reach, daring them to lean out farther than they should. Jamie D'Antona aired out his arm, whipping balls that started out low over the crowd then rose with wicked backspin into the upper decks. Charlie Thoms told him he might want to cool it, that he was bound to hurt someone—or blow out his arm. At the same moment several A's noticed a sleek woman in a jogging bra, and bombarded her with little white balls. They rained Styrofoam balls on a svelte target walking down Main Street in, bizarrely, an evening gown and spiked heels. "We wore those chicks out," said Hindman afterward. Once in a while a player even tossed a ball to a kid and smiled at him, but for most of the A's, acting like heroes was a lower priority than their own brand of civic courtship. The cheering drifted with them, disappeared in the heat and commotion.

The float rolled around another bend, into the heart of downtown. Yet another sea of waving flags washed over the players. Spectators were now stacked ten and twelve rows deep on both sides of the street—families, partyers, tanned women in big sunglasses, old guys in Bermuda shorts. Horns and noisemakers whistled and clanged. Schoolkids screamed for the A's, raised both arms and gave double thumbs up. Ahead of the A's, other floats added to the noise, the celebration. A fire engine's siren screamed over the low *ahh-ooo-ggaah* of an antique car horn and the notes of fifes and drums, military brass bands. The elaborate floats mixed in with the homespun, the 4-H club and fishermen's wives. This was the Fourth of July in an American town, hot, loud, sweet. Chatham was throwing a party, and everyone had come.

The massive crowd rippled out ahead of the A's float, went on out of sight beyond the next curve. The players finally understood the magnitude of this parade, the team's part in Chatham's summer. They started flipping cups and water bottles to the kids and families, hoarded the balls, threw out fewer and finally ran out of them in front of the Chatham Hardware store, five minutes from the end of the route.

At the western edge of Main Street, nearing the rotary, some distance opened up between the A's float and the four that trailed it. Hundreds of people spilled into the gap, thinking the parade was done. They blocked Main Street from curb to curb, walking behind the A's, and the players saw more people wading in beyond them, and along the sidewalks and lawns and down the slope from the First Congregational Church, so that it felt as if the team were being carried along in a river of red, white, and blue. The stories hadn't prepared them for *this*. At the Mobil station kids screeched and laughed in the cold water of sprinklers propped up on tires. The smell of rubber and hot, wet asphalt mixed with the spray. All-American day. Hot dogs on the grill at Charlie and Ginor's. After that, when the day exhaled and the light turned cooler, there would be a baseball game at Veterans Field against an old rival, the Orleans Cardinals, with Tim Stauffer on the mound. The rest of the season looked like a fairy tale waiting to unfold.

D'Antona, Colt Morton, and a few others hopped off the float and walked ahead to Nick's. D'Antona breezed right in and got a meatball sub going on the grill, using some sage sausage his folks had brought from Connecticut for Mimi and Billy. Morton put a Styrofoam ball on the counter and said to Mimi, "This is for you—I know you couldn't make the parade."

Downtown, the crowd shuffled along in the heat, squeezed into the shade, slowly dispersed. Ice cream cones dripped on the sidewalk. Little kids held Chatham A's baseballs tight in their gloves. Other balls, with players' cell phone numbers on them, rode the wave of spectators. One of the A's was bound to get lucky.

TIM STAUFFER WATCHED some TV and grabbed an hour of sleep in the dark cave of his basement room. He and outfielder Ryan Johnson were staying with a family a town away in Harwich, fifteen minutes' drive from the Chatham ball field. The house was actually closer to the fields in both Harwich and Brewster, but Stauffer didn't mind. He liked chilling out before he pitched. The cool quiet of the basement suited him. His simple, colorless pregame routine focused him. He'd made sure to get a good night's sleep the night before. He'd stopped by Charlie Thoms's barbecue, but hadn't stayed long; he tried to keep out of the sun on the days he was pitching—the heat sapped his energy—and he'd already spent a fair amount of time outside during the parade. He ate a light meal two hours before game time.

Except for the team's losing record, the summer had been everything Stauffer had hoped for. He had taken a chance coming to Chatham. In the middle of his brilliant spring season at Richmond, he had been invited to try out with Team USA, the international traveling team made up of the very best of the best collegians. The thought of representing his country, especially after 9/11, had thrilled him. Team USA would tour California, Ohio, and New England, and play in tournaments in Japan and the Netherlands before competing in August in the world university baseball championships in Messina, Italy.

Schiffner had seen Stauffer's name on the list of invited ballplayers, and asked Oriole scout Jimmy Howard to phone Stauffer's parents. Howard had made the call, spelling out the advantages of playing in the Cape Cod League: a more relaxed travel schedule, more major league scouts, tougher competition. A few nights later, in early April, Schiffner had talked with Stauffer on the phone for more than an hour. Schiffner was fair. He described former Chatham players who, after turning down Team USA offers, had still become high draft picks and major leaguers—but in the end he did say that Tim couldn't make a wrong decision. Team USA was both a spectacular honor and showcase.

While Stauffer pondered his decision, Schiffner went out of his way to attend the Atlantic Ten Conference tournament, sitting in freezing weather in Norwich, Connecticut, with Stauffer's parents. Schiffner's gentle, dogged recruiting might have made a difference—Rick and Becky Stauffer were persuaded. Tim took it upon himself to talk with players who'd earlier faced the decision. He heard, over and over, that Team USA was more prestigious, but that the competition on the Cape was, in fact, a lot better than what Team USA faced. More scouts watched the Cape. The international team's travel schedule was brutal. Stauffer would throw 146 innings that spring at Richmond and travel a ton. He liked the idea of setting his bags down in one place for the summer. At the end of April he turned down Team USA. He came to Chatham still not sure he'd made the right decision.

But he had liked the town at once. Everybody he ran into followed the A's. The place seemed shiny, fresh. As he put it, "Everything had a new-car smell." And the competition was good—he was challenged up and down the opposing lineups, no room for coasting—and he'd pitched well. He found Schiffner laid-back, a good guy to play for. Schiffner had recently insisted that he do all his running with the other pitchers, which was fine. Other than that he'd been left on his own, which was fine, too. He watched the growing number of scouts and sensed their interest in him. A couple of them had talked casually with him; others had asked him to fill out questionnaires or psychological profiles. Agents approached him after games, eagerly offering their services. It hadn't taken long to know he'd made the right call.

The A's emphasized winning less than did the team he'd played for in the New England Collegiate Baseball League. That was okay; he'd been there. Chatham was the difference between a regular-season team and an all-star team—except that on Cape Cod the all-star teams played a forty-four-game schedule.

He relaxed in the cool darkness of his basement room, the day sweltering outside him. The A's may have been in last place, but Tim Stauffer was where he wanted to be.

By seven o'clock the temperature had fallen into the low eighties. Red, white, and blue bunting draped the length of the outfield fence. The evening sky, its cottony clouds edged in pink, glowed with the timeless, feel-good sense of a Maxfield Parrish painting. In the sultry air, a thousand people sat on the metal bleachers behind home plate, and more kept coming, filling the sidelines and the surrounding grassy embankments with lawn chairs and picnic blankets: fifteen hundred, two thousand, twenty-five hundred people. Adolescent girls and good-looking families and genial retirees in faded polo shirts and rumpled cotton hats, well-heeled women in sandals and hats with floppy brims. Young kids filled the playground out past the right-field foul line, their parents and nannies keeping one eye on them, the other on the players out on the field. Teenagers shuffled in packs along the outskirts of the crowd behind the row of hawthornes that ran along the top section of bleachers and which gave the park part of its charm. Host families looked on with parental pride. Tim's mother, Becky Stauffer, stood atop the rise behind home plate, next to the Oriole scout, Jimmy Howard, too nervous to sit. Joe and Karin D'Antona, worried about their son's disappointing season, sat in the bleachers not far away.

Some of the older fans looked out and recalled Fourth of Julys past, recalled Charlie Hough and Thurman Munson back in the sixties, and Albert Belle and Jeff Bagwell back—when? Could it already be fifteen years since Bags played here, four hundred major league home runs ago? Time ran together, circled back. Layers of a community overlapped.

Chatham's fire chief threw out the first pitch, and everybody cheered. The A's, in dazzling white uniforms, sprinted out to their positions, took their hats off, and faced the flag. The three umpires stood shoulder to shoulder, dressed for the occasion in a red shirt, a white shirt, a blue shirt. The visiting Orleans Cardinals stood at attention in front of the first-base dugout in bright red uniform tops, white bottoms. Red, white, and blue everywhere on the field of green. The members of a men's singing group called the Hyannis Sound leaned toward a microphone behind home plate and crooned the national anthem. The smell of freshly cut grass, pine tar, and Coppertone wafted with the slightest touch of salt air across the field. The scene was pure baseball, the essence of summer.

Stauffer gave up a weakly grounded single to the second man he faced. With two outs, he threw a changeup with the runner stealing. Colt Morton pegged a strike to shortstop Chad Orvella to nail the runner at second, and the A's were pumped. In the press box Paul Galop turned up a Brooks and Dunn country and western tune and sent it out over the PA:

> *Only in America!*
> *Dreamin' in red, white, and blue!*
> *Only in America!*
> *Where we dream as big as we want to.*

Michael Moon batted first for the A's and pulled the second pitch he saw over the bunting on the right-field fence for a home run. Jamie D'Antona cracked a double to deep center, and a couple of pitches later he scored, and the dugout turned electric. From the bleachers Big Joe D'Antona yelled, "Way to go, Buzz!"

Stauffer felt loose, easy. He mowed Cardinals down in the second, and again in the third. Under the bright lights the white uniforms of the Chatham A's gleamed. Between outs, staying sharp, the players caught with soft hands, glided, whipped the ball around the infield. Paul Galop had fun with the music, played pounding choruses from

"Born to be Wild," "Brown Eyed Girl," the Allman Brothers' "Ramblin' Man." In the fourth Stauffer got an out on a fly ball and another on a weak grounder, then struck out a batter on a wicked curve ball, and the sacred night was turning into a party.

IN THE FIFTH the Cardinals finally nicked Stauffer for a run. The Orleans fans clapped and whistled, got into the act. Fourth of July games between these two teams were always special, the towns so close that visiting fans turned out en masse. No teams drew more fans than Chatham and Orleans, and the crowds multiplied when the two met. Schiffner got a kick out of seeing the attendance estimates that Chatham and Orleans reported to the league. Both inflated their numbers, he thought, trying to outdo each other. Part of the bragging rights. Confirming attendance at games was impossible, because there were no ticket sales. Admission to Cape Cod League games was free.

The traditional Fourth of July game, the rivalry, and the free admission harked back to the old days of town ball, an era when crowds—and the players themselves—were mostly local. Organized baseball had been played on Cape Cod since the late 1800s. The Cape Cod Baseball League, unconcerned about technicalities, stole 1885 for its official founding date, pointing to a faded publicity poster at the Baseball Hall of Fame that announced a Fourth of July game that year between Barnstable and Sandwich. Local historians, unconcerned about publicity, considered 1923 the league's true starting point. Still old enough. That year, four towns—Chatham, Falmouth, Hyannis, and Osterville—announced a twelve-game schedule for July and August, and the phrase "Cape Cod Baseball League" appeared in print for the first time.

Those early teams included local and summering college boys and a sprinkling of natives, high schoolers, ex–big leaguers, and semipro journeymen hoping for one more shot at the majors. In the 1920s, tough, hard-drinking country boys from working-class backgrounds dominated major league rosters. On the Cape, though, teams were filled with players from New England schools such as Boston College, Springfield College, Brown, and Dartmouth. "It may have been a blue-collar sport throughout the rest of the country," wrote Christopher Price in *Baseball by the Beach*, a history of the league, "but it was the sport of bluebloods on Cape Cod."

By the end of the twenties, Cape teams played forty games a summer and challenged the Boston Twilight League's reputation as the nation's best semipro league. The first Cape alumni made their marks in the major leagues, including the future Hall of Famers Mickey Cochrane and Pie Traynor. The league expanded, organized its teams into two divisions, ebbed and flowed through the Depression and World War II. Chatham won seven consecutive Lower Cape League titles in the 1930s, setting a tone that has carried through several generations. Only Orleans challenged Chatham's supremacy, winning seven championships during one run from 1947 to 1957. For a couple of years the major league Red Sox supported Chatham teams, sending used uniforms down from Boston.

In 1965 the Cape Cod Baseball League became one of nine summer leagues certified by the National Collegiate Athletic Association. With the NCAA imprimatur (and money), came the requirements that defined the modern era. Cape Cod players could no longer be paid to play, as they had been for decades. Instead, teams provided host families and day jobs at going rates for real labor. Rosters could include only college-eligible players, which ended the eclectic makeup of teams and, in time, accelerated the evolution of the league from a mostly local one into a wholly national one. Local rivalries softened, became more polite, almost quaint. The extra intensity of the Chatham-Orleans games persisted only because the towns stood side by side yet differed markedly. Chatham was Nantucket; Orleans, Martha's Vineyard. Chatham was Republican, green polo shirts and pink pants, Range Rovers, and 225-horsepower Yamahas on Grady-White speedboats. Orleans was Democrat, fishing shirts and khakis, old Wagoneers, fifty-horse Mercuries on aluminum Grummans. This wasn't Texas high school football, though, where towns lived and died with the success of their teams and put great pressure on the kids to win. This was summer baseball. The Chatham-Orleans rivalry didn't define the communities; it reminded the residents that they were still part of communities.

Everything about the new amateur incarnation—from its coaches to its recruitment of top players, from its marketing to its financial underpinnings—pointed the league in a more professional direction.

When the Cape League received its first major grant in 1965, a *Cape Cod Times* editorial asked, "What Will League Do with Ten Thousand Dollars?" By 1994, the annual grant, funded by Major League Baseball but administered through the NCAA—had grown to $85,000. But that year, a strike-shortened season and a canceled World Series led the Cape League's chief source of income, the major leagues, to cut its funding to zero. The league launched an aggressive publicity campaign called "Preserve the Tradition," and corporations such as Ocean Spray and Bank Boston stepped up. Judy Walden Scarafile, a charismatic president who'd started her work for the league in the seventies as a junior in college, scoring for fifteen bucks a game, rallied support. Her energy pushed and refined the league's fundraising. By 2002 the annual budget had passed $350,000, with nearly thirty big corporate sponsors and foundations kicking in. The Cape League covered the costs of its teams' umpires, bats, and five hundred dozen baseballs. It paid for widespread publicity, including a Web site that registered four million hits in 2002. It created a hall of fame with a permanent exhibition at the Heritage Plantation Museum in Sandwich. Scarafile also worked with individual teams on local fundraising, merchandising, advertising. After years of squeezing in unpaid forty-hour weeks around her job at a local pharmacy, Scarafile had recently drawn her first paycheck from the league, as the newly created "director of corporate development." Quietly—as far as the general public was concerned—the Cape Cod Baseball League had become big business. Its economic machinery would have surprised a lot of fans sitting in lawn chairs out there on those summer nights, watching baseball for free.

The trappings surrounding the professional game, meanwhile, had changed. Major league teams played in domed stadiums, on artificial grass, tried out garish, brightly colored uniforms, experimented with orange baseballs, brought golf carts in from the bullpens, trotted out silly mascots. Agents, contracts, and ballooning salaries grabbed headlines in the sports pages. Minor league clubs turned into promotion-filled "family-entertainment venues," with car raffles and between-inning contests promoted more than the games themselves.

But in what *Yankee* magazine's editor, Judson Hale, called "the most stubborn region of the country," on the Cape the old guard and old-school values worked to hold the game at the center of the experience. A new generation of volunteers—Judy Scarafile, Paul Galop, Wareham's general manager, John Wylde—understood the power of Cape Cod's nostalgia. The wooden bats were part of it, and the lawn chairs, and the simplicity. In Chatham, an old-fashioned wooden sandwich board sat propped at the rotary, announcing the evening's game—just as sandwich boards did in the nine other towns that fielded teams on the Cape. At Chatham's Fourth of July game, most of the fans were washashores or summer visitors, but the game put them on a longer historical continuum. They could look out on that green field and feel a kinship with those who'd looked out fifty, sixty years earlier and seen essentially the same thing.

STAUFFER PUFFED OUT his cheeks, gave the ball a little flip from his glove to his pitching hand—it was one of his few quirks, something a kid might do. The game, now 2–1, Chatham, turned tense. He went back to it, snagged the last out of the fifth inning on a ground ball right back at him, easy as you like. The Chatham fans, relieved, cheered.

Behind home plate, Stauffer's mother, Becky, relaxed her clenched hands. She was always on edge when her son pitched. Her husband, Rick, was the same. It was killing him not to be here. He was back in Saratoga Springs managing the supermarket—the holiday weekend was too important for him to be able to get away. He would say later, "Timmy's fine—he's always been the guy they've gone to in big games. He doesn't seem bothered by them anymore. I used to be the same way when I pitched for St. Joe's. But I had some control over the outcome then. It's only now that I'm a parent and can't do anything that I'm a wreck."

Stauffer struck out two batters in the sixth, but he was wilting in the warm night air. A blister opened up on the side of his middle finger. He refused to put a Band-Aid on it, preferring to feel the ball raw rather than have his touch muted, even if it meant throwing fewer curves. His pitches wandered higher in the strike zone.

In the bottom of the inning the A's loaded the bases with no outs. Michael Moon ripped a single up the middle to put Chatham ahead 3–1, and everything Schiffner had imagined and hoped for was coming true. The game, for Orleans, was on the line. With one out, Jeremy Cleveland took a strike, then another. Now, both sides of the crowd rode on every pitch. The Chatham players stood up in the dugout, shouted encouragement. In the on-deck circle, Jamie D'Antona looked into the stands and noticed a little bull mastiff. "Hey, Schiff!" he yelled. "Did you see that dog?" Colt Morton stared at D'Antona and shook his head, incredulous that D'Antona could be distracted at such a moment.

Cleveland struck out, and now it was up to D'Antona to put the game away. Like Stauffer, he'd come through in plenty of big situations before. At Wake Forest he'd been a money player, an RBI machine, even though, if anything, the more tense the situation, the less he seemed to bear down. He'd already hit a double and a single that night. In the stands, his dad's voice cut through the crowd noise, "Stay balanced, Buzz! Keep your hands back!" D'Antona had grown up with that low, raspy voice in his head. He said he could hear it at Wake, even with his dad back in Connecticut. He found it more comforting than irritating. The son worked the count to three balls and two strikes. The next pitch came in low, out of the strike zone.

The runners sprinted from the bases, off with the pitch. D'Antona swung and missed to end the inning.

Stauffer worked his way through the seventh, striking out another batter, but he'd thrown close to a hundred pitches and was laboring, working harder for each out. During the stretch between innings, as the teams changed positions, Paul Galop asked the crowd to rise. He put on Kate Smith's recording of "God Bless America," and for a minute, all the layers came together—the years, the towns, the scouts and the parents and the volunteers, the young and the old, the fans and the coaches, the players who cared deeply about winning a summer-league game and those who didn't. It would have been a perfect moment to end the night.

Stauffer carried a 4–1 lead into the eighth. He struck out Brandon Boggs, a celebrated switch-hitting outfielder from Georgia Tech, to start the inning. The second batter, a lithe, smooth shortstop from Mississippi State, flied out to right. The A's were four outs away. Then Stauffer lost a batter—missed high, his third walk, and the Orleans fans ratcheted up the noise. Schiffner signaled down to the bullpen for Zane Carlson to loosen. Carlson was Schiffner's automatic closer from Baylor. Two summers ago he'd pitched for Team USA as a freshman, then last summer for Chatham. He and Dave Bush from Wake Forest had formed an almost unhittable combination out of the A's' bullpen. Schiffner called them "Thunder and Lightning." Together, the pair gave up just four earned runs in forty-eight innings of pitching. Carlson, using a nasty, darting slider, saved twelve games for Chatham, four shy of the league record.

He had pitched through sharp pain all of that summer—throbbing pain localized in the center of his biceps, pain that spread and numbed his whole arm, making it impossible to lift his arm for hours after he'd pitched. The pain wouldn't go away even after he rested and started throwing again at Baylor. He had MRIs, several exams, and nothing showed up. Finally, he visited John Conway, the Texas Rangers' team physician. Conway had a hunch that nerve damage might be causing the pain, but could offer only fifty-fifty odds that surgery would fix or even find the problem. Carlson decided against the surgery. But the pain became more intense. He shut his season down—took a medical redshirt, so he wouldn't lose a season of eligibility at Baylor—and went under the knife in early April. Conway discovered muscle fibers that had built up like scar tissue around the biceps's central nerve, pinching it and pinching the blood supply to the arm. He trimmed the mass of fibers, relieving the pressure. (A shiny, red, three-inch-long scar now lined the inside of Carlson's right biceps.) The repair worked. After a couple of months of rehab, Carlson pitched without pain for the first time in two years. His fastball, which had stalled out at eighty-five before the operation, now hovered near ninety, and his slider was as dirty as ever. He'd saved four games already this summer, allowing just three hits and no runs in the seven innings he'd pitched so far.

Stauffer gave up a hard single to left, and Schiffner hopped out of the dugout and strode to the mound. Stauffer had thrown 105 pitches. "Great job, Tim," Schiffner said. "We'll get Zane in here to finish it off." Stauffer didn't disagree. It had been a long, hot day. He said, "Okay," and jogged off the field staring straight ahead, not walking slowly with his head down, as many pitchers did, not moping, not drawing attention to himself. He carefully hopped over the chalked baseline—another small quirk—and shook hands with the A's players on the bench as the crowd applauded his effort. He grabbed a seat near the trainer, Daisy Kovach. As he watched from the dugout, Kovach taped a bag of ice to his hard-used shoulder.

Carlson, like Stauffer, was an overpowering pitcher, but the two couldn't have been more different in style. Carlson was small by comparison, gritty, emotional, impatient. He took almost no time to set and throw—again and again he rocked quickly and fired with everything he had. If pitches seemed to flow effortlessly out of Stauffer's motion, they shot out of Carlson's with exploding adrenaline. You could almost feel the strain on his arm, his back, even his head, which snapped sideways with the effort of every pitch. The scouts saw some negatives in Carlson's mechanics, but he wrung every ounce out of his 175 pounds, and energized a game every time he entered it.

He walked the first man he faced, loading the bases.

The second batter, Steven Garrabrants, Arizona State's second baseman, drilled a sharp single to left-center. Chatham's center-fielder Tim Layden, the most recent replacement on the roster, new to the team but not yet a part of it, played the ball badly, and it rolled all the way to the fence. Three runners scored, and just like that, Stauffer's work—the parade, the big crowd, the expected turn-around—was for naught. The game was still tied, but everything sagged. Jamie D'Antona had a shot in the bottom of the eighth with two outs and a runner on third, and he struck out, again. In the ninth Carlson coughed up two more walks and a triple, and Orleans won the game 6–4.

OVER THE COURSE of a baseball season it was impossible to know in the moment when a team had played a pivotal game. Momentum was crucial but fickle. The A's had it, had it when they needed it, and let it slip away when everything seemed perfectly aligned. Twenty-six games remained—still time to make a run at the play-offs, time to break out of slumps, time to put up some numbers and impress scouts—but something in the season had shifted with the loss. The players knew it. Stauffer stalked off toward the bullpen and stood by himself for a moment. The other players walked slowly toward their huddle in left field. Just for a second Stauffer turned his back and looked out toward the bunting and the tall trees, concealing what-ever emotion he felt, then jogged back to his teammates. In the hud-dle Schiffner spoke briefly, not angrily, said they were "getting closer," then left his players to themselves. They pulled in tight, mur-mured for a moment, lifted their hands together and said, "One, two, three, *tomorrow*." But their hearts weren't in it.

Long after the players left the field, Fincher was still there, drag-ging the infield dirt with the golf cart, cleaning up the dugout. He'd been on his feet since 7:00 that morning. He didn't notice Michael Moon sitting on a folding chair in the shadows down near the Chatham bullpen—Moon, who at times cared more about this team than any other player, who at other times didn't care enough to run out a ground ball. Moon, who could bear down and hit in the clutch one moment and then forget to cover second base the next.

Stauffer was already showering back at his house in Harwich, getting ready for a late dinner with his mom.

Fincher threw his duffel together, drove the cart down to the equipment shed, and headed home. He left Moon sitting in the shadows, alone with his thoughts.

SEVEN

The Universal Soldier

T HE NEWS OF TED WILLIAMS'S DEATH the day after that July
Fourth touched many in New England. Williams had been a
hero to generations of Red Sox fans, and his legend had only grown
larger since the majestic home run he'd hit in his final at-bat at Fenway Park in 1960. The citizens of Red Sox Nation—from the potato
fields of northern Maine to the Champlain Islands of Vermont to the
bars in Woonsocket, Rhode Island—read in their papers about the
passing of an era. On July 5, 2002, flags flew at half-mast at baseball
fields across Cape Cod. In Orleans, a Friday-night crowd of three
thousand was asked to fall silent for a moment before the national
anthem was sung.

In his postgame talk that night, John Schiffner remembered
Williams. The A's had played poorly and lost again to their next-door
rivals, their sixth loss in a row. "I've got two stories I want to tell you.
The first one is about Ted Williams, who you know died today at
eighty-three. Williams was the best hitter of his time because he
wanted it more than anybody else. People still talk about what it was
like to hear him take batting practice." Schiffner assumed a stance,
and became Williams swinging a bat. "I'm fucking Ted Williams"—
crack!—"and you're not going to"—*crack!*—"fucking get me out"—
crack!

"The other story is about Joe DiMaggio. DiMaggio's team was up
eleven to three, once, and he gave a hundred percent running out a

routine ground ball. After the game, a reporter asked him why he had run so hard on the grounder. DiMaggio said, 'I ran hard because there might have been one person in the stands who hadn't seen me play before. I didn't want to cheat that person.'

"Look, I'm not giving up on you guys, but this is going to be my last speech. I don't have anything left to say. We'll keep working with you; we'll help every day when you come to us with questions; we'll keep trying to help you improve. But this is on you, now.

"Losing streaks are good in one sense. They show you what you need to do to improve. And that's why you're here: to go back to your schools as better ballplayers. They also teach humility, which is something you can bring back with you, not a bad thing.

"You're having trouble with confidence right now. But remember who you are: twenty-three of the best college baseball players in the country. Remember why you're here, every at-bat, every play in the field. Remember how good you are.

"Can this team spoil some other teams' play-off hopes? Maybe. Can we still sneak into the play-offs? Maybe. It's up to you."

The players pulled in close while Schiffner walked away. "One, two, three, BEER!" they chanted.

THE A'S PARTIED that night on the long, wind-swept beach below the Chatham Lighthouse. At night the beach seemed to fall off from the Overlook into blackness. It spread along the base of a high bluff where tourists parked by day and looked out at the famous break in the barrier beach. A steep set of weathered wooden stairs descended through the darkness to the sand. Most of the players took their sneakers off at the bottom, setting them at the edge of the beach grass.

D'Antona, one of the first to arrive, wore overalls over bare skin and a knitted winter cap. He'd brought the firewood, as usual—fourteen bucks' worth, two bundles from the Getty station up in town. The sand, pale gray once D'Antona's eyes had adjusted to the dark, dropped gradually away from him, down fifty yards or so to the ragged white edge that dissolved and reemerged with the surf. He trudged on, alongside Aaron Trolia, away from town, away from the bluff and the parking lot, out onto an undulating pile of sand that stretched three empty miles ahead of them.

As they walked, they occasionally passed shadowy figures clustered in small groups. Most of the people on the beach at that late hour were teenagers, local pals, couples slipping off into the dark. Every ten seconds, two quick, powerful beams of white light flashed over them through the thin fog, from the turning lantern of the Coast Guard light station up across the street from the Overlook. The beams momentarily lit up the shadows, revealed faces. "That you, Moonie?" D'Antona said to a shadow, and a few minutes later, "Hey! R.J.! Sweet!"

The bonfires had become a weekly ritual. D'Antona, usually the ringleader, sprang for the wood, brought the matches, remembered the flashlight. He set the fires, policed the beer cans that piled up around them, made sure the coals were dead and buried with sand at the end.

D'Antona dug out a pit and laid up the firewood far down the beach, where the sand dipped behind a long dune tufted in beach grass, out of view and a quarter-mile from any Chatham cop who might have stopped at the sight of cars parked after midnight at the Overlook. Fires on the beach were illegal. D'Antona lit a cigarette from the flames licking at the wood, then rubbed his hands together against the chill breeze.

By a twenty-year-old's definition of fun, some of the bonfires had been a blast—lots of guys, a bunch of girls, plenty of cheap beer, craziness (one night some players had swiped the jeans of a skinny-dipping woman and tossed them on the fire). But that night's was quieter, a couple of A's lurking at the edge of the firelight smoking joints, a handful of D'Antona's high school buddies visiting from Connecticut. A wedding party wound down at the Chatham Beach and Tennis Club, up by the Overlook where the road curved away from the sand. In the distance, high above the bonfire, the wedding tent glowed elegantly in the fog. Strains of a jazz band mixed with the wind and the waves curling onto the shore. Long milky beams from the lighthouse swept through the fog, the whole scene surreal, like something out of *Gatsby*.

Blake Hanan had showed up briefly, to show team unity. He wasn't drinking, so didn't stay long—he headed back to the Troys' house, to play Pictionary with Orvella and Colt Morton and the Troy family. Diane Troy had urged the players to try the game, instead of spending so much time in front of a video screen. The late-night Pictionary games had become intense, competitive. Hanan and Orvella usually won, and bragged about it. By the end of the season other players would join in the games to try and beat them.

Stauffer came to the beach but turned in early. He had the ability to be one of the guys even as he kept a focus that set him apart. He'd been doing it ever since grade school. His essay on right choices and sacrifices had won a D.A.R.E. contest in fifth grade. He wasn't about to jeopardize his performance on the Cape for the sake of some stupid group behavior. But he knew how to pick his shots. He felt comfortable nursing a beer instead of plowing through several, or going to parties and leaving early. The others stayed late, even though D'Antona had to show up at South Cape at 7:00 A.M., and the guys working the clinic had to show at 8:30.

The next morning, Cleveland, Yates, and Carlson, on the youth field next to Veterans, squinted bleary-eyed into the sun with a crowd of eager kids waiting to get going. Yates had swatted his ringing alarm clock to the floor after three or four hours' sleep. He'd looked over and seen D'Antona's bed already empty.

"Stauffer got the sleep," said Carlson. "He should lead the early drills. I say we push the auto-Stauffer button."

There were other nighttime watering holes. The Wake Forest guys led a gang over to the Irish Pub in West Harwich on Tuesday nights for Karaoke. For the older players there was the bar at The Squire, Chatham's classic beer bar downtown. In Schiffner's day, in Harwich, it had been quarter-beer nights at the Improper Bostonian.

The players on Cape Cod were discovering more than where they stood on the diamond. They were learning about themselves, how much they could drink, how little sleep they could get by on, how much they could take, how far they could push it.

Schools of bluefish began to move inshore along the southern beaches. The first highbush blueberries sweetened around the freshwater swamps. The hot, dry weather burned on. After the soaking rain of the first three days of the season, not a quarter-inch had fallen on the Lower Cape. In Emery Pond, a shallow basin rimmed by cattails and pickerel weed where D'Antona plugged for bass and sunfish, the water had fallen to its lowest level in memory. It was being pumped out to keep a small adjacent cranberry bog wet. The towns of Harwich and Brewster had already put in water restrictions, and Orleans was talking about an outright ban on watering, threatening the lush grass of Eldredge Park.

The players worked their morning jobs, cruised Lighthouse Beach after lunch, hot in the sun though the water had barely reached sixty degrees in Nantucket Sound. They trudged along the sand, packs of trim, tanned athletes in baggy, flower-print shorts and wraparound Oakley sunglasses. Blake Hanan's body, cut like a boxer's, stood out.

Hanan worked out four days a week at Willy's Gym in Orleans, along with ballplayers from other teams on the lower Cape. The most serious fitness center in the area, Willy's had a special relationship with the Cape Cod League. Cape players could lift the whole summer there for a discounted rate of a hundred dollars. Early in each season Charlie Thoms found out which Chatham players weren't working out. He'd ask around, and if money seemed to be the obstacle, he'd call Willy's, and the owner, Leslie Finley, would waive the fee. Schiffner always plugged the gym as he welcomed his teams. It became part of the place, like Nick's Deli, like Lighthouse Beach.

Unlike the other A's lifting on their own that summer, Hanan followed a rigorous program he'd brought from school—a weight routine along with extensive sprinting drills. Hanan didn't work a day job. He wasn't going to let anything interfere with his training. He got good sleep, ate well, took his daily protein supplement, did his sprints, pumped iron. D'Antona's lack of commitment irritated him.

When Thomas Pauly had first seen D'Antona on a beach in a pair of swimming trunks, he said to himself, *You gotta be kidding me. That's JAMIE D'ANTONA?* D'Antona's thick neck sloped into big shoulders, but his body had the softness that usually came in middle age. His chest and midsection looked slack, had no definition at all. "You gotta lose those love handles, Boss," Adam Yates told him. D'Antona was broad-beamed, thick in the legs, like a wide-body forward in basketball whose best skill was boxing out underneath the hoop. He ran like Groucho Marx walked. Some scouts classified him as a "bad-body player," a big negative in some books. He liked to play at 200 pounds, 205, but he also loved cooking and eating. His weight might push to 220, and he'd go on SlimFast for two meals a day and get the weight back down, then he'd go back to eating whatever he wanted. He cared more about how he hit than how his body looked.

Conditioning didn't mean much to D'Antona, not yet. That was one reason he liked playing for George Greer. Most of Wake Forest's training focused on the game itself, not, as D'Antona sniffed, on "stuff they do on a football field." He hated running long distances. He lifted weights with the team at Wake only when he had to, and met the minimum requirements. One of the strongest college power hitters in the nation, he could lift more weight than only half the pitchers on his team and maybe 20 percent of the regular players.

Almost all of the other A's worked on their bodies that summer. For some of the pitchers, that meant little beyond the running Schiffner asked and isometric arm exercises with a wide rubber strap, but that was more than D'Antona did. The straps had become ubiquitous in recent years; you'd find them in players' duffels and hanging in dugouts for visiting teams to use. Most of the position players—the hitters—lifted weights to maintain their strength. The fall and winter workouts, back in the weight rooms at school, would build the mass, put on the muscle. It was hard to get big while staying flexible and fresh for games. But get big was what almost all of them wanted to do.

The new guy from A&M, Ben Himes, was big. He had taken his first batting practice in a cut-off T-shirt that revealed rippling biceps and forearms. Six foot five, he had a military haircut, slitty light-gray eyes, high cheekbones, and a head a bit small for his lean, broad-shouldered physique. Schiffner had watched him walking off the plane in Providence and immediately thought "bad face," a disquieting notion Schiffner had picked up from reading *Dollar Sign on the Muscle*, a book about professional scouting. Old-school veteran scouts who'd viewed thousands of prospects believed in something called "the good face"—it had to do with a square jaw and a clear, direct gaze that major leaguers seemed to share. At one time scouts even included the term in their official reports. *Strong right-handed batter. Tall, durable-looking body. Has the good face.* One scout said the good face was difficult to describe, but that you could look around a major league locker room and know instantly you were seeing athletes, not accountants. The "bad face" took many forms. Schiffner had seen something in Ben Himes's face he didn't trust.

As Himes took his first swings in the batting cage, though, the players weren't looking at his face. His wrists were whip-quick; he turned on a pitch and hammered a long home run, then slashed a vicious line drive off the right-field fence. The players in the dugout noticed. Himes had barely said a word, had hardly changed expression since he'd arrived. He seemed unnaturally focused. He'd practically crushed D'Antona's fingers when the two shook hands upon meeting. In the dugout D'Antona said, "He's a Universal Soldier," a reference to the Jean-Claude Van Damme action film featuring dead soldiers reanimated as unstoppable superhuman cyborgs. The nickname Universal Soldier had stuck, joining Ryan Johnson's R.J. and Michael Moon's Moonie. (Tim Layden had become Osama, as in Osama Tim Layden. The bullpen catcher, Jim Kais, a freshman who wore the A's uniform but didn't play in games, went by Hib, a proper baseball nickname. Schiffner and Fincher were Schiff and Finch to everyone. Nicknames were part of the game.)

Himes could run, too—he pumped his legs and arms smoothly, his body leaning slightly forward, and he threw powerfully. Shagging fly balls during batting practice, he sprinted toward a ball hit into the right-center field gap. In the dugout Moonie mimicked the electronic beeping of a radar-tracking device: Himes's computer locking in on the coordinates. "Where'd this guy come from?" asked Jeremy Cleveland. "Forget that," said D'Antona. "Who made him up? I'd like to order some of the parts."

His first time batting in a game, Himes had pulled a long foul ball over the fence, halfway up the embankment behind right field. The players in the dugout howled. "C'mon guys—that's a foul ball," Schiffner said. Then Himes just missed, hitting slightly under the ball. He flew out deep to center. He returned to the dugout and cracked just the hint of a smile. He knew he'd just barely missed a monster home run. D'Antona noticed and said, "Good. He is not a robot." But the moniker "Universal" was still apt. Schiffner even used it on the lineup sheets he taped to the dugout wall.

As if to prove he was indeed made of flesh and blood, Universal fractured his finger after eight unproductive games and went home early. D'Antona was disappointed. He'd wanted to see what the guy might do if the A's ever got into a brawl.

THE A's LOOKED dead and lost again at home. A pack of eight or ten scouts had watched, studying the A's despite the losing streak. Some struggling players—catcher Chris Iannetta, the brick mason's son, for one—had lost sight of everything else and become withdrawn, brooding. He sat by himself in the dugout with a clenched jaw.

The next afternoon, on the drive to Bourne, the players saw the legendary Cape Cod traffic up close. On the Mid-Cape Highway both westbound lanes were backed up all the way to Exit 6 in Barnstable, fifteen miles from the Sagamore Bridge. The players sat with windows down. They blasted their radios and inched through the steamy, hazy air, smelled asphalt baking in the heat. They scanned the next lane for good-looking girls, occasionally saw bikini tops, bare feet sticking out of passenger-side windows—Cape Cod in the summer was all about bodies, and not just athletes'. The drive to the field in Bourne, normally fifty minutes, took two and a half hours. The delay cost the A's batting practice, and then infield practice. They arrived just in time for the first pitch.

A sparse crowd had turned out for the four o'clock start. The Bourne Braves, one of the poorest organizations in the league, drew a fraction of the fans that Chatham did. The field behind the Coady School had once been an embarrassment to the league. It had lacked a sprinkler system, among other things, so that by mid-season the infield grass turned brown, the basepaths as dry as powder. Even after the Braves had completed some much-needed renovations, though, the best thing Schiffner could say about the field was "It has nice dugouts." Nobody who had been around for a while complained.

The Bourne team could do nothing to fix the field's orientation, though, which was wrong for baseball. Late-afternoon batters looked into the sun dropping into Buzzards Bay beyond the Cape Cod Canal. A few years ago Chatham had carried a shutout here into the late innings. The plate umpire halted the game for forty-five minutes because the sun's glare bothered the batters. Schiffner lost his cool and was subsequently ejected. The umpires then let the teams play so far into the dark that nobody could see. Chatham, along with other teams, filed a complaint with the league, and after that, games in Bourne started earlier.

The bullpen in Bourne included a small set of benches out beyond the chain-link fence in right field. Daniel Moore, sporting a pale, newly shaved head, sat next to Stauffer, who had joined in and dyed his crew cut yellow. Dyed hair might not be his style, but he'd joined in for the troop morale, knowing his hair wouldn't be blonde for long. He'd trim his crew cut a couple more times before school.

The game dragged on in the late afternoon sun. Moore and Stauffer hopped down to the bottom bullpen's bench, and ducked behind a sponsor's banner. Out of sight of Schiffner and Myers, they leaned in close and played "Push-Push" on the digital display of Stauffer's cell phone. It wasn't Play Station II, but it helped pass the time.

The bullpen in Bourne was uncomfortable and isolated—too far from the crowd for girl watching, with terrible sight lines for the game. The other bullpen pitchers did what they often did, talked and pondered.

Blake Hanan's body had become a source of speculation. Players talked openly about steroids. They shared the widespread belief that many major league hitters took them. That spring, Ken Caminiti had publicly admitted he'd been on anabolic steroids during his MVP year of 1996 when he played for the San Diego Padres. Caminiti, thirty-three that year, had never hit more than twenty-six home runs in a single season. That season, after injuring his shoulder and turning to steroids, he hit twenty-eight home runs after the all-star break alone. He'd told *Sports Illustrated* that half of the current players in the majors used them, a figure that shocked even those close to the game.

The subject of performance-enhancing drugs in baseball had long been a matter for rumor and speculation. In the 1980s, players around the American League winked at "Canseco milkshakes," the steroid-laced drinks they believed powered the incredibly muscular slugger José Canseco. But even into the early 1990s, when the average all-star weighed less than 200 pounds, most insiders considered Canseco an outlier, someone playing with fire. One day at Nick's, a few of the 2002 Chatham players hooted watching a snippet of the '94 major league all-star game on the ESPN Classic channel. They couldn't believe how skinny the old ballplayers looked—Ozzie Smith, Tony Gwynn, the young Barry Bonds—and how much major league bodies had changed in just eight years. Big-league hitters had gone on a power spree over that time. Roger Maris's single-season home-run record, which had stood since 1961, was shattered and shattered again. The mythic sixty-home-run level—reached only twice before 1997—had been passed six times in the past four years. The average weight of the 2001 major league all-star had risen to 211 pounds. The A's could see as well as anybody that all of the gain had been muscle.

The whispers had grown into a public debate, placing the game's integrity and time-honored statistics at stake. With Caminiti's admission, the debate burst into the headlines and onto op-ed pages around the country. One of the sticking points in the ugly, ongoing labor dispute that summer between the players' union and major league owners involved random drug testing. The NFL, NBA, and International Olympic Committee all tested for steroids, but the Major League Baseball Players' Association balked, claiming that it was invasion of privacy. In the end the association agreed to a watered-down anonymous testing program that almost everyone outside the game considered a joke.

The same week that the A's lost two straight to the Orleans Cardinals, *USA Today* published a multipart special report on steroid use in baseball and how it was filtering down through lower levels of the sport. In the past half dozen years, more than the record books had changed—the culture surrounding the game had changed. Major league players at every position were huge, ripped. No longer were the José Cansecos considered outliers. No longer were steroids believed to be black magic, fire. They'd been around long enough that many young players accepted them as part of the package, as part of what it took to make it.

The A's hitters—D'Antona, Ryan Johnson—struggled with the reality. At college programs such as Wake Forest, and even at Siena, where Blake Hanan played, ballplayers experimented with over-the-counter supplements like Hydroxicut and ephedra—before ephedra was banned in 2004 by the FDA. The powders or pills promised to enable users to burn fat more efficiently, convert fat to muscle, help them lose weight. Some college players—not many—had moved on to anabolic steroids. The *NCAA 2001 Substance Abuse Report* listed steroid use among Division I baseball players at 2.3 percent—the fringe, for now, but health experts worried. (College baseball, without the corrupting big money of football and basketball, avoided many of the shameful, scandalous behavior that marked those other sports, including the prevalence of drug use.) Some conferences and individual schools drug-tested their own baseball players, and the NCAA tested all of the teams in the post-season tournament. But orally taken fat-soluble steroids stayed in a user's system only a matter of weeks. Athletes could cycle steroids in the off-season to bulk up and be clean in time for the testing. Longer-term users, particularly body builders, injected steroids directly into muscle tissue. The slower-releasing anabolics were more easily tolerated by the body, though they could be detectable for many months after the injection. The list of substances banned by the NCAA looked like a pharmaceutical catalogue. The players had other names: "juice," "Arnolds," "stackers," "'roids," "vitamin S."

You couldn't tell by looking at him now, but D'Antona had tried creatine in Alaska the previous summer. The legal substance—a powder D'Antona mixed with water—speeded the production of amino acids. It increased strength and the explosiveness needed for sprinting, and it had made a difference. But D'Antona had to count hours between dosages, monitor the times he ate and what he ate. The regimen for safe use felt too rigid and complicated, and it scared him. The stuff tasted awful. He'd abandoned it after a few weeks.

Steroids—synthetically produced testosterone, a male hormone—upped the ante. They came in two kinds: anabolic (growing or building) and androgenic (masculinizing). In essence, the two kinds had the same affect on an athlete's body: They promoted muscle growth. Athletes on steroids recovered more quickly from intense workouts; some felt a sharper, more aggressive attitude. But steroids were linked with a litany of health problems, particularly in young users, from liver damage and heart arrhythmias to aggression, depression, high blood pressure, impotence, several kinds of cancer, even death. It would be years before studies would confirm the health implications, but one startling fact was worrying major league front offices already. Ligament and joint injuries, long common among football players, had exploded in baseball over the past five years. Muscles were becoming too strong for their supporting infrastructure.

The hitters spoke little about the possible health risks, or about the minor problem of steroids' being illegal. They'd either missed or ignored the growing media attention. D'Antona knew coaches who discouraged using them but, he said, "Maybe that's why they're coaching, not playing." But all of the A's talked about the inevitable decision many of them would face: When it came down to it, when advancement as a pro was on the line and others were getting juiced around you, would you take the next step to steroids? What if a coach or trainer in single-A suggested it might be in your best interest to get on a "program"? What if you'd finally made the forty-man spring training roster, and some little pills might make the difference between making it or washing out? What if the guy next to you was as big as a house, and he was coming after your job and your million-dollar paycheck? When would you reach that point?

The bullpen guys passed time musing on such things. Getting jacked on steroids didn't help pitchers as much—though some inevitably tried, the new culture having seeped into every corner of the clubhouses and locker rooms. They sounded resentful talking about the prevalence, the unfairness. The field they all dreamed of pitching on had tilted in the hitters' favor. The pitchers wondered if any of their teammates had reached the point already. Maybe Universal. Maybe Hanan. They sometimes made jokes when Hanan's name came up, said things like, "Hey, never give up the dream, baby!"

Blake Hanan, by all appearances, took better care of his body than anybody else on the A's. He didn't admit to using steroids, only said that "he would if it ever came down to it." He'd gained twenty-five pounds since starting college, all of it muscle. He was young enough that gains like that didn't raise a flag. College-aged players were still filling out; they had room to grow. That same kind of transformation would, at age thirty-three, be a dead giveaway.

The pitchers didn't know for sure, but, God, some of those bodies were hard.

TWENTY-FIVE YEARS ago, during John Schiffner's playing days in the Cape League, everybody on the teams worked a day job. And a lot of those jobs were physical: house painting, dish washing, mowing lawns. The percentage of players working day jobs on the Cape, though, had steadily declined. On some teams in 2002, only half of the players chose to work, even though the jobs, by and large, had turned soft. Players came from wealthier families now. The need for physical conditioning had grown more intense each year, and players and parents, both, recognized the proper focus of the summer. Some adults around Chatham grumbled about the diminishing work ethic among today's young people. Charlie Thoms and John Schiffner encouraged the Chatham players to take day jobs—the responsibility helped teach discipline, gave a reason to get up in the morning (and therefore go to bed at night), fostered camaraderie. Schiffner, who had been there before, knew how valuable the experience could be. Even the guys doing the youth clinics—with easy work, leading the kids' stretching, turning drills into games like egg-toss-with-a-baseball and five-way-pickle—learned life lessons. The kids in those camps adored the A's players, mobbed them after home games, wrote letters to them in the off-season, returned the next year hoping to see them. The kids gave the players a taste of celebrity, but also contact with families, a sense of making a difference in someone's life, a sense of the wider world.

Still, not all of the A's players were up for it. Steve LeFaivre, working a lame job stocking shelves at CVS, lasted less than a week. He didn't even tell his boss he was quitting; he asked Simon Williams to do it for him. LeFaivre had never worked a job in his life. "I don't know," he said. "I guess I'm not into the whole waking-up-early thing." Williams and Mike MacDonald, the Maine players who bailed out of the South Cape Seafood jobs, didn't make it through the summer at CVS, either.

Others paced themselves, took days off when they were tired. Almost all of them begged time off when the league had scheduled no games. That gave them the chance to shoot up to Provincetown to check out the gay scene, or take the ferry to Nantucket and back. Some of the A's day-tripped to Boston. A lot of them competitively played miniature golf. Other teams had other diversions. At Harwich that summer, one host family kept a powerboat on Long Pond, and high-speed tubing became the sport of choice for the Harwich Mariners. At low tide in Brewster, the shallow waters of Cape Cod Bay opened up a half mile of mudflat. The Whitecaps marked out bases and an outfield fence and played sodden, massive games of whiffleball.

On an off day in early July Tim Stauffer finally took his golf clubs out of the trunk. He and a friend from home shot a couple of rounds at the Hyannis Country Club. On the same day, Jamie D'Antona simply showed up early at South Cape Seafood and read through another heavy day on the order list. Chatham Bars Inn alone wanted two hundred lobsters. D'Antona drove one of the South Cape delivery trucks, a boxy twenty-four-foot Mitsubishi FH-2000 diesel, and played the radio loud. He drove aggressively, paying attention partly to the road and partly to the muscle cars he saw, singing out "Sweet!" at every 'Vette or vintage Camaro. The truck he drove was a beast, but D'Antona swung it in and out of side alleys and tight lots, parking willy-nilly across multiple spaces, driving like he owned it. He felt tough handling a rig big enough to need a backup beeper.

While his teammates were relaxing and working out, pampering their bodies, D'Antona hopped to his work—at the Blue Coral, where the narrow driveway entered blind onto Chatham's Main Street and D'Antona had to back the truck out into traffic; at Moby Dick's; at the Beachcomber, a classic, open-air oyster bar on the headlands in Wellfleet. He bounced in through the service entrances and talked with everyone he saw. Everyone knew him and liked him: He was gregarious, enthusiastic, even when doing rugged lifting. At the Flying Fish Café, not yet 10:30 but the sun already sweltering, someone offered him a Coke and he said, "Hell, yeah!" He usually stopped midroute at a Cumberland Farms on 6A for a soda or bottle of water and a Hostess blueberry pie, breakfast on the run. Then

J.T.'s. Marley's. Swinging around through Brewster he arched and twisted his torso. "Friggin' back," he said. The pain had settled in; he couldn't get comfortable driving. Sheryl Crow's "Soak up the Sun" came on and D'Antona cranked the radio louder, sang along. Castaways. The Friendly Fisherman. The Clam Bar. At Lambert's, another big account, someone pointed to some fresh tuna sushi in the glass display case and said, "Take some if you want."

"You're asking the wrong guy if he wants food," said D'Antona, and joyfully scooped up a couple of pieces. Avril Lavigne came over the radio—*Why you have to go and make things so complicated?*—and D'Antona finished the route listening to what could have been his theme song. He was at Nick's by 2:30, fixing his own meatball sub on the grill and helping Mimi with the late lunch crowd.

He had slowly brought his average up but still struggled, striking out a lot, making errors at third. But he struggled less than Blake Hanan did, less than Universal Soldier, less than Steve LeFaivre and Colt Morton—Colt, who went to church every Sunday and didn't smoke or drink, who lifted weights religiously, who'd been born, his mother had said, with the maturity of a thirty-year-old. Wake Forest coach George Greer, who had seen a lot of ballplayers, asked Schiffner once, "Who would you rather have up with the bases loaded and two outs, a guy who goes to the bar after the game, or a guy who goes to the ice-cream shop?"

The A's took batting practice before the game at home against Cotuit, a game the A's finally won, after eight straight losses. The echo of Ted Williams reverberated, the skinny nineteen-year-old "Splinter" who'd grown into a two-hundred-pound legend, without weights or drugs. The early-arriving scouts looked on.

D'Antona stood in and—*crack!*—started smashing balls into the distant outfield, and—*crack!*—it made you wonder if natural talent was enough to separate the men—*crack!*—from the boys. Or if sleep and lifting and clean living—*crack!*—even fucking mattered.

EIGHT

Something Like a Family

H IS BACK WAS KILLING HIM. Some days he couldn't stand up
straight without wincing. Before games he strapped on a TENS
unit to stimulate the nerves, try and ease the pain. But Jamie D'Antona was still throwing fifty-pound fish totes around at a day job he
didn't need. "Hey, the league gave me a job," he said. "I'm not going
to complain about it." He had paid off the speeding ticket and was
covering his expenses without asking for anything from home, but he
hadn't chipped away at his debt. He was still lifting with his back instead of his legs.

Joe and Karin D'Antona drove out to Chatham for a week to
watch their son play. They urged him to find easier work or quit—to
worry about his baseball, not money. Joe, a bear of a man, not tall but
heavy-set, had a strong grip and strong opinions. Since chemo treatments ended he had recovered most of his weight and all of his hair,
along with his quick laugh. He stood out in a crowd, olive-skinned,
animated. Jamie got his temperament from him. At the Hyannis
game before the Fourth, Joe D'Antona had sat in back of the plate in
a lemon-yellow golf shirt, sunglasses, and a straw hat, shouting out
instructions every time his son came to bat. His hoarse voice had cut
through the noise of the crowd. "Keep your weight back, Buzz!"
"Stay balanced, Buzz!" He couldn't help himself. He'd always been
there with Jamie, had coached him from a young age, had sat
through so many hours of batting lessons at Joe Benanto's cages that

he'd come to know that beautiful swing almost as well as Jamie did himself.

Jamie said he didn't mind the constant advice—but he didn't always follow it. "Me and my dad, we're both stubborn," he said. "We butt heads like it's our job." The two argued about hitting, about fishing, cooking, things they were both passionate about. Sometimes they argued just to get each other going. "I don't know why he doesn't listen to me," said Joe. "I guess he has to make his own mistakes. Just like I did."

The older D'Antona had been a catcher at Southern Connecticut State and had drawn the eye of professional scouts. He'd become a coach on Jamie's Little League team. Baseball dads in Trumbull could be a nightmare, he knew, and he'd wanted to protect his boy from their wrong-headed notions.

Joe had flown out to Alaska the previous summer for ten days to catch some games and to fish with Jamie. They'd gotten into some big salmon and had a great time together. But Joe's back had been bothering him. Jamie had thought he didn't look himself.

Jamie had nine days at home between the end of Alaska and school. On the second morning there he was awakened by his dad. Joe needed a lift to the hospital, for blood tests or something. Then Joe said, "No matter what happens, make sure you take care of the family," and Jamie knew for the first time that something was seriously wrong. He turned from his father, confused, and cried. He drove his dad to the hospital without speaking. From the hospital Jamie called his mother at work. She joined him, and the doctor asked, "Does anybody else in the family have cancer?" It was the first time Jamie had heard the word spoken.

Joe D'Antona had non-Hodgkin's lymphoma, localized around the kidney. They'd caught it early, the doctor thought. It was treatable with chemo and radiation. Jamie spent the next seven days with his dad at the hospital, scared and angry. Angry in general, and angry at his parents for the way they'd let him find out. Joe hadn't even mentioned it during their ten days together in Alaska. D'Antona returned to Wake Forest for his sophomore year. George Greer noticed the distractedness, had D'Antona over to dinner, looked out for him. Jamie hadn't talked to his father about the disease since.

Joe and Karin traveled to a lot of games at Wake Forest, flying several times each season between Connecticut and North Carolina. Over the past year, though, Joe had felt his son slipping away, needing his father less and less as he built a life at college. During the visits, Jamie, too busy with his friends, didn't make much time to see his parents. He didn't acknowledge them at the games. He'd practically stopped calling home, stopped asking his dad for advice, even stopped checking to see how his beloved pug, Otis, was doing. Jamie's growing independence was a natural part of growing up, of course, and for Joe, a part of letting go. But the transition coincided painfully with Joe's illness and Jamie's splashy entrance on the national college baseball scene. "He becomes a big star at Wake Forest and look at him," said Joe, "already big-leaguing his own family."

GEORGE GREER, like all college baseball coaches, had to fight for his players' allegiance at Wake Forest. He felt players needed to answer to one coach, one program. But Greer caught it coming and going—from fans, alumni, and especially the parents of his players, parents who, it had to be said, knew their kids better than he did. The occupational hazard worsened around parents whose kids had a shot at being drafted—when so much was at stake—and worst of all when a kid's father had played college or pro ball himself, as many had. (*My kid's a pull hitter—why are you making him hit the other way? Why'd you move my kid to second? Scouts don't look at second basemen! How can you pitch THAT kid ahead of my boy? Why teach him to throw overhand when he's thrown three-quarters his whole life and done just fine, thank you?* The fusillade of small and large grievances was endless.) A parent's voice in a kid's ear, Greer thought, was one voice too many—it confused, distracted. The game was hard enough. The last thing he wanted a baseball player to do was to think too much as the ball whistled toward him.

Joe D'Antona respected Greer. "George Greer and his staff have forgotten more baseball than I'll ever know," Joe said. "He's done an awful lot for Jamie's game." But Joe was ambivalent. In the same breath he pointed out that Greer had spent his entire career around aluminum bats. His teaching might have served winning with metal bats, but did it serve Jamie's swing, or Jamie's professional development? Joe's eye was on the major leagues. Anybody not heading Jamie that way didn't have his interests at heart. Joe had let Greer know as much.

In Chatham, Joe saw some old complaints showing up in Jamie's swing. Instead of keeping his weight back and quickly snapping his hips to trigger the swing, Jamie was sliding his weight into the pitch as he swung, relying more on linear force than the more explosive rotational force. Jamie's back foot wasn't pivoting and giving purchase; it was light on the ground, "flopping all over the place," Joe said, disgustedly. The swing's arc had shifted from an almost-flat plane to a pronounced uppercut, to generate greater lift, as Greer taught at school. That swing might be fine during batting practice, and against ACC pitching, Joe thought—especially with a metal bat. And it probably produced more distance and home runs for Jamie at Wake Forest. But with a wooden bat against top-drawer pitchers, that swing took too long, and its upward arc intersected just a fraction of the pitched ball's trajectory. That narrow tolerance too often produced strikeouts and pop flies. He wanted his son to get back to the swing he had worked so hard perfecting.

Joe had shown up early one afternoon at Veterans Field, and walked with Jamie down to the batting cage in left field to try and recapture the old sweetness. Schiffner looked out at the old man standing in the batting cage while Jamie took cuts off a tee, and was none too pleased. Schiffner saw his authority being undermined, in public, on his field. He saw a pushy father mistrusting Chatham coaches. He lumped Mr. D'Antona with other overinvolved fathers he'd dealt with. His favorite example was Kyle Snyder's dad, a hotshot brain surgeon in Florida. Schiffner had recruited Snyder, a power pitcher with the promise to become a high draft pick, in 1998. Before Dr. Snyder let his son play in Chatham, though, he'd insisted that the A's mail a uniform down to Florida ahead of time, to make sure it fit his son properly. He flew by private jet to Chatham and inspected the house where his son would live, then checked out the trainer at the Chatham Health Center. This summer was too important to Kyle's future to leave to chance, said the dad. "That kid had to deal with way too many demons," said Charlie Thoms. Snyder, whether helped or hurt by his father's involvement, went to Chatham and kept going. He'd make it to The Show in 2003, with the Kansas City Royals.

Michael Moon's father had paid his son's private hitting instructor to fly in from California for a few days, to keep Michael on track. Blake Hanan's father, Jim, had searched the Internet for eyeglasses to help Blake see the ball better under the lights. (Blake had blamed his strikeouts on poor night vision.) Jim Hanan had a double interest in his son's playing on Cape Cod. He had grown up in Falmouth, on Buzzard's Bay. He'd played baseball, but wasn't good enough for the Cape League. He had worked in his family's restaurant, though, alongside busboys from the Falmouth Commodores. Some nights Jim slipped out early and caught the last inning or two of a Commodores game. The players, the league, had seemed fantastic to him. He hoped to have a son who might play there. Jim had answered Schiffner's call to Blake the previous summer. Without even asking Blake, he'd said, "Yes, of course! Blake would love to play for the A's."

In the stands, Jim Hanan chatted affably with other parents. He talked positively about Blake, about what a thrill it was to play in this league, about how much fun the summer had been. He'd taken three trips to the Cape already to watch Blake play. Every moment, he said, had been a gift. But privately he bristled. He blamed the politics of the league for his son's lack of playing time. The Cape's reputation, he reasoned, depended on players from big-name colleges. Coaches had to cater to those relationships. Schiffner naturally would favor the name-school players over guys like Blake, regardless of ability.

Schiffner's approach generally invited little parental disagreement. He made sure all of his players got a chance to show their stuff—even if not as much as some parents wished. His assistants worked with the players at the players' request. The coaches gently pointed things out. To relax and be confident. To throw strikes, get ahead in the count. To see the ball and hit it. Parents didn't find a lot to argue with in such general instruction. Except that when your kid was hitting .210 with scouts watching, it was tempting to blame the coach. When a kid was failing for the first time in his life, a parent couldn't easily sit by and not try to help.

Joe D'Antona didn't know that Jamie was stubbornly overswinging, trying to kill the ball to impress the scouts, against the wishes of the Chatham coaches. Schiffner watched the father out in the batting cage talking with his son, and—childless himself—saw the arrogance, not the love.

D'ANTONA'S HOUSE PARENTS in Chatham, Paul and Laurie Galop, had hosted ballplayers since '94. They never mentioned it to Jamie, but they'd specifically asked for him. Laurie's mother had lived with cancer for fourteen years before passing away. Paul had told Charlie Thoms. "In case Jamie's having a bad day," he said, "we might be able to talk to him." Paul had grown up in New Jersey and thought he could relate to D'Antona. "The kids from Jersey, the City, the New York side of Connecticut, they can be a little mouthy, a little rough around the edges. I've been there, done that."

Unlike some newer host families, the Galops knew how little time the ballplayers might spend with their kids—they didn't expect surrogate big brothers or beach sitters. "Most of these guys," said Paul, "they get up at seven o'clock and take a shower. Then they come back after lunch and take a shower, or a nap, and then they lift or go to the beach and come back and take a shower before the game. Then they go to their game, and come home at nine-thirty, ten o'clock and take a shower, then go out. They take a lot of showers. We just try to be around for them whenever they need us."

The Galops didn't lay out a home-cooked meal every night, didn't take players sailing, as Charlie Thoms did, nor out pulling lobster traps, as Chad Orvella's house dad did. When was there time? Laurie, a third-grade teacher during the school year, handled the A's' merchandise business with her daughter, Kate; they worked the tent at the home games. She set up early at the field and didn't get home most nights until ten-thirty. Paul assessed loans all day at a bank in Yarmouth and put in extra hours as the A's' treasurer and P.A. announcer. He chaired the league's hall-of-fame committee and was moving toward ever-higher positions in the league's administration.

The Galops had moved to Chatham in 1980. The A's ran on a budget then of less than $30,000 a year. There was no merchandise, no food other than that supplied by a "roach coach" that rolled into the parking lot during home games. Paul and Laurie had bought a little store downtown that sold sporting goods. One of the directors of the Chatham A's came around and said to Paul, "Do you like baseball? You might want to get involved here. It's a great league, and a great team, and they buy their uniforms from you." At his first meeting of the Chatham Athletic Association in the old firehouse, Galop was struck by the makeup of the crowd—former national sales managers, retired corporate bigwigs. "A roomful of George Steinbrenner wannabes," he recalled. "Powerful people with strong personalities, and everybody had something to say."

An A's coach came by to pick up an order at the store, and Paul recognized him from high school ball back in Morris County, New Jersey.

Paul said, "John Schiffner?"

Schiffner said, "Paul Galop? What the hell are you doing here?"

And the Galops got involved. Paul became the A's treasurer in '95, and inherited hundreds of dollars' worth of bills and $36 in the checking account. He and Laurie threw in seventy-five bucks and paid an electric bill. But things were changing. The association's decision to rehire John Schiffner as manager following Chatham's last-place finish had split the directorate. Many of the old guard quit over the decision. The faction included most of the people who had fretted about the team's growing budget. The association had gone without team stationery, recruited players only from east of the Mississippi to save travel costs, said nay to most ideas that required investment. In their place emerged a new breed of doers, people like Paul and Laurie Galop, Charlie Thoms, and Peter Troy, a skilled administrator with an entrepreneurial spirit who ran a nationally known school for autistic kids.

The new group raised revenues instead of cutting costs. (Early on, someone suggested passing the hat for donations twice each game, as they did with the collection plate in the Catholic church. But the board in Chatham, mostly Protestant, nixed the idea.) Peter Troy and Paul Galop focused first on the yearbook, which cost the team five grand a year and brought in only six or seven. The two men approached the Chatham Bars Inn, and came away with an annual donation, up front, for the cost of printing—from then on ads would be pure profit. They aggressively recruited volunteers, sold advertising, eventually increasing earnings of "the book" to more than $25,000. The donors' list grew to eight pages. The new board pushed merchandise hard, brought food concessions in-house, promoted the local youth clinic every chance they got. Nearly seven hundred kids went through the seven weeks' of clinics that summer of 2002, earning the A's more than $30,000 after expenses. The food concession below the press box (Paul's mom, Agnes, ran the register) took in another thirty grand. Merchandise sales went crazy. At the start of the season, fifty-two fish totes held the inventory Laurie and Kate would sell that summer from the tent behind home plate: miniature A's bats, bumper stickers, key chains, coffee mugs, pens, caps, fleece pullovers, canvas bags, towels, sweat shirts, thirteen styles of T-shirts. The T-shirt designs were inspired—Paul and Laurie came up with new slogans every winter. "Chatham Athletics: Diamond Specialists Since 1923"; "Cape League IS Baseball"; "100% Pure Baseball"; one

SOMETHING LIKE A FAMILY

design was a take-off on a MasterCard ad campaign—it featured a
"Chatham A's game card" on the front of the shirt, and on the back:

ADMISSION: FREE
PARKING: FREE
AUTOGRAPHS: FREE
EVENING AT VETERANS FIELD: PRICELESS

By the end of the season only two fish totes and a few dozen un-
sold hats remained, and sales topped $95,000, about as much sold by
the other nine teams combined. The team's revenues for the fiscal
year would top a quarter of a million dollars. The checkbook balance,
$36 when Paul Galop took over, would climb to nearly $150,000. By
2002, Chatham had become the New York Yankees of the Cape Cod
Baseball League: prosperous, hated, emulated, envied. Mary Hen-
derson, the president of the Harwich organization, once sniffed,
"You guys could cut grass and put it in a baggie and sell Chatham
grass for ten bucks." The commitment of the A's top volunteers ran
year-round.

"We're not committed," said Laurie Galop. "We should *be* committed."

"We've created a monster," said Paul.

At home, the Galops grabbed time with the players as they could,
rehashing the games late at night—Paul loved that part of the day—
and cherished the moments. They'd hung framed pictures on the living room wall of every player they'd hosted, and kept in touch with
many by e-mail or phone. They could walk a visitor through eight
summers of stories, in detail, as if they'd happened yesterday. The two
had never forgotten how much it had meant to their son, Pete, when
their players, one year, came and watched one of his Little League
games. Both Paul and Laurie told dozens of tales of boys being boys—
they'd found stolen baseball bats beneath one player's bed; found girls
in their players' beds; found a player asleep in a rolled-up living-room
carpet; found a *mushroom* growing in the damp, wet-towel-filled

downstairs bathroom. One summer a neighbor below them called to complain about water balloons raining down from the direction of the Galops' back deck. "Can't be us," said Paul. "We're a good hundred yards from your place." Then he looked out on his deck and saw two players launching balloons skyward from a homemade catapult. Another time he and Laurie had driven home after dropping Kate at summer camp, and discovered two hundred kids partying. A Chatham cop, Joe Fennell, showed up and said to Paul, "You know, they sent me up here, but I couldn't believe it was your house."

"I can't believe it's my house either," Paul had answered.

A player named Gabe Alvarez, who went on to play shortstop with the Tigers, pointed a video camera at Fennell and said, "Officer, we'd like to get a few words. What do you think of this party?"

"Turn that thing off!" Fennell commanded.

Alvarez came back a few minutes later and said, "Now, back to you officer. What do you think? Never mind. Camera back on me!"

After that, whenever Paul and Laurie saw Alvarez on TV, one of them would say, "Camera back on me!"

The stories were fun—the brushes with celebrity added luster to their lives, too, and reflected some glory—but there was a deeper level to ballplayers living with host families. The athletes, some for the first time, were a hundred or a thousand miles from home, living with strangers who might be difficult, overweening, wonderful, generous. Coping with unfamiliarity was part of the players' coming of age. Host families exposed the players to different lives, to couples who were long-married and in love and had no idea they were role models; to other couples who were wealthy and distant; to single moms, even, who tried to sleep with them. (The seduction scenes in the movie *Summer Catch* angered a lot of adults around Chatham, but they were based on true events, as Thoms and Schiffner reluctantly admitted. One woman's name had been stricken from the housing list in recent years and a current one was suspect. What coming-of-age memories would *those* players carry?) The intensity worked on families, too. On kid sisters who got first crushes. On young boys who looked up to the boarders as heroes. On families, some years, who got intimate introductions to people of a different class or race.

Over time the Galops had learned to read twenty-year-old athletes. "Boys in men's bodies," Laurie called them. But they had trouble agreeing about Jamie D'Antona. Laurie thought he showed flashes of maturity but was a long way from growing up—she didn't appreciate his mouthiness, the way he picked nits and argued with Kate, the two going at each other like brother and sister. At one point that summer, Kate got sick, and D'Antona ragged on her mercilessly—called her a lazy bum, told her to get her butt off the couch and stop faking it. Then that night D'Antona heard Pete Galop's voice come over the P.A., not Paul's. He felt like an idiot when he found out that Pete's dad had driven Kate to the hospital for an emergency appendectomy.

Laurie said, "I got tired those first couple of weeks of Jamie's woe-is-me routine. I came back one night and Jamie was standing in the kitchen, banging his head right on the counter and saying, 'I suck, I suck.' I said, 'Yeah, you do suck. And it's about time you sucked it up around here. There are people who work their asses off all winter long for you guys, and the least you can do is go out and play like you mean it.' Pete and his girlfriend watched the whole thing from the living room. I thought she was going to fall off the sofa when she heard me. But my whole relationship with Jamie changed. We became closer after that."

Paul said, "Jamie is very New Jersey—very Type A, probably ADHD. He talks so fast he can't even get his sentences out. I think his father's illness is weighing on him. I've talked a little bit with him about it, but Jamie is always scattered, bouncing from one subject to another. His energy is exhausting. But he's a good kid, he's got a good heart. He works his butt off. He reminds me of Eric Byrnes, who lived with us the summer we had the two Erics, who's up with the Oakland A's right now. Both those guys have so much focus it's unbelievable. When Jamie gets a taste of something, he's going to run with it. You watch."

Just before his parents left, D'Antona quit working Saturdays for South Cape Seafood and asked for a couple of days off. The TENS unit wasn't making much difference. Maybe rest would. He'd struck out twenty-nine times in twenty-four games. Schiffner had moved him up and down the lineup, searching for a combination that would ignite the A's. As a whole, the team was batting .199, lower than every other league team but one.

D'Antona was settling into a summer routine, but the days blurred together: up at six-thirty and to work at South Cape, then lunch and work at Nick's, early B.P. at three-thirty (when the team was at home) or on the road for away games, ball games every night, the beach or Charlie Thoms's or the bar in the VFW basement for an hour or two of drinking or hanging out afterward, then up early to do it again. (Billy and Mimi had introduced D'Antona to the bar at the VFW. It was one of the few places in Chatham where an underage guy could get a drink.) D'Antona lived life by extremes, going full tilt or crashed on the couch. At Wake Forest, he liked nothing better than to come back to the apartment after a hard game and lie on the floor and let his dog, Hunter, lick his face for fifteen or twenty minutes. His house-mate at the Galops', Adam Yates, who saw more of D'Antona crashed than the other players did, knew D'Antona's hectic hours, but couldn't figure out why. D'Antona never stopped to do laundry, never cleaned his room. "Here, let me show you," Yates said to a fan in Falmouth one night who had asked what it was like to room with Jamie. Yates rooted around in the dirt for a few scraps of trash—a crushed paper cup, some gum wrappers, an old piece of athletic tape—and made a pile. Then he drew a neat square in the dirt right next to it. "My side of the room," he said, pointing at the square. "Jamie's," he said, pointing at the trash. "No wait," he said, and scuffed more debris and dirt onto the pile. "There."

When D'Antona did have some rare free time, he kicked back in a paddleboat, took his shirt off, and spent hours fishing at Emery Pond, usually with Aaron Trolia. Troila didn't like fishing all that much, but he liked being around D'Antona.

Trolia, a burly pitcher who would be transferring to Clemson from a community college in Washington State in the fall, was a party guy. He was one of the four players who eventually squeezed into the basement apartment at Charlie and Ginor's, the newspaper ad having turned up no new host families. His first night there, Thoms had wandered into the kitchen and found Trolia there, poking into cupboards. "Do you guys have any shot glasses?" Trolia had asked, and Thoms knew what was in store downstairs. (The next day Thoms moved the clean-living Colt Morton to the spare bedroom upstairs, away from the four pitchers down below.) Win or lose, Trolia was having the summer of his life. The Chatham A's were, by far, the best team he'd ever been a part of. He was the only player who'd gotten lucky after the Fourth of July parade. A college student working as a chambermaid at the Hawthorne motel had caught a ball with his number on it, and called. She now joined him and D'Antona at the bonfires, regularly bringing a couple of coworkers with her.

D'Antona was one of those guys who generated fun. And D'Antona's star power made Trolia a somebody. The choice of friends, for D'Antona, was revealing. At Wake Forest he shared an apartment and socialized with the second-tier players. It was easier for D'Antona to leave the game at the field that way, easier to talk about something other than baseball, to not get caught up in it. He liked hanging out with guys who weren't so serious. From a distance, though, D'Antona's friends had the look of an entourage. Most Chatham players liked him and thought he was fun. By the end of the summer, few besides Trolia felt close to him.

Against Harwich on July 13, D'Antona batted seventh, as low as he'd batted on any team. Before the A's took the field, the starters drew in together and painted eye black on each other's faces—Ryan Johnson's idea, a gesture aimed at getting into Brad Ziegler's head. Ziegler was pitching against them for the third time in a month. None of the A's said a word about the eye black, they just wore it as an inside joke. Most of the people at the field that night didn't even notice.

Ziegler wore his eye-black, as usual. He entered the game having thrown twenty-seven innings that season without a walk—a league record he lengthened with every new batter. He had shut out the A's in his two previous starts, and had held D'Antona hitless in seven at bats. By chance, again, he was pitching opposite his former Chatham housemate, Fraser Dizard. The grudge the returning A's players held against Ziegler had spread to the newer guys, and now there were two shutouts in addition to repay. The ill will added an undercurrent of tension in the A's dugout.

Ziegler lived in a different world. His Christian faith anchored him, as ever. Alongside his autograph on balls and bats he scribbled *1st John 5:5,* hoping youngsters would look it up. *Who is he that overcometh the world, but he that believeth that Jesus is the Son of God?* But Ziegler's life had changed. He'd married the previous fall, and had adult responsibilities that the A's players still deferred. He'd enrolled at a small college that summer just off the Cape for an education class that Southwest Missouri didn't offer, and so was living forty miles from his home ball field in Harwich, halfway to his class. The class took three evenings a week, and Ziegler's coach had arranged the pitching schedule around them. Ziegler planned to give pro ball a run, but he knew that even successful major league careers didn't last long. He was preparing for a future of teaching and coaching in college. He fit his day job in by starting at 5:00 A.M. at the Hyannis Country Club. His wife worked at a toy store to help make ends meet. The previous Friday they'd been hit with a $300 towing bill on top of a $1,500 estimate for transmission repair.

As he mowed the A's down in the first inning, and then again in the second, he appeared to be the epitome of self-control. He threw without apparent emotion, and he threw hard; his sidearm fastball was at eighty-four, eighty-five, and his overhand a few miles faster than that. He wasn't afraid to throw inside and move a batter off the plate. But Ziegler battled demons. He'd been ejected from games more than once, and struggled constantly with his anger. Before every pitch he said two silent prayers: *Please help me control my temper. Please let nobody get hurt on this pitch.*

In the third inning, his streak of innings without a walk now at twenty-nine, Ziegler got too careful. Gradually, almost subconsciously, he'd started worrying more about giving up a walk than getting outs. He was relying too much on his fastball. The A's finally got to him. Five straight eye-blacked batters touched him for hits, and Chatham scored five runs. The guys in the bullpen went nuts. Ziegler had given up just four runs in the five other games he'd pitched.

The outburst woke him up. He turned aggressive, worked the edges of the plate, and, in his words, "started pitching again." He walked Chad Orvella in the fifth, and instead of getting angry he felt the burden of the need for perfection lifted. He gave up just one hit after that and looked, if anything, more dominant than in his previous two games against Chatham. Toward the end, Ziegler volunteered to finish the game because his team had used three relievers the prior night, and he knew they could use the breather. He finished strong, throwing 125 pitches. He struck out D'Antona once and held him hitless. He hadn't noticed the A's players' eye-black. Someone told him about it days later, and he smiled when he heard it.

Fraser Dizard logged the win for the A's. He gave up four hits and two runs before he reached his hundred-pitch limit in the sixth, and—as far as he was concerned—something far more important: For the first time since his elbow injury that spring, he'd aired out his arm without pain. Larry Doughty, the national cross-checker for the Milwaukee Brewers, picked up Dizard's fastball at ninety miles per hour. It was a little early for such a high-level scout to be on the Cape, but Doughty had come out to watch Team USA's swing through the New England Collegiate Baseball League, and was being efficient. A couple of Brewer scouts had done advance work, thinning the prospect list Doughty worked from. Next to Fraser

Dizard's name Doughty wrote: *Good arm action. Fluid, throws with a lot of ease. Seems to be savvy—knows how to get hitters out. Release points inconsistent early but settled into good consistency. Good movement. Very good change up. Arm action should get even better as he pitches more.*

Dizard returned after the game to his host family's place on Mill Pond Road, a gracious shingled house with landscaped grounds, in-ground pool, and a watery view of sailboats moored in the sheltered harbor of Mill Pond. The nervousness he'd felt since arriving had lessened with each game he pitched—now that he'd finally cut loose and felt no pain, he felt weightless, ecstatic. He fell asleep that night in a double bed in his wood-paneled room on the second floor. Outside, a thin crescent moon shone on the sailboats in Mill Pond, a scene as fragile as glass.

NEAR THE END of his parents' visit, Jamie D'Antona spied a "Help Wanted" sign at a tackle shop on Route 28 between Chatham and Orleans. The owner wasn't in, but D'Antona chatted with the guy's friend for half an hour. The friend left a note for Joe Fitzback, the owner: "Great guy. Friendly. Knowledgeable. Should hire him." A day later D'Antona quit at South Cape Seafood and took the new job. He fit the opening perfectly—he worked mornings in the store, talked with customers about gear and techniques and where the fish were biting, and worked the register. He wouldn't need to lift anything heavier than a saltwater rod.

He'd opened up to his parents again, letting them in. He promised to call home. He wasn't done needing them yet. "It hurts like hell watching Jamie struggle so much," said Joe D'Antona. "But, at least for a while, it's nice to have our son back."

Two days later Fraser Dizard's father was diagnosed with a brain tumor. His summer over, Dizard flew home to Washington right away, leaving behind his Bronco and all his belongings. Some things are bigger than baseball.

NINE

Waiting for Hindman

THE HEAT RELENTED FOR A DAY, but the drought continued. Halfway through July, on a cool, humid afternoon, Scott Hindman walked to the mound of the Cape Cod Tech High School baseball field in Brewster. The grass around him had browned in patches. The sprinkler system had broken just after the school's maintenance chief had left for vacation. Nobody else knew how to fix the thing. The wind whipped across the field out of the southwest, at Hindman's back, swirling minicyclones of infield dust. The dry field looked shabby.

Hindman walked on his toes, head tipped slightly back. He led with his chest, nose in the air. His left arm hung stiffly, bent at the injured elbow. He'd been unable to straighten it fully since the ligament surgery almost two years ago. He'd thrown only ten innings on the Cape, but the Anaheim Angels had seen enough. They wanted to sign him and get him out to Provo, Utah, to their rookie team in the Pioneer League. Hindman wanted a lot more money than they were offering. He was in no hurry. He liked living in the basement of Charlie Thoms's house, at the center of the team's social life. He liked fooling around in the bullpen. One night at Harwich, with the A's in need of a late-inning rally, Hindman had furiously rubbed together two pieces of a broken bat. He'd managed to produce a few wisps of smoke, but no fire. The bullpen guys were always doing stuff like that, and Hindman was often behind it. In Chatham one night he talked Thomas

Pauly into ordering a large pepperoni pizza on his cell phone, delivered right there to the bullpen. Another night at home, the pitchers messed with the little kids who hung by the fence waiting for autographs. Hindman said, "Hey! Do us a favor! We need a box of curve balls. Can you go over to the Cotuit bullpen and ask if we can borrow theirs?" The little kids came back, and earnestly apologized. "They said they don't have any, but they were wondering if they could borrow your left-handed fungo bat." And back and forth they went ("the key to the batter's box," and so on), the youngsters trying to please their heroes. "We wore those kids out," Hindman said afterwards.

He told his teammates he'd be happy staying in Chatham all season even if he didn't throw another inning. Over the past several days, though, the Angels had turned up the heat.

Behind the chain-link backstop in Brewster, a platoon of scouts aimed their radar guns at Hindman. Among the scouts was Guy Mader, one of Anaheim's two cross-checkers. In the hierarchy of the Angels' scouting department, Mader stood right below the director, Donny Rowland, who ran the show from Anaheim. In the normal migration of scouts, Mader was a week or so early. National cross-checkers tended to arrive right around the league's all-star game at the end of July, after the area scouts had completed dozens of evaluations and regional supervisors had narrowed the higher-ups' focus. The overlapping layers put two and three sets of eyes on the most-favored prospects, each level bringing wider perspective to the evaluation. Mader lived a few hours away, in Tewksbury, Massachusetts, though, and he'd come not for routine reasons, but to put pressure on Scott Hindman.

The Angels had started working on Hindman right after the draft. Their mid-Atlantic scout, Tom Burns, had driven up from Pennsylvania and caught Hindman's second appearance. Burns hadn't been assigned to the Cape that summer, but Princeton fell in his home territory. Burns had pushed hard for Hindman with the Angels' front office, and he remained the contact man between the team and the player.

Hindman had pitched only briefly that night, against Orleans. He'd struggled to find a rhythm, throwing two pitches out of the strike zone for every dirty slider or low fastball strike. He'd left the bases loaded for Adam Yates, who got out of the jam with no runs and preserved for Hindman stats that looked good on paper. After the game, Hindman, still in uniform, had driven straight to Burns's room at the Chatham Motel on Route 28. Hindman was pissed at having been selected in the twenty-second round. He'd been led to believe he'd go in the top ten, where he felt he belonged.

He came off as cocky, but Scott Hindman was not a typical Cape League baseball player. He was a history major with a 3.5 grade-point average at Princeton. He approached his negotiation with the Angels as he did any research project. He knew how major league clubs treated a $25,000 investment and how they treated a $200,000 one, the nurturing and patience and benefit of the doubt growing with the dollars. In the bottom half of the draft, the biggest value in the contract wasn't even money but the thin crack it opened into the doorway of professional baseball. Most players drafted in the low rounds began and ended their careers as "organizational players," bodies kept on minor league teams just to fill out the rosters. Once players started their minor league careers, they all received the same flat salary, 850 bucks a month to start in short-season A ball, and inched up each rung of the ladder from there. Judging by salaries, all minor leaguers played on the same level field. But guys who signed for a thousand bucks in the thirty-eighth round carried that label like an anchor throughout their professional careers, no matter how well they performed.

Hindman knew that *Baseball America* had pegged him at number 120 on its projected draft list—around the start of the fifth round— and as the fifteenth highest rated left-handed pitcher in the country. He knew how coveted left-handed pitchers were. A left-hander's breaking ball veered away from left-handed batters—a distinct advantage. Yet in a country where 10 percent of the population was left-handed, only a small minority of that minority had the talent to pitch in the major leagues. A major league team, hungry for lefties, typically carried only two or three on its roster, each of them a precious commodity. Hindman had tracked down the signing bonuses for similar positions in the past few drafts, and for the other top left-handers in his class who had already signed. He was adept in the library, on the Internet, on the phone.

He talked about himself with his teammates, describing where he stood in the universe of amateur draft-eligible pitchers, dropping references and statistics so casually that he sounded like a bullshitter. But the guy had done his homework.

He couldn't factor in the uncertain shape of his left elbow, of course, but that was for the Angels to decide, not him. He wasn't going to tell them that his arm hadn't felt right in four years. That he'd forgotten what it was like to throw without pain.

He had talked with scouts. Most struck him as slick and aggressive. He'd looked at some of them and thought, *You know, I'm a hell of a lot smarter than you.* But he liked Burns, and regarded him more as a friend than as an Angels employee. The two didn't dicker about the bonus that night, though Burns assured Hindman that the Angels certainly weren't thinking about twenty-second-round money. They had simply gambled that his injury would scare off other teams. They'd waited as long as they dared. They could talk money—regardless of his draft slot—after he'd shown his arm in the Cape Cod League.

The Angels' East Coast supervisor had driven into Chatham unannounced a couple of weeks later on the chance he'd see Hindman pitch in relief, a dicey bet which the scout lost. After the second game he watched, the scout pulled Hindman aside and the two of them walked down by the equipment shed behind the left-field fence. They talked while teenage girls spread out among the players for autographs and little kids tore around the base paths, pretending to be major leaguers. The fans packed up their blankets and lawn chairs, unaware of the two figures out there in the shadows.

The scout tried to tear down Hindman's expectations, remind him he was a risk. The two were still talking long after the lights had gone out.

"He tried to be a hard-ass," said Hindman afterwards. "He offered $60,000 to sign and $40,000 for school, and I told him, 'No way.' I wasn't being a prick, but they were pricking me." What the scout had failed to understand was that Scott Hindman felt he had the world by the balls, no matter what happened. Hindman was the kind of guy who could pick and choose among opportunities, who made this run at baseball seem like another adventure along the way. Most players had no idea what their lives would look like after baseball. They prayed they'd be drafted, didn't even think about the alternative, or the end. Baseball was not only the center of their lives but the sum total. If those players washed out, as most would before reaching the majors, they'd look back and see failure. Hindman would be off on the next adventure, surrounded by smart, interesting people who'd find his baseball career exotic. When he became a partner in a law firm or the head of some foundation, the fact that he'd played pro ball would simply be another cool facet of his successful past.

Hindman had retained an agent named Barry Meister, who was big in the sports world—his marquee clients included the Arizona Diamondback's all-star pitcher, Randy Johnson. Hiring an agent violated NCAA rules. To protect Hindman's amateur status as a college player, in case he didn't sign, Meister served only as an "adviser," and was disallowed from doing Hindman's bidding with the big-league club. The distinction was a technicality that often went ignored. Advisers routinely spoke on the phone, and sometimes in person, with scouts and scouting directors—particularly when representing players at the high end of the draft. Since 1981, when Yale's Ron Darling was the only top draft pick to hire an agent, the number of agents in the game had proliferated alongside the burgeoning salaries and bonuses. Among the top fifty players drafted in 2002, only four were negotiating contacts on their own—all the rest had agents. Some observers said the draft had become agent-driven and blamed agents for the inflation of signing bonuses. Teams could no longer draft the best player available. They drafted the best player they could afford, which often meant passing over a prospect simply because a powerful agent had set too high a demand for his client's "package." Since the 2000 draft, in an effort to rein in owners who couldn't rein in themselves, Major League Baseball's commissioner's office has recommended signing levels for every draft slot in the first few rounds. In theory, the recommendations established benchmarks that were fair and public, which took some of the negotiating power away from agents. In practice, teams still paid out bonuses "above slot" without penalty.

The big-name agents and the mega-agencies, the Scott Borases and the IMGs, looked at the scouting reports and cherry-picked the highest likely draft choices. They worked the phones, typically calling the players' parents at home. A 4 percent commission on a half-million-dollar pick meant twenty grand—and that was just the start if the client went on to the majors. Other agents, competing for the unrepresented, showed up at fields on Cape Cod, getting a read on players and approaching parents in the stands to sell their services. Some of the agents, with radar guns and stopwatches, were hard to tell from the young scouts.

Hindman's connections to Meister ran deep: Meister was, like Hindman, from Chicago and had kids in schools Hindman had pitched against. He was a friend of Princeton's coach, Scott Bradley, and had represented Chris Young, a Princeton pitcher drafted by the Pittsburgh Pirates in the third round in 2000.

The Pirates had promised Young a minimum of five hundred grand—good money but well below the market rate—and told him to go to the Cape and prove how good he was against top-level talent. Bradley had worked the pipeline to Chatham. Every time Chris Young pitched for the A's that season the Pirates upped their offer by tens or even hundreds of thousands of dollars. And every time they called, Young told them to treat him like a third-round pick and he'd consider it. That summer, Team USA played an exhibition game in Chatham against a Cape Cod League all-star team. That single game—with five thousand fans crowded into every seat and open space around Veterans Field, with more than one hundred big league scouts looking on, with pageantry that included a military fly-over and pregame parachutists—was perhaps the greatest concentration ever of one year's college talent. Knowing he'd throw only two innings that day, Chris Young didn't pace himself. He let it fly against the élite hitters of Team USA, and stifled them. He pitched impressively through the end of the summer, and signed for $1.75 million. Hindman wasn't looking at that kind of money, but he liked the precedent. Meister had deftly advised Young—whose two-sport eligibility issues also affected his N.B.A. prospects—and he understood how important the education part of the package was to Princeton athletes. Meister advised Hindman to hold out for a hundred fifty grand, plus school: fifth-round money.

Guy Mader, down from Tewksbury, had introduced himself to Hindman in Bourne—the day the A's spent so long in hot traffic—before his second start. Hindman had pitched three showy innings and lit up the radar guns with tailing fastballs in the low nineties. One scout clocked a pitch at ninety-five and turned to another and said, "Ninety-five? Did you get ninety-*five?*"

Four days later Mader showed up at Hindman's next appearance, at home, in relief against Wareham. Against NCAA rules, he treated Hindman to a meal at the Squire. The two didn't talk numbers, but Hindman could sense things starting to move. His next game was the one in Brewster. Mader was there again.

IN THE WIND and swirling dust, Hindman kept the ball low and got the first three batters on groundballs. Only one pitch was stung—to D'Antona at third, who stayed down on it and picked it soft as cotton; his defense was coming around. Hindman threw seven fastballs that inning, all between eighty-nine and ninety-one miles an hour. More important to Mader, they had life in them, sinking down and away from right-handed batters. His slider broke sharply. In the second inning Hindman fell behind a couple of batters, and walked Anthony Gwynn. He stood like a pro pitcher out there: broad shoulders, wide hips, thick legs on a tall frame. His arm still didn't feel loose or springy, but he'd regained the air of cockiness missing in his earlier starts. His subtle mannerisms had authority. He quickly scraped dirt from the pitching rubber with his cleats, he leaned forward and snapped his glove in front of him, almost impatient for the catcher's return throws. It was a practiced, not wholly genuine, gesture. Hindman had heard that scouts liked to see pitchers hungry to get the ball back and make the next pitch. That was one difference between him and Stauffer, who showed hunger because he *was* hungry.

Halfway through Hindman's delivery, though, a slight hitch interrupted the flow of the motion. It stopped his arm from getting full, smooth extension, and in that instant Hindman looked unpolished, unsophisticated. Bobby Myers, the A's pitching coach, thought Hindman had "high school mechanics." Scouts saw the same thing, but overlooked flaws they knew could be corrected. The scouts focused on the sinking movement of his major-league-speed fastball, and a wicked slider that some big league pitchers never mastered. If anything, his imperfect form was a plus—it left room for yet more improvement, left some room to project. As long as his arm was sound.

With Gwynn on first, Hindman threw a fastball—from the stretch position, a quicker, more compact motion pitchers use with runners on base—that topped ninety, even without the whip of a full windup. Behind the backstop, the East Coast supervisor from the Kansas City Royals said, "He has a good arm. He's inconsistent right now—he throws two good curve balls followed by a bad one. He gets behind hitters then finishes strong. That's probably a result of not being totally comfortable with his body and his motion. Once he gets comfortable, he should be solid." The scout knew how many innings Hindman had pitched on the Cape that season, when he'd last pitched—impressive, given that he also knew another big league club already controlled Hindman's future.

Guy Mader watched impassively.

Hindman finished the inning without giving up a hit. In the third his inconsistency continued: He struck out the Brewster shortstop on a nearly unhittable slider, but hit a batter and walked another. With the bases loaded and two outs, he fell behind three balls and no strikes to Brewster's number five hitter, a burly Hawaiian from Brigham Young University named Kainoa Obrey. Hindman fired in a called strike, and then another, then got Obrey to hit a routine ground ball to shortstop. At the last moment, the ball took a crazy hop sideways off the dry dirt, and Chad Orvella dived to his left, speared the ball, and flipped it to Blake Hanan covering second. The flip came too late to catch the runner, but Hanan turned and threw to first—another head's-up play—and nipped the slow-moving Kainoa Obrey. Hindman escaped without giving up a run.

In the fourth inning, the P.A. welcomed Gus Quattlebaum to the game. It was a down-home tradition at some ball fields to acknowledge former Cape players in the stands. Quattlebaum had played in Chatham in '96. He was a good-looking guy whom teammates had called "G.Q." He stood with the scouts behind home plate, doing area work for the New York Yankees. With Quattlebaum, Mader, and the others looking on, Hindman gave up a harmless groundball single sandwiched between three quick outs, and finished his audition in style: four innings, one hit, no runs.

After Hindman's exit, half of the scouts took off for an evening game between Harwich and Orleans, but Guy Mader stayed till the end. Chatham won 1–0, a combined four-hit shutout. Mader saw the same qualities that Tom Burns had advertised: a "plus" fastball with movement, a quality breaking pitch that was a work in progress, a feel for a changeup, one of the easier pitches for minor league instructors to improve. Hindman had a power arm and three potential major league pitches, which meant he could be groomed for starting and relieving, both.

Mader shook Hindman's hand, congratulated him, and said that the Angels would love to get something done this next week. Hindman had taped ice around his shoulder and elbow. The elbow felt numb even without the ice. He smiled and said he would, too.

SCOTT HINDMAN HAD grown up in a landscaped neighborhood of doctors and lawyers and CEOs in suburban Inverness, Illinois, northwest of Chicago. His mother was an elementary school principal, his father, vice-president of a Fortune 500 company. His background told part of the story of the game's changing demographics. At the professional level, the game evolved along with the country from rural, working-class roots. Over the twentieth century, rosters changed in concert with the American population's migration south and west, the growing black population, the explosion of Hispanic immigration, and, more recently, the wave of immigrants from Asia. Of the 1,218 players who appeared on big league rosters in 2002, nearly 25 percent were foreign-born. The Anaheim Angels, without an especially aggressive international focus, employed scouts in Japan, Mexico, the Dominican Republic, and Venezuela.

The United States, meanwhile, had become a country of suburbs, and that's where American ballplayers came from. The teenager shuffling in from the mall wearing baggy pants and Walkman earphones had replaced the barefoot country boy showing up for a try-out with hay in his hair. Almost all of the 2002 Chatham A's came from suburbia.

The Cape Cod Baseball League mirrored the demographics of the game on a couple of levels. Increasingly, major league teams were recruiting from colleges, not high schools. College players had more growth and experience, had longer track records, and were less expensive for big league clubs to draft and develop, something that poorer, small-market franchises especially appreciated. It was easier to project the course of their development into the future. ("College players don't necessarily have more emotional maturity," pointed out one scout, "but at least we've had three years longer to figure them out.") Some teams—notably the successful, low-budget Oakland Athletics, whose passion for college players would be chronicled in

Michael Lewis's bestseller *Moneyball*—relied on collegians for their top draft choices. The number of scouts on Cape Cod in the summer had risen in recent years, with the tide.

The players in the Cape Cod League reflected not professional but college baseball. Chatham didn't carry a single black or Latino player on its 2002 roster. The town had hosted just fourteen black players since 1990. It was tempting to look at the racial diversity of a major league team and at the all-white town of Chatham, and see a disconnect. But Chatham's numbers mirrored the Cape League's. Despite the league's promotion of famous African-American alumni Mo Vaughn, Albert Belle, and Frank Thomas, only a handful of minorities played on the Cape each summer. In Chatham, coaches and volunteers hardly thought about race—it seemed to be a nonexistent issue. Some of the veteran volunteers in town, though, knew families who had refused to house black athletes. Some recalled an ugly incident, from not that long ago, where a host family had told a black player he had to use the house's outdoor shower.

For the most part, though, it was not a situation where black players avoided the Cape because of any bigotry or isolation they'd feel in New England. None of the summer leagues—the Coastal Plain League, the Central Illinois League, the Jayhawk League—had high minority numbers. It was simply the story of college baseball. The *NCAA Ethnicity Report* listed 626 black players among the 9,392 Division I baseball players in the academic year 2000–2001, and just 528 Latinos. Those totals included the nation's sixteen historically black colleges—and the best of those black programs, Southern College in Florida, barely ranked in the top half of the 273 programs in Division I. At the University of Texas, which had won the national championship in Omaha in June, just two players on the thirty-man roster were black.

Major league baseball better reflected changing American demographics than did the college game, but it drew its diversity from different worlds. Black players were typically drafted directly out of high schools, often from inner cities; Latino players came from high schools in the U.S. and high schools (and special baseball academies supported by Major League Baseball) in the Caribbean and Latin America; Asian players, usually, were hand-picked from the very highest professional levels in Japan and South Korea and were moved directly to major league teams. Overall, the number of black players in the game was declining. Major league baseball was becoming more international and more suburban at the same time.

On the Cape, players didn't make a big deal about race. The only player on the A's who seemed to give any thought to the subject was Scott Hindman, who studied African-American history at Princeton, purely out of curiosity. His senior thesis explored umpiring in the old Negro leagues.

Tim Moss, a black infielder in Wareham, had been drawn to the Cape by the baseball and the movie *Summer Catch*. "It's not bad here," he said. "Last year I played in Nebraska." He knew of the other black players in the league but hadn't gone out of his way to befriend them. Dant'e Brinkley, a black outfielder for Harwich, had a sense of humor about the whole thing. He stepped back into the dugout after being called out on strikes and said, "Just another case of a white man keeping a black man down." He reached third base in Orleans one night, and said "Hey, bro'!" to the Cardinals' black third baseman, Myron Leslie. Leslie ignored him. "C'mon, man," said Brinkley. "We're *free*."

BEFORE HIS ARM went dead during the final game of his senior year in high school, Scott Hindman had been rated as the top pitching prospect in Illinois. His résumé sparkled. As a twelve-year-old, he'd pitched on a select travel team whose split-quads, playing a dizzying five-month schedule, won 145 games and lost twelve. He'd pitched in the prestigious "Area Code Games" and in the Pan-American Games in Venezuela. Cincinnati had taken a long shot on him, drafting him in the forty-eighth round ("Like number fourteen-hundred-something," said Hindman. "It was a joke."), even though Hindman's parents had warned teams not to draft their college-

bound son. Athletics and academics ran in the family. Hindman's father had played football at Colgate; his brother played baseball at
Columbia.

Hindman had thrown a pile of innings in high school—probably
too many—and he hoped that his arm needed only rest. He took the
summer off. Then, having rejected full scholarships from Duke and
Northwestern, he enrolled at Princeton. He came in as one of the
highest-profile recruits the Ivy League had seen in years.

In his first game as a Princeton freshman, during the spring trip at
Old Dominion, he blew out his elbow—actually felt something snap
this time, and then it felt like his arm wasn't there. That summer, Dr.
Jeffrey Bechler, an orthopedic surgeon at the Rutgers University
Medical Center, grafted ligaments from Hindman's right forearm
onto the medial collateral ligament that had ruptured in his left
elbow. The reconstruction, called "Tommy John surgery" after the
major league pitcher who first had it done, in 1974, had seemed like
a medical miracle at that time. Dr. Frank Jobe, who performed that
first procedure, gave John 100-to-1 odds against pitching again. John
went on to pitch in the big leagues for fourteen more years. In the
intervening years the surgery had become commonplace among
young pitchers. Anaheim scout Tom Burns didn't even consider it a
negative. It relieved the worry about a future ligament problem. He
talked about "Tommy John" as if it were preventive surgery.

In high school, Hindman had reached eighty-eight miles an hour
with his fastball—very fast, but not astonishing. By the time he
started throwing again, after sitting out his sophomore season at
Princeton, he had grown an inch and a half, to six foot three, and had
gained thirty pounds of muscle. As he worked into shape over the
winter of his junior year and started throwing for real again, his
elbow felt okay. His fastball had jumped to ninety-three miles per
hour. He'd thrown only sporadically that spring for coach Scott
Bradley, who wanted to bring Hindman back slowly—and who also
wouldn't trust a rehabbing pitcher in the chase for the Ivy League
title. Hindman struck out thirteen batters in just seven innings, but

walked eleven. His earned-run average of 15.43 was so high that it looked like a typo. He couldn't get his arm to feel right.

This past June, Tom Burns had called Hindman at home in Illinois and told him the Angels had drafted him. Burns said they'd like him to pitch in the Cape Cod League before talking money, though. The Angels had arranged a spot for him at Yarmouth-Dennis. Hindman immediately called Scott Bradley. Bradley didn't know Scott Pickler, the Y-D coach, but he knew that John Schiffner in Chatham would handle Hindman gently. Bradley called Schiffner and found him needing an arm he'd just lost to the draft. Hindman had arrived in Chatham two days later, in time for the first practice.

GUY MADER HAD seen enough. He phoned his boss in Anaheim and gave his report. As Hindman would later tell it, Donny Rowland, the Angels scouting director, called Tom Burns and said, "Get out to Chatham and don't come home until you sign him."

Hindman might have been flattering himself in the telling—he dramatized the stories he told about himself—or he might have misread the pressure Burns felt on the Tuesday following the Brewster game, the two of them finally talking money over lunch at the Squire. Burns covered a tough territory for pro prospects. Amateur players from California, Florida, and Texas dominated the draft each year. Powerful college conferences grew out of the fertile, sun-drenched ground of the Southeast, the Southwest, the West Coast. Burns had a chance to sell only a few mid-Atlantic guys each year to the front office. He'd given his all in his predraft presentations on Hindman. He'd put a lot on the line in selling Rowland on the soundness of Hindman's arm. The Angels had sent four people to the Cape to confirm Burns's faith. Burns was putting a lot of pressure on himself to close the deal. He'd signed just one other player that summer—a high school outfielder from Harrisburg, Pennsylvania, in the thirty-fifth round.

Burns must have felt a twinge of doubt as he sat down to lunch at the Squire. He had talked with Schiffner, and was aware of Hindman's reluctance to pitch that summer. Burns knew that the normal rehab time for "Tommy John" ranged from twelve to twenty months. It had now been twenty-three months since Hindman's surgery. He'd pitched impressively on the Cape, but he had taken longer than he should have between appearances. Over one stretch, Hindman had pitched only three times in twenty-four days. Either his arm was still damaged, or he was afraid to pitch, and either way Burns saw a flashing light. During their first conversation, at Burns's motel room, Burns had looked Hindman in the eye and asked him about it. Hindman had explained that he was simply easing back into a routine, intentionally keeping on a safe schedule. The explanation reassured Burns, who liked and wanted to trust Hindman anyway.

At the Squire, Burns offered $80,000 plus school, and Hindman said no. Burns looked crushed by the directness of the response. He didn't even bother to finish lunch.

Hindman spent the afternoon and evening with his teammates. He was out ahead of them now, not dreaming of a shot at pro ball but negotiating one. The A's organization had set up a bus trip to Fenway Park for that night's game between the Red Sox and the Tampa Bay Devil Rays. It was the annual "Cape Cod League Night" at Fenway, and a lot of teams made the outing. The two Chatham players selected for the league all-star game, Tim Stauffer and first baseman Jeremy Cleveland, would be honored on the field before the game.

Hindman sat in the back of the bus with Everson and Pauly. The pitchers played word games on the bus to pass the time, just as they did in the bullpen during the early innings some nights. Hindman liked one where the pitchers substituted the word "vagina" for a word in a famous book or movie title, as in *The Old Man and the Vagina* or *Full-Metal Vagina*. That kept them going for two or three innings one night in Chatham. Just when they thought they were done with it Everson or Pauly shouted out a new one that trumped the earlier ones, and everybody cracked up again. A few days earlier Osama had introduced a hard game they played at Duke called "Road Trip." On the bus trip to Fenway, Hindman finally figured out the key—the first letters of the cities on the trip spelled out the name of a sports team in the mystery city he needed to identify.

Across the aisle, D'Antona and Trolia passed around a soda spiked with Jack Daniels and played cards. D'Antona was wearing a pork-pie hat; he stuck the jokers in the hatband and dealt. Chris Shea sat in on the game. He'd been a temporary player on the team at the start of the season. Schiffner had brought him back from the local Cranberry League to replace Fraser Dizard, now home with his ailing father in Washington State. Between Chatham and Boston Hindman made two calls to his adviser, Barry Meister, by cell phone.

At Fenway the A's sat in a block in the right-field grandstand. Thomas Pauly kept gaping around—the color, the bright light, the emerald green of the grass—and saying, "This is awesome. This is fucking awesome." He'd seen a few spring training games in Florida but, incredibly, had never visited a big-league park before. D'Antona, Trolia, and Chris Shea cheered the Cape League all-stars parading around the outfield warning track. Their names and pictures flashed on the mega-scoreboard above the bleachers. Some of the all-stars carried video cameras; others pantomimed leaping catches against the Green Monster, Boston's towering left-field wall. The three A's hung in to see Sox pitcher Derek Lowe throw a couple of innings, then they headed over to the Cask 'n' Flagon and spent the evening shooting pool and buying each other rounds. Stauffer and Cleveland left their all-star section after an hour and hung out with the A's in right field. Hindman talked with his agent again on the cell phone. The Angels had come up to a hundred plus school. But Meister told Hindman to keep holding out. In the top of the ninth, Red Sox closer Ugueth Urbina strolled to the mound to nail down Lowe's 4–0 shutout. In the A's section, Daniel Moore said, "I feel an implosion coming . . ." He said, "C'mon—let's get something going! Old-guy hats!" He leaned back, tipped his baseball hat forward slightly, and folded his arms across his chest. He looked remarkably like the old-time scouts covering games on the Cape. Hindman, Pauly, and a few others assumed the position, and Tampa Bay's luck changed. The Devil Rays scored off Urbina. Moore pursed his lips and nodded—the chief scout, quietly approving what was unfolding. Tampa Bay scored again, and again. The A's pitchers, disrespectful of the home team's mythology and hold over its local fans, laughed, then laughed harder. By the end they were all leaning back in old-guy hats, laughing hysterically and high-fiving the Devil Rays' 6–4 comeback victory.

It was hard to say, in that exact moment, which of the Chatham A's felt higher on life. In this summer of summers, Thomas Pauly was enthralled. Seeing Fenway Park in person felt like coming into the light. He knew then that he wanted more than anything to pitch in the majors. *I could like this. This is awesome.* He couldn't stop thinking it. Jamie D'Antona stood in a bar just beyond Fenway's famous left-field wall, pounding one last beer. He'd started his work at the Top Rod tackle shop. The new job was the best. His back felt better already. He was with a couple of buddies who looked up to him as if he were a god. He was light-headed and twenty years old and laughing, and anything might happen. Tim Stauffer sat with the chosen few of the Cape Cod Baseball League, having just been honored on the hallowed ground of Fenway Park before thirty thousand fans. In his dreams he always pitched in this very ballpark, before these very fans. His dream was not just within sight. It was within reach. Scott Hindman sat laughing, wearing an old-guy hat that had helped turn around a major league game—just the kind of goofball fun he loved. He was surrounded by players on a team, but was above them, had already entered a world they still only hoped for. With an arm that didn't feel right, he had one of the country's most powerful sports agents on his cell phone's speed dial, and was staring down the entire scouting department of the Anaheim Angels.

As usual, Hindman started his Wednesday at eight o'clock, vacuuming the carpet of the Chatham Library. He liked his carpet-cleaning job with the business's owner, John Reisner. The job was a plum. Reisner doted on him, brought him into million-dollar homes with deepwater views, treated him to lunch every day. That morning, Reisner drove them away in his white Toyota pickup, his little yippy dog in between them. They had just one house to clean, a big place on the water in South Orleans. Reisner had a habit of philosophizing. He'd say, in a thick Boston accent, "You know, that's *just* like baseball." or "See that? *Just like baseball*." Hindman had gotten a lot of mileage out of imitating him, but he enjoyed Reisner. Hindman skipped lunch with his boss that day, though, and met Tom Burns at the Chatham Motel a little after noon.

Burns said, "I called Donny, and he said he'd go to a hundred plus school."

Hindman was ready with his answer. "Nope. I'm going back to Princeton," he said.

"Well, give me a minute," said Burns.

He went into the other room, made a phone call, and came back a couple of minutes later.

"Okay. One-ten, plus school."

Hindman didn't budge. Burns asked him to think about it, maybe talk it over with Schiffner, see what he thought.

The leverage points in a baseball contract negotiation were murky. Major League Baseball violated so many free-market principles that few standard business rules applied. The Angels held exclusive rights to sign Hindman until he stepped into a classroom again that fall. If they failed to sign him, the chances were good that a different team would draft him the following year. If they signed Hindman, they would control his rights for his first six years in the minor leagues and, if he made the majors, his first seven years overall. (After that, Hindman could become a free agent and see what his true market value really was.) If the Angels held the stronger position, they also had a strong long-term incentive not to let him get away for the sake of a few thousand dollars. Players had only one real bargaining chip: They could return to school and enter a subsequent draft. That chip, a powerful one for top high school prospects, lost value in college. Hindman had one more season of eligibility at Princeton. If he

returned and was drafted as a senior, with no chips left, he'd be looking at a signing bonus about half what a junior would command at
the same draft slot. Of course, after a great senior year, with more
teams competing for his services, he could get drafted in a signifi-
cantly higher round.

A few hours after lunch at the Squire, on a hot, blue-sky afternoon, the A's stretched in left field before their game against
Yarmouth-Dennis. Hindman wandered with Schiffner over to the
fence near the third-base dugout. Early-arriving fans who looked
that way saw Schiffner stand with his arms folded, get animated, gesture with both hands, shake his head emphatically, nod. Hindman
stood leaning against the fence, an arm slung over the top railing and
his other hand on a cocked hip. From a distance he looked bored, or
cool, probably both.

Schiffner told Hindman that he knew the Angels were putting
pressure on him, and thought it bordered on abuse. Schiffner had
gotten a threatening phone call from one of their scouts in the Midwest, who assumed Schiffner was the one telling Hindman to hold
out. If Schiffner didn't stop "tampering with Hindman," the scout
said he'd have Major League Baseball pull funding from the Cape
League. Schiffner had exploded on him for that kind of horseshit—
then immediately rang the Angels' GM and told him to back the
scout off.

"Today was a fifty-thousand-dollar day," Hindman said to
Schiffner. "I think they'll go to two hundred plus school tonight, and
I'll probably sign tomorrow."

"You should think about it," said Schiffner. "If you go back to
Princeton and have a strong season, you might be looking at four
hundred thousand in the draft next year."

"Look," said Hindman, "the money isn't really the issue. I'm going
to go to law school. I'll probably get a corporate job somewhere and
start at a hundred fifty grand."

The response caught Schiffner by surprise. He opened his eyes
wide, started to say something, then stopped. He'd been furious at

Hindman's attitude, at his irreverence, his selfishness. He'd scheduled Hindman to start the following night's game against Harwich,
and didn't want to imagine his pitching staff if Hindman signed and
took off—Fraser Dizard and Mike MacDonald were both gone already. And then he understood Hindman's secret for the first time:
Hindman didn't need the money. He didn't even need baseball. He
wasn't like nearly every one of the players Schiffner had known,
wasn't like a kid, say, from South Carolina or Ole Miss. He was a *history* major from *Princeton* with good enough grades to snag an Ivy
League law school. He was a man with a plan.

"Good point," said Schiffner.

Schiffner whistled for Bobby Myers, who ambled over and joined
them. Schiffner explained the situation. Myers immediately grasped
all of it, including the feeling of being hung out to dry. He stuck his
hand out to Hindman and said, coolly, "Good luck."

In the bottom of the first inning that night against Yarmouth-Dennis, Hindman sat on a folding chair down in the bullpen, joking with
the other pitchers. But it was his turn, as the next-day's scheduled
starter, to sit in the dugout, charting the game's pitches. Wind kicked
up dust across the field, swirled around the dugout steps. Myers
looked around and didn't see him. "Where's Hindman?" he shouted.
He grabbed Hib, the bullpen catcher. "Go get Hindman and tell him
he still has to chart. He's not a big leaguer yet. And you can tell him
I said that!"

Hindman soon appeared. He grabbed a pen and started filling out
the pitching chart. He looked studious, thoughtful, wrote with confident strokes, looked completely at home with a pen and paper. Even
with a clipboard, you could tell he was different from the others.

That night Barry Meister stepped in for the first time and negotiated directly with the Angels. He called Hindman's cell phone at
eleven the next morning and said the best Rowland would do was
$125,000 plus $45,000 for school. He said Rowland had agreed to let
Hindman go back to Princeton in the fall and graduate on time. The
school portion would essentially be cash, because with Hindman it

wasn't theoretical, he'd use it—in fact it was better than cash because it would be nontaxable. Meister considered it a fair deal: a package worth 170 grand, pretty good money even for the fifth round. Hindman's mind raced. He trusted Meister, but he'd been set on more, and hated backing down. He knew there weren't ten other left-handers in the draft who could throw ninety. He knew, also, that this might be his last chance.

He took the offer.

Within minutes Tom Burns was driving from the Chatham Motel over to Hindman's with the papers. On the picnic table in back of Charlie Thoms's house, on a hot, sunny, perfect summer day, Scott Hindman took out a pen, and with confident strokes signed his name to a contract and became a professional baseball player.

He showed up at the field that evening out of uniform. The instant he turned pro he became ineligible to pitch in the Cape Cod League. He could have waited another day, and pitched for the A's once more. Schiffner felt jilted. The two would remember the summer very differently. Hindman, who had gone to Chatham assuming that Schiffner had signed off on the agenda, would tell stories of the hijinks and let people know that, excepting one inning in Bourne when he gave up four runs, he'd pitched thirteen innings in the Cape Cod League and allowed only one run—when his center-fielder pulled a hamstring and muffed a line drive. The facts were there; you could look them up. Schiffner, who thought he was getting a pitcher for the summer, would remember Hindman's selfishness, his refusal to pitch any more than once a week, his walking nine guys and hitting four others and continually falling behind hitters and putting them on base. Schiffner would remember that Scott Hindman had bolted on that final day, when he'd been needed to start.

Daniel Moore volunteered to pitch in Hindman's place against Harwich, and threw two scoreless innings. Myers and Schiffner turned to Thomas Pauly, hoping he could come up with a few decent innings before turning the game over to someone else.

Pauly, after his disastrous game against Y-D at home, had been buried in the bullpen. Schiffner had called on him for a couple of innings here and there, and Pauly had pitched well—but in the no-man's land of mop-up relief, it took extra time and extraspecial pitching to crawl into the light and be noticed again. In Brewster three days earlier, Pauly had quietly thrown four shutout innings, after most of the scouts had left. One of his fastballs, though, had lit up the radar guns at ninety-six miles an hour—friggin' gas, D'Antona called it, friggin' *cheddar*. A scout later mentioned it to Schiffner. Only one Cape pitcher that summer threw a faster pitch. Schiffner widened his eyes when he heard it. He knew Pauly threw fast but not *that* fast.

Pauly had been working on the changeup that Bobby Myers had shown him back before Myers had written him off as just some clown from the Ivy League. Everson had shown him a new way of holding his two-seamer, and Pauly's fastball had added a sharper, sinking tail to the outside corner. He'd been gaining confidence in the pitches. Against Harwich, subbing for Hindman, he finally let loose in a game with every pitch he could throw.

The first batter he faced topped a weak grounder back to him, and Pauly fielded the ball quickly and threw it to first, no nonsense. He struck out the second man, looking. He shut out the crowd noise, the doubts. The voice in his head quieted. He walked a man on a close call, and didn't let the umpire's call rattle him. He went right after the next batter, and sawed him off with an inside fastball, getting a weak ground ball to first. He struck out another batter in the fourth, with low fastballs that sank off the edge of the plate, then two in the fifth, two in the sixth. He mixed his pitches, kept hitters off-balance, got stronger as he went. His slider bit and dropped—"dirty" was the word the players used for it, "filthy." He'd shown flashes of incredible stuff before, but he hadn't shown such command. He struck out the side in the seventh. After six innings he'd struck out ten and hadn't given up a hit. For the first time he hadn't grinned or shrugged on a single play. His arm felt fluid, good. No, it felt great. He could have pitched six more.

Jamie D'Antona, his back feeling fine, had three hits in the game, including a double. The A's won 5–0 easily, without Scott Hindman.

That night Hindman picked up three cases of beer and celebrated with his former teammates back at Charlie and Ginor's apartment. When Ginor came down the next morning at seven to wake him, a half hour before his bus to the airport was leaving, she found beer cans all over the place. Trolia was in bed with a girlfriend. Everson was in bed with a girlfriend. D'Antona was passed out on the couch. And there was Hindman, passed out, clothes and gear scattered everywhere. He hadn't yet packed. He gathered his pile and stuffed it into a duffel, and left without saying good-bye. One of the last things he'd said at the party was, "I just made $17,000 for every inning I pitched in college. That's insane."

TEN

All-Stars

BECKY AND RICK STAUFFER ARRIVED two hours early for the
Cape Cod Baseball League all-star game at Whitehouse Field in
Harwich in late July. Cars already filled the large lot behind the high
school, and the stream kept coming, spilling into a lot across the
street. The field lay hidden behind a tall, parklike stand of pines,
which people flowed into through worn footpaths—an odd sight,
people disappearing into the woods in small groups, like cult members called by some unseen force. The trails converged on a central
path by the merchandise area behind home plate. The Stauffers
waded into a parting sea of fans who filled the metal bleachers near
the dugout where Tim Stauffer and the Eastern Division all-stars
would be sitting.

The first five hundred kids in had received little American flags,
which bobbed here and there against the bunting and the patriotic
theme of this year's game. Fans had already staked out standing room
around the perimeter of the outfield fence. Lawn chairs dotted the
sandy rise in back of left and center fields, on a lift of land barely high
enough to afford a view over the fence. Low rain clouds threatened,
and a chilly, humid breeze blew out toward left field. The field lights
glowed. Writing about Ted Williams's final game at an overcast Fenway Park, John Updike had described ballpark lights as "always a wan
sight in the daytime, like the burning headlights of a funeral proces-
sion." But here in Harwich the mood was festive, red, white, and blue.

The all-star game, each year, took place more than three-quarters of the way through the league's season. In earlier times the league had put up its best players against the cream of the Atlantic Collegiate Baseball League in all-star games at Fenway Park, Shea Stadium, and Yankee Stadium. In recent years the league had kept the annual event in the family, with the venue rotating among Cape League fields. Limping along in last place with nine games left in the season, Chatham had placed just two players on the Eastern Division's twenty-one man squad.

The Western Division all-stars rapped out hits during their round of batting practice. Peter Gammons, the veteran *Boston Globe* sportswriter and resident baseball guru at ESPN, stood behind the batting cage chatting with a couple of Bourne Braves. Gammons owned a summer place in Bourne. He caught a few games on the Cape every summer and helped the struggling Bourne franchise with fundraising. He had written about his love for this league—its simplicity, the opportunity to see great baseball up close before players became celebrities. His shock of silver hair had become widely recognized, thanks to ESPN's "SportsCenter" program, and well-wishers interrupted him as he took in the batting practice. Mike Pagliarulo, a former Chatham player who'd gone on to play third base for the New York Yankees, saw Schiffner out on the field and walked out to say hi. Their greeting blurred into the color and commotion surrounding the field, but it showed Schiffner's power. He knew big shots who came over to greet *him*. Because he'd won the Eastern Division title the year before, Schiffner managed the East's all-star squad. Pagliarulo would do color on Fox's television broadcast—a Cape League first. Gammons wandered over and joined the conversation. Reunions happened on Cape League ball fields all summer long, but this was the evening the stars came out.

Atop the third-base dugout, the East's all-stars sat facing the crowd in a long line, their backs to the field, their legs dangling over the edge of the dugout roof. Tim Stauffer, in a bright red pregame

T-shirt and bright red cap, reached out with his teammates to the stream of autograph seekers that trickled past at knee level. The line stretched back to the bleachers down the left-field line and curled back on itself, kids with programs, balls, bats, caps to sign, even little American flags, anything that would hold a signature.

Becky Stauffer looked out on the wonderful scene and felt like a wreck. Before coming to the field, she and Rick had attended the luncheon the league threw for the all-stars and their families and host families. Tim beamed, looked extra happy. But she still felt anxious. Today's game could be critical for Tim's career, and here she was forced to sit, squeezed tight into a crowded bleacher, with the game still a couple of hours away. Rick was as nervous as Becky. He preferred to stand and pace. Even at the games where he could pace he chewed through packages of Rolaids.

Becky worried that Tim's earned run average was the highest for any pitcher on either team. Rick explained that Tim had allowed only two extra-base hits all summer, that six of the runs charged to him had been given up after he'd left the game, that he'd pitched well— better than his respectable 3.02 earned run average suggested—and deserved to be here.

In fact, Stauffer had been a lock to make the team. In a morning meeting in Yarmouthport ten days before the game, the five Eastern Division field managers had drawn up the roster at the league commissioner's house. They went around the room and picked off the obvious choices first, each manager throwing out one name that required little or no selling. Schiffner had said, "Tim Stauffer," and four heads nodded agreement. No debate. The coaches understood that pitching statistics can mislead in a short season. An unlucky inning here or there, one bad outing (as Thomas Pauly knew) scrambled a pitcher's numbers. Stauffer's earned run average had been hurt by a couple of bullpen collapses and Chatham's mediocre outfield play. The opposing managers knew what their players said after facing Stauffer. They knew what their players thought when

188 o THE LAST BEST LEAGUE

Chatham approached on the schedule. The players didn't fear any Chatham mystique. Said one Brewster player, "We just look in the paper for the pitching matchups and hope we're not facing Stauffer."

The Chatham players had their own way of honoring Stauffer. It had come in a roundabout way. Eric Everson had tired of hearing Osama's bragging about fistfights and gang members he supposedly knew on Long Island. "Yeah, he's a bad-ass," Everson said, which led to a discussion in the bullpen about the definition of bad-ass. The pitchers eventually agreed that bad-asses were posers—guys who walked or talked tougher than they were. *Undeniable* bad-asses, though, were the rare guys who actually could back it up. And *undeniable* became a synonym for anything that was tough, studly, legit. Universal was undeniable, they agreed, and so was Tim Stauffer.

Some of Stauffer's statistics, of course, spoke for themselves. Heading into the all-star game he had fifty-three strikeouts in forty-seven innings, the second-highest mark in a league stacked with undeniably bad-ass pitchers.

Nevertheless, Becky Stauffer was right—this game was crucial to Tim's draft prospects. This was the showcase event of the biggest showcase league in the country. Television and radio stations and the Internet were all broadcasting the game; local papers in the Northeast, including *The Saratogian* from Stauffer's hometown, had sent reporters. The migration of scouts had peaked. Thirty major league teams had sent an average of four representatives each to watch, and to judge.

DURING THE RAMBLING pregame ceremonies, firemen and policemen ("local heroes") from the ten Cape League towns paraded on the field along with the players. A U.S. Army color guard added pomp to the singing of the national anthem. The crowd quieted to honor Wally Pontiff, an infielder for Brewster and Wareham over the past two summers who had died earlier that week from an undiagnosed heart abnormality, just when he was on the verge of signing a pro contract with the Oakland Athletics. His Brewster Whitecaps jersey hung in the East dugout as a silent tribute, his Wareham Gatemen jersey in the West's.

Wareham's Matt Murton won the pregame home run derby. Jamie D'Antona had been snubbed by not being picked for the contest. None of the Eastern Division coaches doubted his power or credentials, but a couple of them didn't like his attitude on the field, and they made him pay for it. At that morning meeting in Yarmouthport, Schiffner had read the mood in the room, and decided not to push for his slugger. Afterwards he said that D'Antona had been screwed.

Three generations of the Merullo family—all Cape League alumni—threw out a four-barreled ceremonial "first pitch," each Merullo with his own ball and all-star catcher. The iconic Lenny Merullo, Sr., eighty-five years old, had been a Cape League player in the thirties, a major leaguer, and, for the past three decades, a scout with the Major League Scouting Bureau. In that one life you could see all that this league had been and had become. A reporter for the *Cape Cod Times* had asked Merullo what the biggest change in the game had been since his playing days, and he said, "The equipment is better. The influence of the big gloves is the biggest thing." Lenny Sr. had spoken the night before at the small banquet for Stauffer and the other all-stars at a private home on the Harwich waterfront. Grandson Matt Merullo, himself an ex-big leaguer, scouted from Connecticut for the Arizona Diamondbacks. He'd scouted Jamie D'Antona in high school.

The poet Donald Hall once said that baseball is fathers playing catch with sons. Here on a ball field in Harwich, Massachusetts, Cape Cod baseball Merullo fathers and sons stood with their sons, with littler ones watching. The league stitched generations together across the timeless white lines of a green field.

STAUFFER VIEWED THE start of the game from the dugout. He knew he'd pitch the top of the fifth inning if everything went as planned. All-star games didn't always follow the script, though—as the West batters proved right away. Bourne's Trey Webb, a shortstop from Baylor, flared a single to left-center. With one out, Cotuit's third baseman, Brian Snyder of Stetson, lifted a fastball up into the breeze and over the left-field fence, and the West had scored one more run than starter Brian Rogers had given up in thirty-eight innings he'd thrown that summer for Orleans.

A's players and coaches stood in a bunch along the back of the third-base dugout, watching over the lip of the roof. Colt Morton—with his tanned good looks, brightly striped T-shirt, and sandals—had the air of an athlete on vacation. Chad Orvella, in a faded untucked T-shirt and a Red Sox cap turned backwards, was the baseball equivalent of a gym rat. D'Antona was missing. He'd worked that morning at the tackle shop and was off fishing for bass at Emery Pond. He had better things to do than watch other people play, and none of the A's seemed to miss him.

After the opening salvo, the teams settled into the Cape Cod League pitchers' battle that fans expected. Stauffer entered, as planned, in the top of the fifth, his team trailing 3–1. By now every big league team had built a comprehensive file on him, with details probably varying only slightly from club to club. But teams constantly searched for angles, for some way to get closer to the elusive ability to accurately predict the future. They also approached the draft with varied philosophies, and with different budgets. The Pittsburgh Pirates had long favored speedy high school and Latino players. The Texas Rangers were strong on size and raw athleticism. The Yankees liked hitters. The Oakland Athletics and other new-school teams ran statistics.

That fall the Anaheim Angels would win the World Series behind the gritty play of its shortstop, David Eckstein. Eckstein stood just under five feet eight inches tall, but he stood for something larger. He compensated for a weak throwing arm by grabbing the ball with three fingers, softball style, taking quick little shuffle steps, cocking his arm back almost to his hamstrings, and heaving the ball across the diamond. All he did was throw people out. As the Angels leadoff hitter, Eckstein batted from an unorthodox stance, but he rarely struck out, rarely swung at pitches outside of the zone. All he did was get on base.

By the end of the World Series Eckstein's story had become almost institutionalized: He had walked on as an unrecruited freshman at the University of Florida and had made himself an all-conference player, and then an All-American. He had been picked in the nineteenth round of the '97 draft and had been given a thousand bucks for signing, and again he worked harder than anybody around him, simply willing himself to the next level, and then the next, and then the majors. He was a bad-body player with no "plus" big league tools except his drive. He was the latest example of a player succeeding against conventional wisdom, and soon scouts were working "the Ecks factor" into their scouting reports, using David Eckstein as a point of comparison more frequently than they used any other player in the majors. Eckstein gave hope to a new generation of Blake Hanans.

But when it came to pitchers, clubs tended to homogenize their approach: All of them liked size, left-handers, and raw speed. However, some clubs were more willing than others to risk a high pick on a high school prospect, and clubs differed when considering injuries or choosing between a risky pitcher with a "higher upside" and a more polished, more easily projected pitcher with a lower ceiling.

The presence of scouting directors and general managers at the all-star game signaled higher stakes. Those men oversaw not only the drafting of amateur talent but the evaluation of their own major and minor league systems and those of all twenty-nine other clubs as well for possible trades. With such broad responsibilities, they didn't casually hand out their time. They couldn't possibly see the hundreds of amateur prospects under scrutiny each year. But they'd see players the club's scouts considered first-round. Major League Baseball was big business, and no decision maker wanted to make a mistake on a seven-figure investment.

Personal opinions still counted, especially when deciding among prospects that looked equal on paper. As draft day neared, and teams arranged their draft boards, it wasn't uncommon for some director or GM to say, "I don't know. I saw him on the Cape last summer and didn't have a good feeling about him." Or, "I saw him twice on the Cape, and I think there's something special there."

Stauffer had tried to approach this game as he did any other. He'd grown used to pitching in front of scouts, knew what it was like to pitch with runners on base and a dozen radar guns pointed at him. Now the pressure was rising: From here on, he would be looked at through many lenses, from multiple angles. The question was no longer whether he was a legit prospect. The question was whether he was a $2 million first-round selection, or a $700,000 second-rounder, or a $400,000 third-rounder. Those numbers trickled through the roped-off scouts' section of Whitehouse Field as Tim Stauffer finished his warm-up tosses, preparing to face the meat of the Western Division all-star batting order.

The breeze had died and, along with it, the threat of showers. The evening had turned thick, warm, comfortable. Becky and Rick Stauffer felt the nerves and shifted in their seats.

Stauffer got ahead in the count on Cotuit's Brian Snyder, who'd added a single since his two-run homer in the first. Stauffer's motion looked methodical, effortless. The scouts noticed his head, perfectly still, his eyes focused on the catcher's target even as his arm whipped through its delivery. They noticed that he didn't fall off to the side after making the pitch, as some pitchers did who overthrew the ball. Stauffer landed square to the plate. On one-and-two, he shook off a sign and threw a changeup, fooling Snyder, who slapped the ball on two hops to third for an easy out. A gutsy pitch, and one he'd had the confidence to call himself. Against the West's cleanup hitter, Cotuit's Lee Mitchell, Stauffer threw a ninety-three-mile-an-hour fastball at the knees, and Mitchell got his bat on it, topping a grounder up the middle for a seeing-eye base hit. Stauffer got the ball back quickly. He turned to his stretch position, kicked dirt from in front of the rubber, and looked in for the sign. He checked the runner, and threw a strike to Vasili Spanos, a husky right-handed power hitter from Indiana. The scouts checked their stopwatches. Time to the plate: 1.2 seconds, right around where they liked a pitcher's time of delivery from the stretch. Thomas Pauly had the quickest time to the plate of any A's pitcher, 1.02. Aaron Trolia's 1.7, the slowest on the team, would be reason alone for him to wash out. Compared to Stauffer, Trolia gave up more than twelve feet of running length to a base stealer. If Trolia didn't shave his delivery time, runners with major league speed would steal against him at will.

On the next pitch Spanos hit a hard ground ball back at Stauffer. Stauffer—in a perfect defensive position—stabbed it, wheeled, and threw a strike over the second-base bag to the shortstop, who finished off the one-six-three double play, and Stauffer was out of the inning just like that. He jogged off the field looking straight ahead, hopping over the third-base line as he went. He'd thrown seven pitches.

In the stands, Becky Stauffer cheered and sighed. She and Rick both laughed, looked a little stunned at how quickly it was over. Later, able to relax and simply watch the game, Rick said, "We'll replay Tim's game on the way back to Saratoga Springs—about fifty-two minutes per pitch! If we get a tape of this for back home, we'll have to tell people they can't get up to get a drink."

The West won 4–1. The scouts, by tradition, voted afterwards on the game's most valuable players. They picked Brian Snyder, with three hits and three runs driven in, as the West's most valuable player. They voted Tim Stauffer the most valuable for the East.

When his name was announced over the loudspeakers, Stauffer was lounging in the dugout, caught off-guard. A couple of teammates pushed him toward the steps to receive the award. He emerged looking back over his shoulder, quizzically, half smiling in embarrassment. *Me? Are you sure?* he seemed to be saying, as if they might be pulling a prank.

The choice surprised almost everybody watching, including Rick and Becky Stauffer, and the stands buzzed. Stauffer had pitched a good inning, but other East pitchers had appeared more dominant, given up no hits, struck out batters. The vote, though, hadn't even been close. The scouts had seen something. Tripp Keister, a Padres scout for the territory including Richmond, voted for Stauffer. "I loved how hard he threw, and how much movement his ball had," he explained. Stauffer's results had been solid, but the scouts had voted on style.

Back in the dugout, Schiffner thought of Adam Bourassa's truly valuable contribution—two hits, three stolen bases, and three strong, startling throws from the outfield to hold or cut down runners—and said, "If I'm Adam Bourassa, I'm pissed."

Brad Ziegler, with sweat beading on the grease of his eye black, stuffed his glove and shoes into a duffel. He'd pitched a scoreless inning himself. "I thought a couple of guys different might have gotten it," he said. "But the scouts all love Stauffer."

THE GAMES AGAINST Wareham always mattered. Regardless of the standings, Schiffner and Thoms liked to beat John Wylde's teams. Officially Wylde wore the hat of the Wareham general manager, but since retiring in 1995 he'd worked virtually full time for the Gatemen, funding much of the team's operating budget and even footing the bill for a series of expensive field renovations. He treated his team as a paternalistic overseer would, and dreamed of the day when the franchise could somehow provide summer jobs for all twenty-three of its players. Wylde's style seemed heavy-handed to Schiffner and Thoms, who referred to him as "the owner" of the Gatemen. Suspicious of his control, they were guilty of spreading stories that followed Wylde around the league: that he purposely built Wareham's infield out of crushed stone dust—a hard, unforgiving, gray surface that differed from every other infield in the league, giving Wareham an unfair home-field advantage; that he took liberties as official league scorer, which explained why Wareham players had captured three league batting titles and four outstanding pitcher awards in the past seven years; that he brought in enough temporary players at the beginning of each season to field A and B teams, so he could personally evaluate players before deciding on his roster (and keep them locked away from other Cape teams in the process); that his checkbook was so deep he could pay for whatever the Wareham club needed.

Wylde, sixty-four, had been educated at Harvard. He'd made his money in the family's steamship agency, Patterson, Wylde & Co., based on the Boston waterfront. He stood six foot nine and cut an even larger figure in a town like Wareham, which lacked the polish and pedigree of Chatham. He had started summering in Wareham as a boy in 1942; he and his wife had moved there for good, from outside of Boston, in 1974. He was the kind of character who inspired gossip in a small town, out of envy or resentment simply because he was "from away."

The stories passed along by Schiffner and Thoms may have twisted the truth, but John Wylde's competitiveness and devotion to the league were intense. He single-handedly organized a league tryout each May, screening nominations from 150 college coaches and scouts. The tryout gave unrecruited players a shot at hooking on with a Cape team; it gave Cape coaches a convenient way to fill out rosters with last-minute replacements. Schiffner didn't think much of the tryout; it took a day of his time, and usually for nothing, though he had picked up the odd player on occasion. As official scorer for the league, Wylde, for free, painstakingly input the results from the five games each night and uploaded them to SportsTicker—a statistics service once owned by Wylde's steamship agency, now owned by ESPN. Recently Wylde had been contacted by designers in Silicon Valley working on a computer scoring program that would improve on The Automated ScoreBook, the software used by the Cape Cod League, Minor League Baseball, and about 90 percent of Division I colleges. Major League Baseball relied on the Elias Sports Bureau in New York. That bureau's sophisticated proprietary software required at least three scorers charting each pitch of every game, a luxury the Cape League could neither justify nor afford. But even relying on lone inexperienced scorers who were paid just thirty dollars a game, Wylde had fooled with features of the program and made the Cape League's scoring more complete than that of any other league in the game short of the majors. He looked forward to the time when every scorer on the Cape charted not only hits and runs and errors but every ball, strike, and foul. (Wareham and Chatham were two of the few clubs to capture that level of detail.) On nights when the Gatemen played out in Chatham or Orleans, Wylde wouldn't finish entering data until three or four in the morning. As if by magic the updated stat sheets from SportsTicker would spit out of fax machines at Charlie Thoms's and the other general managers' houses early the next morning for distribution at that day's games.

 · In the Cape Cod League head coaches recruited their own players. Wylde was the exception; he recruited each of the boys who came to Wareham. As GM he'd established pipelines into Rice, L.S.U., Baylor, and the University of Texas, among other powerhouse programs. In the Northeast he did in person what Schiffner did mostly through contacts and by networking. (Wareham and Chatham typically listed more New England–based players on their rosters than other teams in the league, though never a high number. The country's best college players overwhelmingly played at warm-weather schools.) Thoms said that nobody, anywhere, watched more college baseball games than John Wylde.

Wylde wanted there to be no doubt that the Cape Cod League was the premier summer-league feeder system for the pros. That was part of his drive for the top-notch statistics, which he knew aided professional scouts. He recruited only players who had bona fide major league tools—merely being excellent college players didn't cut it. And he worked ahead, too: He had his list ready by August 15 for the following year, so his field manager could review it before leaving Wareham and heading back to school.

Schiffner often found himself in competition for players that nobody but Wylde seemed to know about. Both Thoms and Schiffner gave him that much: The guy did his homework. And he did a ton for the league at no charge.

Two days after the all-star game, the A's traveled to Wareham for their final meeting of the summer with the Gatemen. Two games below .500, Wareham's record stood second-best in the West, if barely. Had the season ended right then Wareham would have backed into the playoffs with a losing record. Chatham, with a record of fourteen wins, twenty losses, and two ties, lagged five games out of second place and a spot in the Eastern Division play-offs.

After the eight-game losing streak, the A's had been foundering, all but dead in the water. The team had won four of its last five games, though, puffing some wind back into the sails. Schiffner rallied his players, told them they weren't out of it yet. *Maybe...* They would need to win all eight of their remaining games to have a shot.

Tim Stauffer felt weak in the bullpen before the game, not his usual self. He was dripping with sweat when he finished warming up.

From the start Stauffer labored. He felt washed out, even as he threw a couple of fastballs at ninety-four. He missed high—always, with him, a sign of fatigue. Nothing came easily. He uncharacteristically pitched from behind in the count, fielders made errors, putting on more runners, adding more pressure. Over seven innings he gave up eight hits and a walk. But Stauffer hung tough and made the big pitches, and, somehow, walked away unscratched and unscored on.

Between innings he sat with his head hanging down, his uniform heavy with sweat, a towel wrapped around his neck. After seven he was spent. He left the game with the A's leading 2–0.

"Shit today," he said to Daniel Moore. "Sometimes it works."

To Adam Yates he said, "That was fucking disgusting. Seven innings of poo."

Yates answered, "Yeah. Poo and ninety-four."

Yates and Carlson made the lead stand up. Stauffer had done what good pitchers do: win, even without his best stuff. In the team huddle the players felt loose, hot. They'd won five of six. *Maybe . . .* "One, two, three, poo!" they said.

That night Stauffer had trouble sleeping. Even in his basement cave he dripped with sweat. His body ached, his throat hurt when he swallowed. In the morning he dragged himself out to the car. Driving to his job at the baseball clinic, he felt even worse. At eight o'clock the sun beat down, oppressive, heavy. Stauffer couldn't imagine being out in that heat. He turned the car and drove to a doctor's office, instead.

"Strep," the doctor told him.

Stauffer went back to his cave and stayed there, trying to chill.

THE HEAT WAS the worst of the summer. Normally the Cape, with dependable on-shore breezes, stayed ten degrees cooler than inland. But it was 103 degrees in Providence that day, 105 in Boston. Guys who had played out west said they'd take 100 dry degrees out there over 85 or 90 here any day. The promise of relief from the heat had not materialized, as a series of cooling thundershowers had repeatedly skirted the Lower Cape since early June but had not made landfall. Only a few A's showed up for the optional three-thirty batting practice before the game against Hyannis. Chad Orvella's hands were sweating so much that they squished in his leather batting gloves; he couldn't swing without slipping. He walked back to the dugout with his bat under one arm, took off the batting gloves, and wrung them out like a sponge. D'Antona's gray "Wake Forest" T-shirt darkened with sweat halfway into his first round of swings. The players wished Schiffner would allow them to take B.P. in shorts and no shirts, the way the teams did in Orleans and Bourne.

Several facts crystallized that hot evening. Thomas Pauly pitched another outstanding game, six innings in relief of Aaron Trolia. Pauly gave up a bare run—just the second run he'd allowed in his last nineteen innings. His earned-run average had fallen steadily over eight appearances, to a solid 3.46. He'd accomplished something difficult in the process: He'd made a manager and a pitching coach take notice and change their opinions. Schiffner still thought Pauly a head case, still didn't know what to make of him. But he and Myers now considered Pauly a go-to pitcher on a staff that sorely needed one.

Something had also shifted in Pauly's manner. Normally, a player doing well acted looser, joked more. Instead, Pauly grew more serious. On the field he lost the grin and kept his focus. He now pitched and carried himself as though he belonged.

Hyannis won 4–1. There would be no miracle finish for the A's. A slim mathematical possibility might still have existed, in a perfect combination of six A's wins and other teams' losses, but it wasn't going to happen. People on a team had an intuitive sense of when it was over. The previous night, after the win against Wareham, that sense of *maybe* was still there. Today, after losing, it was gone.

SCOUTS FROM THE Boston Red Sox invited a few dozen Cape Cod players to Fenway Park for an exclusive audition on August 1, an off day across the Cape League. The players coming from the A's had talked about it for days. They met at 7:00 A.M. in a supermarket parking lot in East Harwich. Stauffer and Daniel Moore rode in one car. Stauffer was on antibiotics, wiped out, his throat white with puss and so sore he hadn't swallowed solid food for two days. But he was going to Fenway. Chris Iannetta drove with his younger brother in a second car. Colt Morton and Pauly rode in D'Antona's Mercury.

Pauly couldn't believe he was included among the stud prospects of the Cape Cod League, but sensed something special happening with his season. He knew about surfing, knew how it felt when you hit a wave just right and rode it for all it was worth. He was pitching beautifully, blowing people away, but that wasn't all of it. Ingrid Goldberg, the pretty lacrosse player he'd given his number to back in June, had called. After so many weeks of not hearing from her, he hadn't expected the call. But she'd been away with her family. Upon returning to Chatham she rang Pauly up. They went out to dinner at the 400 East Club, took in a movie. They lifted weights together at Willy's Gym. Soon they were going to parties together. Things were working out. He couldn't have been more psyched as the players gathered for the drive to Fenway. Seven A.M. seemed cruel to D'Antona, though, who'd been out drinking with Trolia at the VFW until

1:30 in the morning and was hungover. He felt about as spry as Stauffer looked.

Riding north in D'Antona's car, the players listened to the radio, D'Antona singing along. Colt and Pauly tried to catch some sleep, though they felt cramped in the small car. D'Antona, in the chase vehicle, had no problem keeping up with the others across the bridge and around the Sagamore rotary onto Route 3. Just south of Boston, though, they hit traffic. D'Antona moved quickly to stay in sight of the two cars ahead of him. No one knew the way—none had paid attention during the bus trip. Near the giant propane tanks in South Boston, in crawling interstate traffic, the driver of a Mercedes nosed into the space ahead of D'Antona, thinking D'Antona would give it to him. Instead, D'Antona hit the gas to stay close to Iannetta, and the Mercedes driver swerved back into his own lane, clipping a piece-of-junk station wagon that had slowed in front of him. "Damn!" said D'Antona. "Sorry, bro'." But he kept going, pushed along by the flow.

Off the Chinatown exit, Iannetta and D'Antona, pointing vaguely toward Fenway and, running close on time, ran a yellow light. Moore and Stauffer, on their tail, ran the red. D'Antona looked up to check that they'd made it through, and saw an eighteen-wheeler just miss side-swiping them. "Damn!" he said.

The players' cars wended their way toward the light towers of the park, which loomed above the surrounding brownstone neighborhoods. D'Antona guessed the lights were a half-mile away, but the players turned up and down a few narrow, poorly signed, one-way streets, and the lights appeared again, this time farther away, maybe a mile. They couldn't seem to get any closer, and now they were running late.

Finally they found their way to the right-field side of the park and paid retail at the closest parking lot. They grabbed their stuff out of the trunks and changed right there in the lot. They were all laughing as they walked through the gate off Yawkey Way into the old brick ball yard just a few minutes late. They'd been at the park recently, but it felt different walking in to play.

The free-spirited Red Sox pitcher Bill Lee had a similar first impression of arriving at Fenway Park in 1969. The description he gave in Ken Burns's documentary *Baseball* still rang true in 2002: "Fenway Park, when I first saw it . . . I drove by it. I'd come down Route 90—I got called up from Pittsfield—and I said, 'Well, there it is. Look at that. Beautiful. There's the Green Monster. There's the highway. I'll take a right and a right and I'll end up at the park.' I took a right and a right and I ended up in Cambridge. Then I realized that the Northwest Territories Act hadn't been in effect when Boston was built. I couldn't find the park. And when I finally found it I said, 'This is not a park, this is a factory.' There was the brick façade, and this little red door on Yawkey Way—it was called Jersey Street back then. And then you walk through the gates and you come through that little tunnel and then all of a sudden you see the green. The green of the seats, the green of the Wall, the green of the field, and the little dirt cut-outs, and the proximity of the foul lines to the stands and the closeness of the bullpens to the crowd. And you go down on one knee and bless yourself and you go, 'Thank you God for making me a ballplayer.'"

Buzz Bowers, the semiretired Sox scout who lived on the Cape, greeted the players on the field in bright sunshine. He stood before them in full Red Sox uniform. Bowers said the team had set aside a couple of hours for a light workout—fifteen or twenty swings for the hitters, a couple of rounds of infield, a few minutes of throwing in the bullpen for the pitchers. "We're very appreciative of you guys coming up here on your day off," he said. "We don't want any of you to overdo it, especially you pitchers. We already know what you can do. This is just a chance for us to see your bodies, your mechanics, your arm slots." The Red Sox had hosted such an event every year for the past decade. For what little new information the scouts would glean, the whole thing felt like public relations, or maybe a favor to Bowers, or a perk for the suits in the front office, whose job was building a successful baseball operation but who rarely had time to see stud prospects doing their thing. The innards of the park struck the players as surprisingly old and dingy. The playing field, just as green and close to the seats as Bill Lee said, was perfect.

Colt Morton put on a catching clinic. Behind the plate he caught the ball crisply and fired low bullets to second. The stopwatches had him at 1.85, then 1.80 seconds from "pop to pop," the time between the pitch hitting his glove and his throw hitting the glove of the in-fielder covering—an excellent major league time. During his swings he pounded the Green Monster, whistling line drive after line drive against that high left-field wall. The A's players shagging out in left yelled, "Higher! Higher!" with each pitch, emphatically lifting their arms. They seemed to be the only players enjoying themselves—everyone else had on game faces. Just before B.P. the A's had slipped into the hot, dirty, narrow room inside the Green Monster in back of the huge, hand-operated scoreboard, just to check it out. Thomas Pauly had added his name to the graffiti. The players now fielded Morton's drives off the wall as if they were for real, playing the car-oms, turning, and gunning the ball in to the screen behind second base. Colt obligingly elevated, hammered a couple of line drives off the highest part of the wall, then one into the screen, then two long drives over the screen to end his round. Moore, Pauly, and D'Antona went wild in the outfield and cheered like fans.

D'Antona shook the fuzz from his head, fielded ground balls at third like a machine, and threw hard strikes across the diamond. He charged the last slow roller, picked it bare-handed, and zipped an off-balance throw that cracked into the first baseman's mitt and echoed around the sea of empty seats. Whether it was the true, eas-ily anticipated hops or the confidence that comes with playing on the lush, golf-green grass of a major league infield, D'Antona looked re-born as a third baseman.

In the cage, D'Antona went for broke. He lengthened his swing, tried to crush every ball over the Monster. He fouled pitch after pitch straight back into the netting. With two swings left he hadn't hit five balls fair or taken one deeper than the warning track. Then he blasted a towering shot down the left-field line. The ball hooked and hit halfway up the pole above the wall—fair!—just as Carlton Fisk's had done in the sixth game of the '75 World Series. On his last swing D'Antona launched a rocket over everything—a startling, extraordinary sight. It dwarfed the memory of his previous swings. It dwarfed the hangover, dwarfed the tense ride to the park. It was a hit that thousands of New England kids reenacted in their backyards every year, that D'Antona himself had daydreamed about back in the batting cages in Shelton. Playing with the best hitters of the best summer league in the country, he had, by far, hit the longest home run of the showcase. And D'Antona didn't have to run it out. He could just watch it go.

ELEVEN

A Hard Ninety

JOHN SCHIFFNER HAD SEEN IT EVERY year he was in the league. July melted into August, and players started looking at the calendar, counting the days. They had made their cases, understood the pecking order. Their day jobs wilted with the heat. The scouts had fled. The players lost their fervor for playing six days a week. Bodies ached. Little injuries appeared, enough to merit a day or two off, maybe an early flight home. Even in guys twenty years old, there was the sense of time running out, the distractedness that came when days were numbered and members of the disengaging collective had begun looking beyond them toward other places. Most of the players would have only a couple of weeks after the Cape season before the start of school. Still, games piled up relentlessly, like waves.

Schiffner had seen it mostly in the teams Chatham played against. His teams had won the Eastern Division or the Cape League championship seven years in a row—his stretch runs were usually exciting, the guys playing hard, buying into the idea that the Cape Cod League play-offs were worth delaying vacation a few days. The previous summer Chatham had eliminated a team during the final week of the season, and the losing players had walked through the postgame handshake line saying, "Thank you. Thank you. Thank you."

Schiffner looked at the calendar and looked at his players, wondering what was inside them.

WITH FIVE GAMES left in the season, Chatham showed up in Harwich on yet another hot, sticky afternoon. Harwich, vying for second place, had lost two in a row and needed the win to stay alive. The A's, in last place, had no reason to win beyond pride.

Shortstop Chad Orvella led off the game by pushing a bunt to the right side. The pitcher cut the ball off and flipped it to first, barely beating Orvella's headfirst slide. Orvella was a sweetheart of a kid whose gentle personality was almost feminine, but he was the hardest-working player on the field. He ran "a hard ninety," a respectful phrase players used for those who gave every bit of effort to all ninety feet between home plate and first base, even on hits that would almost surely result in routine outs. The phrase had become shorthand for anyone who went all out, all the time. Orvella was a hard-ninety guy who wasn't afraid to get dirty. He slid headfirst into bases, dived for any ball he might reach. In fact, Schiffner had noticed that Orvella's uniform was always dirty. Halfway through the summer the coaches had started betting on how soon in each game the dirt would show. That evening in Harwich, it took one pitch. "Good ninety!" yelled Schiffner. "Good ninety!"

Schiffner called Orvella "a classic, old-fashioned, East Coast shortstop," referring to Orvella's textbook style of infielding. Orvella laid back slightly on ground balls, slid into position to field the ball squarely in front of him, then set and threw to first. He was quick, catlike, with soft hands and a terrific arm—he'd been a pitcher in high school, and his arm might have helped Schiffner's pitching staff had Schiffner not needed his glove so much. But the shortstops in the majors played a more modern brand of infield. They all fluidly charged the ball, moved through it, threw on the run with their momentum already pushing toward first as they scooped up ground balls. It was a faster style favored by the players from the Dominican Republic and Venezuela, and in the past few years every shortstop at the highest levels played "Latin style," no matter where they came from. Orvella's throwback style cost hundredths and even tenths of a second, and over 162 major league games that might mean tens of runs and a handful of losses that could have been wins.

Orvella had played since May with a broken index finger on his left hand. Four weeks before the ACC tournament he'd taken extra ground balls after practice to break in a new glove. (The glove he'd used since his junior year in high school—his favorite glove—was a rag. He'd taken so many ground balls with it over the years that the padding had disappeared. A hole had opened up in it. Orvella was tired of restringing the leather every few games.) He dived for a ball and rolled over his finger. He knew he'd snapped it, but didn't bother to have it checked. The next day he put a thick foam pad inside the glove. He never mentioned the injury again, unless someone noticed and asked him about it. He popped a couple of Advils before games and kept playing.

Over the summer in Chatham the pain had eased. He'd stopped wrapping the finger. He'd started gripping the bat, again, with all his fingers. Every once in a while, though, a hard throw from Colt Morton hit wrong, and he winced. Or D'Antona, clowning on him, whipped a ball from close by, and Orvella had to make a split-second adjustment and cradle the ball in the webbing of his glove instead of using the pocket, lest the pain make him yelp.

He had lifted weights hard up at Willy's Gym—he'd pushed his bench press to 315 pounds, his squat to 460, incredible weight for someone who weighed 180. He'd worked through the soreness at the start of his summer. But three-quarters of the way through the season he wore down. His legs felt heavy. He stopped lifting. He still took extra hitting each day, but was measuring his energy, conserving it for games. He saw guys getting a day off here and there around him and wanted one himself, but he never asked for it. He didn't know, but Schiffner couldn't stomach an infield defense without Orvella at short.

GEORGE GREER SAT with Martha Schiffner in the stands that night in Harwich. He stayed with the Schiffners whenever he came to the

Cape, usually once or twice each summer. In Greer's sixth decade, his body and features had gone soft. He sat with his hands folded, a straw hat covering his bald head. His round eyeglasses gave him the air of a professor. Judy Walden Scarafile, the league president, walked over and greeted him in the stands. Once or twice Greer got up from his seat between innings and talked to Schiffner through the chain-link fence at the corner of the dugout. But otherwise, for all anybody could tell, he looked like a casual tourist, not a big-name college coach who'd mentored more than two dozen major leaguers.

Greer saw the game at levels that few others could. He watched his players from Wake Forest—Jamie D'Antona, Ryan Johnson, and Steve LeFaivre, players he'd first seen when they were juniors or seniors in high school, players he spent more time with than he did his own family. He saw familiar mannerisms and half-forgotten quirks— the way R.J. still looked old-school—no batting gloves, pant legs tucked high in his socks, the pigeon-toed run, the way LeFaivre swung as hard as he could in the on-deck circle. LeFaivre was an example of a self-made player, Greer thought. Unlike a natural like D'Antona, LeFaivre didn't dare try new things, didn't dare to make adjustments, didn't have the confidence to tinker with what had brought him this far. It would probably keep him from advancing to the pros. Greer also watched John Schiffner, who'd grown into a good friend over twenty-five years.

Greer had coached for nine years in Cotuit. He'd won 213 games, and coached future big leaguers Ron Darling and Terry Steinbach, among others. NCAA rules prohibited him from doing real coaching of his own players during the summer, a rule aimed at keeping programs from practicing baseball year-round. Still, he made notes about things he'd work on when his players returned that fall. He watched with the eyes of someone who'd played in this league himself, for Chatham, back in the mid-sixties, when teams played four or five day games a week and players had evening time and off days to enjoy. The league was serious back then, too—Greer had been a two-time All-American at UConn—but the schedule spread from

June fifteenth to almost Labor Day. The current mid-August end-date was another NCAA mandate, to guarantee at least some down time for the players at the end of the season. But it compressed the season on the Cape. Summers when Greer played felt more relaxed.

Greer watched D'Antona glove a ball in the bottom of the second inning and gun it across the diamond. "You know, he reminds me a lot of Steinbach, when I had Steinbach in Cotuit," Greer said to a friend in a quiet voice. "I wouldn't be surprised if he also ends up as a catcher—he has the size, the arm, the quick release. He has the same drive that Steinbach had. But I'd like to see him develop as much as he can at third base until it's clear he can't play there. He has so much ability." In the third inning Greer watched D'Antona stroke a solid single up the middle and take a big turn at first, and he said, "We've got to work on that flat-footed running gait this fall. And Jamie needs to do some body shaping—strengthen his wrists and forearms, trim his waist and butt and thighs. But his tools are right up there with anybody I've ever coached."

D'Antona fielded flawlessly that night. Simon Williams made a hard running catch in center; Orvella and Hanan turned a clutch double play. In the top of the eighth, down 6–3, the A's didn't pack it in. They loaded the bases, and Michael Moon shot a low line drive past the first baseman down into the right-field corner and legged out a triple, running hard all the way. In the top of the tenth the A's scratched out two more runs, breaking the tie. Zane Carlson and Adam Yates shut Harwich out for three final innings. "That was the old Chatham A's," Schiffner said to Greer afterwards. "They said, 'Screw you—you're not going to beat us, even if you're ahead right now.'"

Blake Hanan walked into Willy's Gym at eleven o'clock the next morning. Mirrors lined two walls of the large, open weight room. The wall facing the parking lot, mostly tinted glass, gave a smoky feeling to the bright haze filtering in from outside. A TV hung from the ceiling above a small refreshment area, tuned silently to ESPN, which seemed to be the only station in the players' world. The base-ball highlights on "SportsCenter" aired each night at 11:00 P.M., then again at 1:00 A.M., then every hour on the hour from 5:00 A.M. till noon. Hanan glanced around the room, recognizing Brewster's Kainoa Obrey and a couple of players from Orleans, and stepped on the scale—164. He hoped to get up over 170 by next season, after working his legs. He guessed he'd lost five inches around his thighs since hurting his knee in February. He opened his beat-up training manual and flipped it onto the floor. Pencil marks filled the curling Xeroxed pages. Rap music pulsed from a sound system. Hanan leaned back into the bench. His biceps and shoulder muscles flexed beneath a cotton T-shirt torn out at the sleeves. His arms looked pumped even before he started.

He was hitting .190, just twelve hits out of sixty-three at-bats. He'd struck out twenty-one times. He explained away the batting average, sliced it into pieces and held up the ones that gave him hope. He told the others that most of his hits had come in his first or second at-bats—showing that his troubles had to do with his eye-sight or the poor field lights of the league. He mentioned that he'd hit the ball hard five times out of eight during one stretch, but had only one hit to show for it. "So batting averages don't really mean that much here," he said. "Not with so few at-bats." He blamed his strikeouts on his lack of playing time and his loss of confidence, which had gotten mixed up with how he needed or didn't need to adjust his swing.

He tried to convince himself that his failure on the Cape stemmed from the problems in his left knee. The iliotibial band on the outside of the joint had tightened, making it painful to bend the knee. Hanan had shortened his natural running stride as a result, and bent more from the waist fielding balls to his backhand. Midway through the season he'd gotten an MRI and a cortisone shot over in Mashpee, and had subsequently scheduled surgery for the end of August.

He had a new plan: He would flow out of the rehab and—tem-pered by his summer in the Cape Cod League—dominate the fall scrimmages at Siena. He vowed to steal forty bases next season as a junior, something no scout could overlook. *Against all odds.*

He had worked out at Willy's with Orvella, Morton, and Hib, but all of the others had shut it down for the summer. On his drive over that morning, Hanan had passed a sign in front of the South Chatham Community Church: *Smooth Seas Don't Make Skillful Sailors.* He grasped the bar and ripped into his bench presses. He was lifting alone now.

THE FIRST ARTICLES on NFL training camps ran in the *Cape Cod Times.* The New England Patriots, unlikely defending Super Bowl champions, had opened their camp in Smithfield, Rhode Island. They dominated the region's sports-talk radio programs. At Veterans Field, before the game against Falmouth, a couple of the visiting players tossed a football back and forth in front of the dugout. The first two weeks of August—the peak of the summer tourist season on Cape Cod—were the busiest time of year for South Cape Seafood, the hardest time to find a parking spot at Nauset Beach, an impossible time to book a room at the Chatham Bars Inn. In August the chilly waters of Cape Cod Bay warmed to tolerable; old-money families took month-long vacations at grandparents' compounds. Labor Day Weekend, still a few weeks away, marked the traditional, psychic end of summer on Cape Cod, when miles and miles of cars inched back over the Canal toward the rest of the year. But baseball was the summer game, and with the Chatham A's winding down, something in the air began to change.

In the press box during the Falmouth game, Charlie Thoms and Krystal Cortez, one of the A's' interns, filled out travel vouchers for the players' trips home. It felt strange to them both, the end coming so suddenly. Thoms recalled how surprised he was at the end of his first year as GM. "It was unbelievable," he said to Cortez. "I came to the last game and saw all these bags piled in the parking lot. Those guys were gone before the lights were out. Summer was over in one minute."

212 o The Last Best League

The A's looked lively, talked it up, seemed to carry momentum from last night's come-from-behind win back here to Chatham. They stood straight during the singing of the national anthem, looked crisp in clean uniforms, didn't slouch. They hit the ball hard, played sure defense. Thoms and Schiffner gave them this: These guys didn't carry themselves as losers. Tied at one in the third, Orvella doubled with two outs and Steve LeFaivre lifted a long homer onto the bank behind the right-center field fence. D'Antona walked leading off the next inning, Orvella got a big base hit with two outs, and the A's scored four to go up 7–1. Between innings, Paul Galop fired up "Let's Twist Again Like We Did Last Summer." The Falmouth Commodores, two points behind Wareham for the second play-off spot in the Western Division, needing this game to stay in the race, turned chippy. They slammed bats down in frustration, barked at the umpires. Orvella robbed a hit with a diving stop of a ground ball up the middle. D'Antona charged a slow roller and made a beautiful bare-handed play. Travis Udvarhelyi, one of Schiffner's late-replacement outfielders, sprinted for a foul ball curling toward the playground and caught it, sliding up against the fence next to the Falmouth bullpen. The Falmouth players drooped, looked demoralized. They shuffled through the handshake line and dragged themselves out to the parking lot while Paul Galop cranked out the Beach Boys behind them.

THE BLUE-BLACK welt that seemed forever on Jamie D'Antona's left shin had faded into dark yellow-brown splotches. Spots from his ankle to the middle of his shin had calcified from repeated bruisings by foul balls. He wore a plastic shin guard when he batted, and probably would for as long as he played. His hamstring had healed completely. He'd lost twelve pounds since coming to the Cape, mostly from skipping breakfast and having no time to sit and eat regular meals. That was no big deal. His weight always swung a lot.

His back felt fine. Almost as soon as he'd stopped working at South Cape he was able to stand, bend over, twist without pain. The game had become fun again. His play had picked up almost immediately after quitting.

Paul and Laurie Galop had seen a change in him as well. He was still scattered, still going a hundred miles an hour, but Laurie would ask him how the game went for him and he'd say something like, "I wish I didn't friggin' strike out with a runner on third, but I did okay. Made some good plays. We won." Once in a while he still said he sucked, but then he seemed to forget about it, just like always. No more banging his head against the counter. He was rolling with the waves again.

He liked his new boss at the Top Rod Fly & Surf Shop. Joe Fitzback had fished on the Cape for thirty years and run charters out of Chatham for the past six. He'd given D'Antona a key to the shop on the first day. After dealing with hundreds of customers in his years as an electrician, Fitzback had come to trust his instincts about people. He'd liked D'Antona immediately. After a few days of watching D'Antona talk with the customers, Fitzback told him he had a job next year if he wanted it. He promised to take D'Antona out for stripers before the baseball season ended. D'Antona liked the casual way Fitzback ran the shop, liked talking fishing and gear. D'Antona never faked something he didn't know. He knew a lot about saltwater fishing and could recommend lures and techniques, but he didn't know the local water, and wasn't embarrassed to say so. He asked questions. He liked looking around the shop when things were quiet. He gave out directions over the phone as if he'd been driving around the area for years—he was one of the few A's who could do that, thanks to the South Cape job. The customers all seemed to be friends of Fitzback's, and they gave the place a comfortable air. D'Antona had loved the South Cape Seafood job, but he wished he'd been there at Top Rod since June.

He was hitting the ball hard again, but he wouldn't have time to hit himself out of the black hole of the first half of the season. His numbers were numbers—he could have sliced them like Blake

Hanan did and found a good story in them. His seventeen runs batted in were the most on the team. His five home runs were among the best in the league. But his average—.227—was paltry by most standards, and that's what people saw first. As the writer Mark Kramer once noted, baseball was a sport where a man's virtue was measured to the third decimal place.

But low batting averages anchored the entire Cape League. D'Antona was hitting twenty points higher than the A's as a team, his average higher than all but Jeremy Cleveland's, Michael Moon's, and Steve LeFaivre's—and he'd pass LeFaivre over the next three games. Since his two-for-twenty-four start, D'Antona had hit close to .270 in the Cape Cod League, a number that was higher than those of half the guys who'd gone on from here to the majors. He hadn't torn up the league, hadn't even put together a string of great games. But he'd hung in there and worked out of a deep rut. D'Antona was hitting to drive the ball again, not worrying about failing. He looked forward again to getting up with men on base. Some of his old swagger crept back in.

Schiffner couldn't explain it—unless it was the back—but D'Antona had played some of the best third base in the league over the past few weeks. He hadn't taken extra ground balls or worked on his footwork. He hadn't suddenly changed his attitude, or finally realized that fielding was something he needed for his future. D'Antona couldn't even say that he felt any more confident than he had at the start. In this game confidence was a huge factor, and it accounted for many of the good and bad streaks that all players went through.

But D'Antona was joking around less on the field. He'd made only two errors in the past thirteen games. He was still making the pretty, aggressive plays. He showed some athleticism one night against Wareham that would have made any league's highlight reel—a ground ball had kicked up and back toward the third base bag as D'Antona slid over toward the shortstop hole. With no time to check his momentum, he flashed out his throwing hand and speared the ball barehanded, just as it was skipping by him, and easily threw the runner out. That was D'Antona, pure. But he was making the routine plays now, too, not just the spectacular ones. Schiffner saw a connection between the A's' turnaround and D'Antona getting out of his funk. D'Antona, for better or worse, was the kind of player who carried a team.

MCKEON FIELD SAT two blocks south of Main Street in Cape Cod's largest town, up from the docks of the Hyannis fishing fleet. A dozen times a day a ferry steamed between the harbor and Nantucket, eighteen miles out to sea. The Cape League franchise here had struggled: struggled to find dedicated volunteers, struggled with low attendance, struggled financially. The team was competitive enough but had won just one league championship in the past twenty years. The size of the town was part of the problem. Unlike other Cape League towns, Hyannis presented the distractions of a small city. The Mets competed for fans with bars and arcades and movie theaters and the shopping mall. (Those distractions took the players' attention away from the game, as well, though they also made recruiting easier.) The organization hadn't built a consistent fan base from the transient commuters and tourists who flowed into Hyannis to work and shop and play by day and then returned to their quieter villages each evening. It wasn't like in Chatham or Cotuit, where baseball played a big part of village life, where attending games was a nightly ritual for summer families. It wasn't like in quieter Orleans, where attending a Cardinals game was on the must-do list of every visitor who came to town.

A bigger part of the problem—though it was harder to put a finger on—was the disconnect between the place the league held in the imagination and the place Hyannis had become. People from away heard "Hyannis" and thought of the Kennedy compound, touch football on the beach. But the growth that had so altered Cape Cod over the past half century had all but paved over Hyannis, which now sprawled with plazas and national chains and looked like everywhere else. It was less a city, really, than a generic suburb with an urban-feeling downtown and water at the edges. Cape Cod League baseball games, with their free admission and wooden bats, trafficked in a less-changed world that functioned on a smaller scale. Elsewhere on the Cape, teams gave fans a hometown, many of whom saw the Cape as a refuge from their own suburban and homogenized neighborhoods back home. People didn't come to Hyannis to put picnic blankets on a hillside.

Hyannis's ball field ranked with Bourne's as the worst in the league. Though that summer's Cape Cod League yearbook bragged about the recent renovations here, McKeon Field looked terrible. The patchy, thin grass reminded D'Antona of the tundra on some of the fields he'd played on in Alaska. The base paths were dusty and badly dished. A three-inch-high seam ran between the infield dirt and thin grass of the outfield. Deep, uneven holes riddled the pitcher's mound in front of the pitching rubber. When the A's first visited here in early July, Bobby Myers had said, "I was warned that some of the fields in this league were poor. I didn't think they'd be embarrassing."

Even though McKeon Field had lights, Hyannis games started at five o'clock, ostensibly to spare the ospreys nesting atop the light tower in center field. During batting practice two adult ospreys chirped and circled above the outfield or sat tall on their branchy nest. Schiffner and other A's volunteers suspected another motive—the ospreys were merely an excuse for keeping the lights off and saving the Hyannis club some nickels. The explanation had an echo of the John Wylde stories in it, as if it ought to be true because it fit with the larger nature of things, and it sounded good, so there was no need to check its accuracy. But if the story was true, or even if it wasn't, the decision to skimp on light was a misguided one. Substantially fewer fans went to the five Cape League fields that lacked lights, and the smaller turnouts meant lower merchandise sales and donations. Falmouth, which also had ospreys nesting on top of one of its light poles, used its lights anyway. The ospreys didn't seem to mind, and Falmouth would draw twelve thousand more fans that summer than Hyannis.

AFTER THIRTEEN APPEARANCES in relief, Thomas Pauly started his first game of the summer. Schiffner told him to go as long as he could. Every inning he gave them would be a gift to the short-armed staff. The coaches had been amazed at the resiliency of Pauly's arm. Scott Bradley had told Schiffner that Pauly's arm was durable enough to start—and Pauly had proved it.

Pressed into longer service by the defections of Schiffner's pitching staff, Pauly had thrown six no-hit innings on the twenty-fifth of July and six more strong innings five days later. Schiffner sent him back out on four days' rest again. The schedule gave Pauly a taste of starting in a standard major league five-man rotation. His arm seemed impervious to the strain.

Compared to most pitchers, he seemed to need no time to warm up. Before one appearance in Brewster, he'd gotten the signal to loosen. He'd thrown eight or nine warm-ups and sat down. "Hey, Boss," Adam Yates said to him. "Coach wants you to be ready."

"I am ready," said Pauly.

"Man, if my coach at school saw me sitting down, he'd be right on my ass. Why don't you keep throwing, just to look like you're staying warm?"

Pauly walked back to the mound. "Okay," he said, and pantomimed throwing without a ball. Catching the invisible return throw. Pitching it again.

"You *are* crazy," Yates said.

Pauly's shoulder sometimes ached after he pitched, or felt tired, but he'd never had arm troubles or any real pain. He had pitched for less than four years—a blessing, Schiffner thought, having seen so many young pitchers come into Chatham with scarred or injured arms. Pauly's inexperience kept him from having the refined mechanics of a Tim Stauffer. Stauffer's arm, for instance, came from the same angle—the same slot—on every pitch, regardless of what pitch he was throwing, or how fast. That ability, rare in a young pitcher, helped Stauffer fool hitters, who couldn't read clues in his motion about what pitch was coming. Pauly occasionally wandered from his normal "high three-quarters" slot. But the two shared a crucial trait. The complex physiology behind throwing a baseball involved a series of accelerations—of the legs, hips, torso, shoulder, arm, elbow, finally wrist—each acceleration building on the previous one as the body uncoiled. When coaches talked about "mechanics," they were talking about how smoothly the accelerations worked together, how efficiently. Some percentage of a thrower's mechanics were taught, some were developed through practice, some were innate. Both Pauly and Stauffer could throw a baseball off a pitcher's mound ninety-four miles per hour, then throw another, and another, and another, and do it as easily as if they were playing catch.

Pauly had what scouts call a "fast arm." His easy motion built into a deceptively fast final acceleration—he was always making hitters rush. His ball got in on them while they were in midstride.

His arm's resiliency had let him get away with the charade of not caring. Playing it cool would be tough to pull off while babying an arm or sticking to a regimen. It was easier when you could saunter into the outfield and casually heave a baseball from foul pole to foul pole. Or when you could pitch on command—no matter when or for how long or on how much rest—with a shrug and say, "Sure. Whatever."

Pauly's summer was turning excellent. He had revised his earlier opinion of where he stood on the team. Now he felt there wasn't any difference between him and the other players, except for his brand of work ethic. "Everyone works hard at baseball," he said. But few of the others threw themselves into everything as Pauly did his carpet-cleaning job, his studies, even stuff he didn't enjoy. Pauly was driven by a different engine.

At the Fenway showcase, the Red Sox scouts had let the pitchers take a few hacks in the batting cage, just for fun. Pauly was the only pitcher to jack one over the Monster. He walked out of the cage, dramatically holding the bat over his head in victory. He let the bat drop, then flung his helmet on the ground with a flourish, and high-fived the pitchers around him, who suddenly regarded him differently.

He'd thrown eighty-one pitches two nights before going to Fenway, but was still buzzing from the home run when he threw in the bullpen in front of the scouts. The major league ball had felt large and hard in his hand, the seams smaller and tighter than the college balls. He liked it. The red clay mound felt hard, perfectly formed. The dirt didn't cake his spikes. His arm felt strong and lively. He pumped up the velocity, hit his marks, threw his slider, threw his change, threw brilliantly. Everything worked, moved, darted. Then he turned goofy—this time not as a mask, but because he'd been feeling cocky, like he could do no wrong. "Want to see my intentional-walk pitch?" he asked one of the scouts looking on. It was an absurd thing to suggest at a showcase, and the scout didn't see the humor. "You make a joke about it," said the scout gruffly, "but that's actually something we spend a lot of time working on." Pauly motioned for the catcher to stand up, and lobbed a soft one in to him. The scout growled, "Okay. That's enough."

Pauly didn't care. He was a stud prospect, doing his thing.

There were no charades in the bullpen now. In Hyannis Pauly took his pregame warm-up pitches seriously and sat down. He put a jacket over his right shoulder to keep it warm, even in the afternoon heat. Sitting next to him, Stauffer, still weak from the strep, looked skinny and pale by comparison. Pauly had stepped out from behind Hindman's shadow and up to the mound, as if he owned it. He was locked in now.

He struck out Hyannis's leadoff man, Danny Putnam. Putnam, a high-profile freshman from Stanford, had played in the Cape League all-star game. Against Pauly he looked overmatched.

Pauly blew away seven of the first eight batters and looked just as sharp as he had the last two times out, if not sharper. He cleanly fielded a ball hit back at him, and made a sure, strong throw to first. He didn't tug at his uniform; he seemed comfortable enough in his body to pay attention to his job. The concentration didn't make him tense or knotted up, as it did some players. In the dugout he talked to teammates, but about the game, about batters. A fan seeing him for the first time might not have even noticed Pauly's demeanor. But to fans who had seen Pauly earlier in the summer, acting goofy and disengaged, he seemed transformed. Confidence was a powerful trait—it made players look bigger, stronger, more intense—and people sensed it in Pauly now even if they couldn't say why. But something crucial had changed: Pauly no longer had to worry about saving face in case he failed. He wasn't going to fail, and he knew it.

With two outs in the third inning, Hyannis scratched Pauly for two runs. The first scored on a weak pop-up dumped into right field. The second scored on a fly ball that should have been caught by the left-fielder, Steve LeFaivre. LeFaivre misjudged the ball, sprinted to make up for the mistake, but then slowed and let the ball fall for a double. Some things hadn't changed. Both runs were charged to Pauly, tough-luck runs. He came back and struck out the side in the fourth, got the side in order in the fifth—he looked great, at the top of his game—then again in the sixth, the seventh—he was cruising, unhittable—then again in the eighth. In the top of the ninth inning, with Pauly keeping the A's in a tight game, Colt Morton launched a three-run jack and gave Chatham a 5–2 lead. Schiffner brought in Zane Carlson to finish it off, just like old times.

Pauly's numbers on the day sparkled—eight innings, four hits, eight strikeouts, no walks. His summer had turned into a coming-out party. Over his last five games he'd been one of the most dominant pitchers in the Cape Cod League, giving up just four runs in twenty-seven innings. This was his final performance of the season. He'd gone out in style, retiring the last sixteen batters he'd faced at the highest level of his playing career. He couldn't wait to get home to his buddies and the beach, couldn't wait to get back to school and see Ingrid, couldn't wait to start pitching again in the fall. He caught a wave that showed no sign of breaking. He was having the ride of his life.

TWELVE

Home

JOE FITZBACK CUT THE MOTOR three-quarters of a mile out to
sea from the Chatham break. At five-thirty in the morning, in the
last hours of low tide, the heavy fog lightened to a pale, milky gray.
Fitzback could see the dark green seawater against the sides of the
boat; a few yards away the water disappeared into the grayness. The
boat wasn't fancy, a no-frills twenty-foot Maritime skiff with a ninety-
horse four-stroke engine. But it had a large cooler for keeping fish,
which Fitzback occasionally brought back for market. His bread and
butter, though, was his charter business. He was finally getting Jamie
D'Antona out for some striper fishing.

D'Antona hadn't bothered to put in his contact lenses at that
hour, and with his round frames and curly hair he looked as if he
might be Fitzback's bookworm nephew, out there in the early-
morning fog only at his uncle's prodding. He wore mesh athletic
shorts and a black, long-sleeved "Wake Forest" T-shirt. He didn't
look like a fisherman at all until he grabbed a rod out of the holder,
and you could tell by the easy way he held it that he knew what he
was doing. Fitzback had rigged the light spinning tackle with a long
wire leader and a small, shiny, silver-colored spoon, which he told
D'Antona to jig along the retrieve. The seas were calm, swelling
gently beneath the boat. D'Antona whipped his rod tip back and let
the spoon fly out into the fog. He heard the whistling of the line
shooting through the guides, and several seconds later the distant

bloop of the lure hitting the water. A minute later he had his first fish on. On his fifth or sixth cast a good fish hit, and D'Antona sang out "Sweeeeet!" as he reeled in, the rod tip bending sharply. D'Antona saw the silver flash of the fish's side alongside the boat—striped bass, and a heavy one. Fitzback hauled it up with a gaff and handed D'Antona a pair of pliers to disgorge the hook. The striper went close to forty-two inches. D'Antona said, "Yep. I'll keep that one."

The two of them fished all morning, changing locations a few times but consistently catching decent-sized striped bass and small sand sharks. Other boats drifted into milky view, even followed Fitzback as he fired up his motor and chugged several hundred yards farther offshore. "That's what they do," said Fitzback. "They haven't put in the time to know where the fish are, so they find someone who has, and then follow him."

D'Antona got excited every time a fish hit, like a kid, and whooped when he and Fitzback had fish on at the same time. After the first one, he gaffed for himself. He callously lobbed the sand sharks back and said, "Go away!" He slipped the smaller stripers back into the water and said, "Go get your big brother!" He talked with Fitzback about fishing in the Keys, in Alaska. He pissed over the side when it came time, and kept on talking. D'Antona acted more like a fishing buddy than the paying clients Fitzback usually had to fish with. Unlike them, D'Antona didn't complain about hunger, about not feeling well, about the lack of comforts on the boat. He didn't ask to change lures to see if they could get into bigger fish; he experimented with the speed of his retrieve, the cadence of his jigging, the depth he let the lure sink to before he brought it back in. When he landed fish on three casts in a row and Fitzback's rod had stayed quiet, he said, "They must be hungry on this side. Try here—I'll move to the back and try out there." He did things himself that Fitzback normally had to do for others.

In the disorienting fog the boat floated in time, in space. D'Antona cast, retrieved, and cast again. Five hours after starting, they set the rods back into the holders. D'Antona couldn't believe how fast the time had gone.

They motored back with D'Antona's limit of one fish, plus ten stripers thirty-four inches or more in the hold for Fitzback. Fitzback kept the skiff inside the bar on their way into Pleasant Bay. Closer to shore, the thinning fog gave a gauzy, ethereal feeling to the big oceanfront houses and the hotel and cabañas of the Chatham Bars Inn. Fitzback idled off the docks of the Chatham fish pier. The warm, humid air smelled salty, fishy, faintly of gasoline. They waited their turn behind other fishermen, docked, then hauled close to two hundred pounds of striped bass up the pier into the storehouse. A clerk entered Fitzback's catch into a ledger. The stripers would go to the Gloucester fish market, at market price. A buck fifty a pound would make its way back to the fisherman, a few hundred extra dollars at the end of the month for Fitzback. At the parking lot at Ryder's Cove, D'Antona lay his fish, unwrapped, on top of some newspapers in the trunk of his Mercury. He drove straight to Nick's to clean it and throw it on the grill.

He felt conflicted about the season's ending. He was tired, more than ready for a rest. He wasn't looking forward, though, to classes back at "Work Forest." He'd felt sad a couple of nights earlier at the good-bye dinner Mimi had thrown at Nick's—she did it each year for her favorite guys. Mimi had cried when she hugged him. D'Antona had just one more day of work at the tackle shop. He was going to miss the people.

BEFORE THE FINAL home game, against the Brewster Whitecaps, Chatham honored its players. John Schiffner, Matt Fincher, and the other coaches lined up between home and third and faced the crowd. Charlie Thoms trotted out through the gate next to the third-base dugout and joined the coaches, and the players on the bench whistled and clapped and shouted, "Awwright, *Charlie!*" Paul Galop read the award winners over the loudspeaker. The coaches had picked Tim Stauffer as the 2002 Outstanding Pitcher. Stauffer jogged out to the line as his name was called, shook the coaches' hands. Thoms, last in line, handed him a specially inscribed wooden bat made by the Barnstable Bat Company.

The air hung over the field, humid, sultry, but the days were shortening. By seven o'clock the lights were on, pink and orange streaking the evening sky behind them. Twenty-five hundred fans joined in the applause, a good crowd right to the end.

Just before the bottom of the sixth inning, Paul Galop publicly thanked the A's fans and volunteers for their support. The players hopped out of the dugout, turned toward the fans, and clapped for them. Schiffner stepped out with his players, looked toward each set of bleachers, and touched his fingers to the tip of his cap. Paul Galop let the moment sink in—it felt tender, spontaneous—then put out "Thank You for Being a Friend" over the P.A.

In the press box, a steady flow of well-wishers stopped in to say good-bye to Thoms, to Galop. The A's press box was always the liveliest in the league. Extra seats lined a short platform that stretched along the back wall of the spare, well-lit room, just above Galop at the microphone and the row of volunteers who worked the scoreboard and did the scoring. League president Judy Scarafile stopped by as did the league's publicist, Missy Alaimo, and other league officials; Russ Charpentier, the long-time sports columnist for the *Cape Cod Times*; members of the Chatham Athletic Association; former A's; random reporters; and friends of the family. Charlie Thoms grabbed a staple gun and a white card with a red *K* on it, the baseball scoring symbol for "strikeout." He leaned out of the wide front opening and stapled the card next to five others lined up along the top of opening—the running strikeout count for A's pitchers.

The game, taut, well played, was tied at 1–1 after six innings. The A's were clearly playing until it was over. Brewster, which had once seemed like a lock to take the second playoff spot in the east, had slumped over the past week and needed to win both its remaining games to get in. The Whitecaps had started their ace against Chatham, a lanky left-hander from Alabama named Taylor Tankersley, who had six wins coming in, the most in the league.

Brewster put its first two batters on base in the seventh. Expecting a bunt, Jamie D'Antona pulled in several steps closer. Anthony Gwynn shot a hard line drive down the third-base line. Positioned so close, D'Antona had almost no time to react. He dived to his left and snared the ball in the webbing of his glove. He scrambled to his knees and fired a bullet across the diamond and doubled the runner off first. *From his knees.* "What was that?" asked Schiffner in the dugout. "What did I just see? . . . Way to go *JAMIE!*"

In the eighth inning the A's, down 2–1, came back. Michael Moon lined a base hit, and Chad Orvella bunted him over to second. The crowd sensed something coming, started clapping in unison. In the dugout, Thomas Pauly and Ryan Johnson pulled out a new kind of rally cap. They folded their A's hats and held them in front of their faces like robber's masks—Pauly, in the dugout instead of the bullpen, his head in the game. Simon Williams stepped into a fast ball from that stubborn crouch of a stance and stroked the ball into right field to score Moonie, running hard from second. Pauly and R.J. laughed and slapped five, their rally caps having brought the good fortune. Charlie's "*K* cards" mounted. Ten of them now fluttered across the top of the press box like flags.

An inning later D'Antona sprang to his backhand again for a ground ball skimming along the baseline. The ball kicked into foul territory just before the bag. D'Antona reacted, speared it with his glove as he slid on his knees, his momentum carrying him past the far side of the third-base coach's box. One out of fifty infielders might have stopped a ball that far into foul territory. Not one in a hundred would do what D'Antona did next. He stopped his slide by sticking out his right leg and jamming in his cleats, pushed off from that low position, and gunned a throw all the way to first to beat the runner. The third-base umpire threw both hands up in the air, signaling the ball foul, but the fans, primed with tension, went nuts anyway. The play was so far beyond the normal range that it electrified the night, put a buzz through the crowd that only gradually subsided. Husbands came back from the food line and wives said, "You missed it." Kids playing catch down by the playground tried to reenact the play, sliding on their knees and throwing, sliding on their knees and throwing. In the dugout, as he had only once or twice that long season, Schiffner said, "Oh . . . my . . . god."

No one went home early. The crowd seemed to swell as the innings marched on. Kids got a bedtime reprieve from their parents. The game was going to extra innings, the summer refused to end.

And that was the heart of it. The game had the awesome ability to stop time. There was no clock in baseball. The players out there on the field were twenty years old, just as they were last year, five years ago, ten. Nothing had changed—that was the illusion. Forget that the big electronic scoreboard in left field was new. Forget that they were playing music at games in Chatham. The following year they would broadcast games on the Internet. Forget that this little old-fashioned club had spent $60,000 in the off-season on field improvement, including replacing turf in the infield with a better mix of seed. That was real grass out there, those were wooden bats. The generations blurred. Mike MacDougal, Mike Lowell, Jeff Bagwell, Thurman Munson. Johnny Schiffner watched from the dugout. These were the same kids out there, chasing the same dream, giving the same gift. There was still a fishing fleet in Chatham. There was still sand. The family was still here.

Zane Carlson strode in from the bullpen to start the tenth inning, with that familiar tense face, that impatience, the team's most valuable player, the all-time Cape Cod Baseball League leader in saves. And now everything was perfect. It was 2001 again; the A's were going to the play-offs. Carlson fired the ball in low and fast, got it back from Chris Iannetta, and fired it in again. He struck out Anthony Gwynn to lead off the inning. Charlie Thoms leaned out of the press-box window and hammered up another red *K*—the thirteenth of the night for A's pitchers, the *K*'s marching across the entire window opening. Carlson threw again, this time a nasty slider in the dirt, and Kainoa Obrey, the Hawaiian from BYU, swung and missed, and the losing streak, the no-hitters, the last-place standing all disappeared.

But then the ball bounced past Iannetta, and everything crashed down. Obrey reached first base on the wild pitch, the strikeout for naught. Carlson walked the next batter. Then, against a .130 hitter who had just ten hits all summer, he gave up a sudden, devastating home run to center field.

The A's players, who'd been standing in the dugout in the ninth inning wearing rally caps and yelling encouragement, were subdued in the tenth. This had been fun, this run they'd made at the end. Knocking out Brewster at home, in front of that last big crowd, the last game most of them would ever play at Veterans Field in Chatham, well, it would have been a great way to end the summer. The fans were still into it—nobody was leaving, there were still three outs to go—but down 5–2, the players slumped. On the bench, Blake Hanan, Hanan of all people, talked about golf. He was trying to round up some guys to play a few rounds on Martha's Vineyard after the season ended. Chris Iannetta, who had struck out twice and let Carlson's low strikeout pitch get by him, sat away from the others, in a funk, beating up on himself, not even watching.

Osama led off the bottom of the tenth with an easy ground ball to second. It should have been an out, but the Brewster second baseman stumbled just as he gathered the ball in, dropped it, picked it up and dropped it again. Colt Morton, the next batter, pulled his head off a breaking ball and struck out—for the fifty-ninth time that season, a new league record for futility. He stared at the pitcher, slowly walked back to the dugout, into the privacy of his teammates, and flung his helmet down in frustration. But Moon walked, and now runners led from two bases. The players on the Chatham bench stood up, came to life. Orvella poked a single through the right side, and now there were three on. Pauly and R.J. put on their robber's masks. The crowd started again—*clap, clap, clap*—the sound starting behind home plate, then spreading—*clap, clap, clap, clap*—

down the lines and over the lawn chairs on the grass and around the banks of the outfield. Simon Williams hit a soft liner to right that fell for a hit, and Osama scored, and now it was 5–3. The players on the bench jumped up out of the dugout to greet him. Palmieri gave Williams a playful slap on the helmet at first base, and Williams made a fist and flexed his arm. With the bases loaded and one out, Brewster brought in a new pitcher and D'Antona stepped in. He'd been here before. He was the man. The one they counted on. The one who had failed in a baseball season for the first time in his life. The clapping grew louder—*CLAP, CLAP, CLAP*—and it was the championship year of '92 again, '96, '98. It was impossible to tell. D'Antona drilled a low line drive to right-center and brought home two of the runs. He scampered down to second when the right-fielder misplayed the ball. Jeremy Cleveland, up with the score tied at five, walked to load the bases, and now players in both dugouts were standing. Some fans behind home plate stood up too, then more, and then all around Veterans Field fans stood and clapped in unison. The noise crackled in the air, echoed out across dark streets and quiet houses. Residents with their windows open to catch the breeze on the warm night could hear the sound a mile away. The glare of the lights cast a glow high above the field, an aura. Brewster brought in another pitcher. He jammed Steve LeFaivre with a fastball, and LeFaivre got wood on it but missed the sweet spot. Off an aluminum bat the ball would have lofted into the outfield for a routine out. But this was a wooden-bat league, a league that gave as much as it took away, and the blooper fell into shallow right field for a base hit, and Simon Williams—with the effortless glide and the major league body and the bad stance and the bum shoulder—sprinted home with the run that won it.

JOHN SCHIFFNER SAID it didn't matter what happened in Orleans in the team's final game of the summer. It was always nice to beat Orleans, especially in their yard, but the comeback against Brewster had been gratifying enough—it showed the players' character. It gave back something to the Chatham fans: something to cheer about and remember the summer by.

He'd remember that summer as a strange one, not a bad one. It didn't come close to the dismal season he'd endured in '94, his first full year as manager of the A's. That was the year he lost three players to Team USA and his team lost twelve games by one run. Both of Schiffner's parents were diagnosed with cancer that same year. A close colleague at Plainfield High, the vice-principal, stepped in front of a truck and killed himself. Two of Schiffner's seniors died in a car accident just before graduation. Nick the Barber, a legendary figure in Chatham and a close friend of Schiffner's, unexpectedly dropped dead. "*That* was a bad year," Schiffner reminded Paul Galop halfway through the summer. "Bad?" said Galop. "They make movies about years like that."

Schiffner knew he'd gambled coming into the 2002 season. The experiment had been worth it, he said, but he wouldn't hold spots for that many juniors again. He'd invite just two players back for 2003, Adam Yates and Zane Carlson. People had consoled Schiffner back in June as he'd lost players off his original roster to the draft, and he had brushed them off. "How can I feel bad?" he asked. "These guys are getting a chance to play pro ball. That's what it's all about. I'm excited for them!" But the injuries were another thing. Schiffner had made fifteen changes to his roster after the first of June. He'd carried a couple of injured players for long stretches of the season. He'd patched together a lineup that had little speed and no true centerfielder, weaknesses that showed up in his team's poor outfield defense. Errors in the infield cost outs, but errors in the outfield cost runs. Three or four games might have ended differently had Ryan Hubbard been running around center field with a healthy back, or had Universal not busted his finger, or had Adam Greenberg not signed. Three games meant six points—one point more than Chatham would have needed to make the play-offs. But that was slicing numbers, and in a division packed as tightly as the Eastern Division was that summer, every coach could have said, *if only. . . .*

Other things made the summer strange. Chatham led the Cape Cod League in home runs, an unlikely mark of a John Schiffner team, though one he'd anticipated that first week of practice. Eight different A's players hit home runs—which meant, possibly, that eight different players were swinging too hard for home runs, because the team's batters also set a league record for strikeouts: 455, an average of eleven strikeouts every game, a frustrating statistic that Schiffner hadn't anticipated and couldn't explain. Chatham's pitching staff struck out more batters than any other team had in history as well, with 406. Schiffner had never seen so many games with so few baserunners.

He couldn't remember a summer that had been so unrelentingly hot and dry. Set it in seventy-two-point type: Fog had not interrupted a game in Chatham for an entire summer. Strange.

ROSE MALLOW BLOOMED in the marshes. The pink flowers, wide as saucers, showy as orchids, lit up the green marshland and then disappeared almost as soon as they'd arrived. The blossoms lasted just one day. Beach plums and blackberries ripened. The foliage on the first tupelos and red maples turned toward fall.

But the heat stuck in there till the end. Just three Orleans Cardinals showed up in the midday sun for that team's early batting practice, and they hit without shirts on. But the humidity had finally broken. By game time that final evening, long shadows stretched across Eldredge Park, and the air felt delicious.

Like Veterans Field in Chatham, Eldredge Park was a gem of a summer ball field whose facets sparkled most when a crowd of two or three thousand people filled the perimeter and brought the field to life. A terraced bank of grass spread from the backstop all the way down the right-field line. On nights with especially good crowds, bright spots of color—particularly the Cardinals' bright red and white—lit up every bit of green along the terraces. The Chatham games always drew well. That night some 3,300 people—a great crowd, a play-off crowd—completely covered the bank. Lawn chairs stretched along the back of the outfield fence and across the raised stage of the band shell in right-center field, and on around behind the bullpens in left.

The traffic along Route 28 traced one edge of the park, not forty feet behind the A's' dugout on the third-base side. The busy road might have made the scene feel pedestrian, unromantic, had it not been for two details in the composition. First, the field lay in a shallow depression, so that Route 28 ran slightly above the level of the playing surface. That small change in elevation gave the field depth, made it special in the way that one or two shadow lines subtly distinguished fine old houses from flatter reproductions. The second detail was the line of lush shade trees that lined both sides of Route 28. The trees arched their canopies out over the road, enclosed it, made it feel less like a highway than a teeming, upper-level concourse of a stadium. The stoplight at the corner of Route 28 and Eldredge Park Way slowed the traffic to a residential-street stroll as it passed the field. Drivers occasionally flashed lights, honked horns, yelled encouragement through rolled-down windows. The road's proximity made the games public, wrapped the field into the community even as it attracted community to the games. Every night, dozens of cars spontaneously pulled into the parking area of the middle school next door, seduced by the lights and all that color out on the field. Only Orleans drew more fans to its games than Chatham.

Before the game, the home team held its own version of year-end awards. The ceremony included a traditional Orleans ritual. Individual players and housemates were announced over the loudspeaker along with the names of their host families. The players greeted their host moms and dads out on the field with hugs or handshakes, then handed them a single red rose.

It seemed fitting that Tim Stauffer should finish it. He also was playing to the very end, which both impressed and surprised Schiffner. Schiffner had misjudged Stauffer. He'd guessed Stauffer would return home long before now. And he would have understood if the pitcher had begged off from this last start. The team was out of the race. Stauffer looked emaciated in his away gray uniform, his belt cinched tight to hold up pants that now looked too big for him. He had lost a dozen pounds in the past week because of the strep. Lord knew he'd pitched enough innings that spring and summer.

His parents, here for Tim's last game on Cape Cod, stood on the short bank in back of the A's' dugout, chatting with Tim's house mother. Blake Hanan's parents had come from upstate New York, Chris Iannetta's from Providence. They all sat or stood along the narrow strip of grass between the field and Route 28. In the small set of bleachers, Paul Galop sat next to his wife, Laurie. The Troys were there. The Ruddocks. Charlie Thoms, of course. Martha Schiffner. A handful of other A's volunteers. One of the fans who followed the team home and away, Bob Sherman, an impish-looking man with a white beard and round glasses, stood next to the bleachers. He'd kept meticulous records of the team's performance over the years, sent away for the players' college media guides, kept a record of roster changes on a spreadsheet on his computer back home in Norwell, across the bridge. He had timed his two-week vacation in Chatham to match the final weeks of the A's season. The Chatham contingent had the feeling of a core family, the A's' inner circle.

Stauffer finished his warm-up pitches in the bullpen out behind the left-field fence and walked in to join the rest of the team. Forty or fifty fans thoughtlessly moved in and spread out blankets and set up lawn chairs right there in the bullpen, right between the pitcher's mound and the home plate, just a few feet from the bench where the A's pitchers looked on, unbelieving. "I guess Stauffer's going nine tonight," said one of the pitchers.

A gang of kids approached the pitchers on the bench and asked them for autographs. "We can only sign until the game starts," Zane Carlson said. "Then you're going to have to leave us alone." Ryan Johnson, not playing tonight because of a sore shoulder, sat next to Carlson. A small, shy kid hung back, and R.J. called him over. "Let's see what it looks like if we trade hats," he said. He dropped his size-eight cap completely over the boy's head, and put the kid's little hat on his own head, where it looked like a toy. The boy laughed hysterically, and R.J. traded back with him, then signed the bill of the boy's cap. It was among the last of hundreds of small acts of kindness that season. The players would have no way of knowing how many kids' summers had been made by that kind of slight contact, how many kids fell in love with baseball as a result.

STAUFFER PITCHED TOUGH. A couple of scouts looked on from behind home plate, or maybe they were agents, it was hard to tell. Most of the scouts' work on the Cape was done; the agents' work was just beginning. Agents approached Rick and Becky Stauffer at games now, and called them at home. This would intensify as next year's draft approached. Would-be agents, even professional money managers, aggressively courted the families of the kids who promised to go high in the draft. Most of the men approaching the Stauffers were polite, but they all wanted a piece of their son's action.

Stauffer had proved he belonged at the very top of the next year's class. He acted unsurprised by his success. Outwardly he had changed little during his ten weeks in Chatham. He was still unusually private. He still spoke to adults in safe, predictable clichés. He still held himself to a higher standard. But the vagueness of his expectations about the draft had clarified. He was aware of the talk swirling around him. He knew that the season had confirmed his blue-chip status. He didn't let it change the way he went at things, but to friends he admitted that he'd be disappointed if he didn't go in the first round of the draft—among the first thirty players chosen in the country. His dream was to pitch for the Boston Red Sox. If not them, he didn't care. "Maybe someplace totally random would be fun," he said, "like San Diego."

In the bottom of the eighth inning, Stauffer gave up two singles to start the inning. Orleans had knotted the score at two, a gift of two errors, an out being given back by Orvella and then a couple of runs given by Simon Williams in center field. Stauffer still threw with the nice, easy motion, but he'd worked hard for his outs that night, and his father said he wished Schiffner would lift Tim and bring in a fresher arm. Yet Stauffer stayed in, and he struck out Mike Rapacioli of St. Bonaventure, one of the few other Atlantic Ten Conference players on the Cape that summer. Stauffer flipped the ball to himself, looked in, and got Myron Leslie—a former teammate of his in New Hampshire—to hit a little tapper to third. D'Antona charged and bare-handed the ball and flung it to first, off-balance, just as he'd done forever, and got the out. But Stauffer lost the next batter on balls, then hit a batter to force in a run. Stauffer's expression didn't change, but he turned his back on home plate and did some hurried landscaping at the rubber with his cleat, staring straight down. He puffed out his cheeks and blew, got set again. He mixed his pitches, worked the count. He ended it by freezing infielder Steve Garrabrants with a curveball for a called strike three—Stauffer's eighth strikeout of the game, his sixty-seventh overall, best in the league. The A's entered their final inning of the summer needing a run to tie. Stauffer, sweaty, exhausted, had thrown 109 pitches. He was done.

With one out in the ninth, Jamie D'Antona ripped at a fastball and fouled it back. His swing felt good, fluid, powerful. He was seeing the ball well. He'd had one hit that game already and crushed one other—a laser to deep center field—that was chased down nearly four hundred feet from the plate. But four pitches sailed wide, and he took a walk. He barreled around to third as a perfectly executed hit-and-run single rolled through to right field, and the A's had the rally caps on in the dugout again, everyone standing and hollering again, everything lined up.

Travis Udvarhelyi, the smooth-swinging outfielder from Grossmont College in California who had come to Chatham when the Universal Soldier went down, had two hits and a sacrifice bunt so far that night. Like Blake Hanan, he'd come to this league out of a small school not knowing where he stood, and he'd discovered he was overmatched at this high level. He'd started that night's game with just a .104 batting average, getting five hits in forty-eight at-bats. But the law of averages guaranteed a good game at least once or twice for him, as well, and this was his shining moment on the Cape.

He sliced a hard ground ball to shortstop and took off. His speed to first, from the left side of the plate, was a very fast 3.9 seconds. But Matt Maniscalco was a pro talent at short, and his soft hands picked up the ball and, smooth as water, flipped it to Garrabrants at second. Garrabrants, an infielder at Arizona State University who had rejected the Minnesota Twins out of high school, deftly turned the pivot as D'Antona steamed toward the plate with the tying run. The throw to first nipped Udvarhelyi by a half step, nailing down the double play.

That's the way the game ended, and in that ending, the story of the entire season: Jamie D'Antona leading a comeback that fell just short; Tim Stauffer pitching impressively but losing, betrayed by a porous defense; Thomas Pauly cheering in the dugout, part of the team, finally giving a rat's ass about winning a summer-league game; the last at-bat left to the replacement of a replacement player who wasn't in the same league as the rest of the competition on that beautiful level ball field.

Van Morrison rang out over loudspeakers into the black night air as the A's gathered one last time in the outfield for a team huddle. Cars streamed by on Route 28, their drivers having no idea of all that had transpired under those bright lights. The final score still lit up the electronic scoreboard in left field. The Cardinals had just won thirty games for the first time ever and were headed for the play-offs. The A's finished their 2002 season with nineteen wins, twenty-three losses, and two ties. The small cadre of A's' fans and family members stood as the players walked past, applauding their players, their heroes, their boys.

Schiffner apologized in advance for choking up, then addressed his players: "I can't thank all of you enough for the way you pulled together and finished this summer. I know a lot of teams that would have collapsed—in fact we saw some of them this week. But you kept coming out and playing hard, and that's all we coaches could ask of you. I wish every one of you success in your next season and in your careers. Make sure if you're ever around Chatham again that you stop by and say hi. I'll probably be here."

Schiffner left them there. He and the other coaches would have their own good-byes the following day—putting the ball field in Chatham to bed for the winter, stacking and storing away equipment, the ritual just as important and poignant as the closing of a summer house or cottage. Then the good-bye dinner at Pate's Restaurant. Schiffner had surprisingly few loose ends to tie up. He needed to make a couple of phone calls, though they could wait a day or two. There was this Lambert kid from Boston College, threw ninety-five, ninety-six . . . Schiffner had heard that Wareham's John Wylde had gotten the jump on him.

The players leaned in close in the huddle, bowed their heads as if in prayer, raised their hands together. Young boys and girls ran around the base baths out on the field, waiting with pens and markers for autographs. "One, two, three, A's!" the players chanted.

They broke apart slowly, mingled, shook hands with each other, distractedly signed the balls and baseball caps offered up to them. Some of the players hugged, quickly, awkwardly. None of them seemed to know exactly what to say. Charlie Thoms tracked them down one by one and handed out address lists and travel vouchers. He and Ginor had already said good-bye to their guys, had given them wooden bats from the Barnstable Bat Company, personalized as keepsakes.

Thomas Pauly and Daniel Moore posed for their house mom's camera. Moore's black Honda Accord waited in the parking lot out past the band shell, where the Orleans players were starting into their postgame sandwiches. Clear plastic storage bins, clothes on hangers, and two fishing rods packed the small back seat of Moore's car. A blue Chatham A's hat sat in the back window. A "MapQuest" printout rested on the dash. He was gone.

Near the third-base dugout, Rick and Becky Stauffer talked quietly, waiting for their son. Bob Sherman, the A's superfan who kept the records, intercepted him first and handed him a ball to sign. "You're my pick this year for future major leaguer," Sherman told him. Another ritual.

Jim Hanan walked over and put his arm around his son, Blake.

Van Morrison kept singing, those lovely long lyrics that never seemed to end. Headlights and red tail lights bobbed in the stream of traffic on 28. Little kids threw tennis balls and played catch on the smooth grass in back of third base. A couple of ten-year-olds pleaded with their parents for just one more run around the bases. The players walked slowly across the outfield toward the parking lot—toward the Irish Pub in West Harwich, toward Pictionary at the Troys' house, toward surgery, toward life.

John and Martha Schiffner, last to leave, lingered with the straggling fans. Schiffner did one final sweep of the dugout. The air was cool. They talked quietly for a moment. Finally, they too walked slowly across the outfield, in silence, toward their last late-night meal of the summer. Then the lights of Eldredge Park cut out, and everything, suddenly, was dark.

The Draft

Two days after the Wareham Gatemen defeated Orleans for the 2002 Cape Cod League championship, *Baseball America* published its annual collegiate summer-league roundup. The editors, leaning on the opinions of scouts, named Tim Stauffer second-team "Summer All-America," even though Stauffer hadn't made the final honorary year-end Cape Cod League all-star team. The publication included Stauffer and Jamie D'Antona among the top thirty Cape Cod League prospects, Stauffer ranked number two. D'Antona, who'd come to the Cape near the top of everybody's list, had fallen to number twenty-seven and was called "easily the biggest disappointment on the Cape this summer. Managers were disappointed in his mental and physical approach." When Schiffner saw the write-up he exploded. "That's horseshit!" he said. "Nobody should say that about a twenty-year-old kid! Not for publication—not with his career at stake. I don't know who said that, but they're way out of line."

At one of the A's games that summer, Wake Forest coach George Greer had watched Jamie D'Antona strike out trying to kill a low and outside pitch. Greer had mused, "I can't tell you how many kids I've seen struggle on the Cape and come back to school as if they've had a wake-up call. They suddenly realize they have only one year left, and they stop doing the kinds of things that nineteen- and twenty-year-old kids do. Jamie will be fine."

D'Antona returned to Wake Forest that fall not sure of the damage he'd done to his draft chances but much clearer about what he needed to do. Greer noticed the change right away. D'Antona had always been one of Greer's hardest-working players when it came to batting, but now he showed up early and stayed late for everything, and grabbed a rake without being asked. He worked diligently in the weight room three days a week, and he did his sprints, his mile runs, without complaint. Through the off-season he worked on footwork at third base, at staying low and fielding with his legs instead of his hands. He hit in the cage with wooden bats and with wood-composite "Baum bats," which simulated the balance and density of solid wood. His game bats would have been easier to hit with, but wood was unforgiving. It didn't let D'Antona get away with anything.

He balanced his checkbook. In November, Joe and Karin D'Antona finally trusted him to stay within a monthly call plan and got Jamie his first cell phone. He used it responsibly—mostly for calling home. He'd settled down with a steady girlfriend, a McDonald's All-America soccer player.

That fall and early winter, personality tests D'Antona had completed for various teams trickled into front offices—more data for the thickening files, more science, another angle. One test, the "Caliper profile," which he'd filled out for George Biron of the Anaheim Angels, was shared with other Caliper clients, including the Detroit Tigers, the Cincinnati Reds, the Chicago Cubs, the Chicago White Sox, and the Houston Astros. The results were startling.

Caliper's founder, Herb Greenberg, who developed the test in the late 1950s as a tool for predicting sales success in the insurance industry, believed that the same measures of competitiveness, self-discipline, self-esteem, and other traits could help evaluate the potential of professional athletes. By 1989 his customer list included clients from all of the major sports and a good number of college athletic programs. Major league clubs paid $195 per report, which consisted of a numerical grading of a prospect's psychological traits, a brief written summary, and a detailed conversation with Greenberg himself, who interpreted and colored the numbers.

Greenberg, a Ph.D. who'd taught psychology before starting his consulting firm, had been blind since age ten. He believed passionately in the ability of his test to see inside a person's character. The questionnaire he'd refined included 150 word problems, number problems, and statements, choices, and comparisons involving personal viewpoints. D'Antona thought many of the questions were bizarre. Many of them asked D'Antona to choose traits that "most" and "least" described him, such as:

A. I get things done more quickly than others.
B. I never get nervous in new situations.
C. I'll tell someone what's on my mind, even if he or she might not like hearing it.
D. Knowing what I know now, I might have lived my life differently.

Once tabulated, the profile graded characteristics such as coachability, ability to be a team player, leadership, self-confidence, and mental toughness.

Caliper employed 175 people at its Princeton headquarters, but Greenberg and four analysts worked all of the sports profiles, usually in focused silence. When D'Antona's test came through, Greenberg yelled, "Hey! Look what we've got here!"

D'Antona scored off the charts on competitiveness and self-confidence and in the high zone for every single positive trait the test measured. Greenberg got on the phone and talked with GMs and scouting directors about the results of the test. He told them D'Antona possessed a rare combination of strengths. The kid was an overachiever who would likely exceed his talent. He showed tremendous drive. He was a quick decision maker, with excellent self-discipline and self-esteem. He would motivate himself, Greenberg told them. He wouldn't be rattled by setbacks. He'd be a hell of a team player—as long as the coaches made it clear that the team

needed him. That's the frame he'd respond to. He'd be coachable—
he wasn't afraid of failing or trying something new, but he was also
stubborn. He marked high on intelligence and leadership. There
were only a few wild cards that could be negatives: D'Antona was
impulsive, impatient, not particularly interested in details. "But
those all deal with maturity," Greenberg told the GMs. "I guarantee
he'll grow out of them."

Greenberg was asked if a player couldn't simply fake the test by
choosing answers that put him in the best light. "Everybody tries to
put his best foot forward," Greenberg answered. "This test shows
which foot, it shows what you're trying to project. The combinations
of questions are set up so it's impossible to claim every virtue and
deny every fault—you've got to choose. You've got to decide which
way you're going to lie. And that's what's revealing." He told the
baseball people he couldn't comment on D'Antona's talent. He had
no idea about that. But he said, "You could tell me Jamie is a college
quarterback and I'd say take him."

Greenberg processed between six and seven hundred tests a year
for major-league clubs, and saw maybe eight or ten that ended in the
highest possible score of 1. Lance Berkman of the Astros had been a
1, as had Jeromy Burnitz and Edgardo Alfonzo of the Mets. And now
D'Antona. Every player who had ever achieved that score on the
Caliper test had gone on to play in the majors.

Unconcerned about how he'd scored on the tests, D'Antona went
out that spring and pounded Atlantic Coast Conference pitching.
Wake Forest faltered from a lofty pre-season ranking and finished
without getting a regional bid to the NCAA tournament, but D'Antona hit .360 overall, with twenty-one home runs and eighty-two runs
batted in. He was named the ACC Player of the Year. He became
Wake Forest's all-time leader in home runs and runs batted in after
just three seasons. He walked more times than he struck out. He reduced his errors from twenty to thirteen—his .926 fielding percentage led all ACC third-basemen. He was named first-team All-
America by two organizations and second-team by a third. The most

recent Wake Forest player to be named first-team All-America had been Dave Bush; Bush's and D'Antona's parallel paths continued.

D'Antona had performed under the constant glare of exposure, thanks to scouts who turned up en masse to study his highly touted teammate, pitcher Kyle Sleeth. (Sleeth had pitched a season on the Cape, in Cotuit, before pitching for Team USA the previous summer.) Every weekend between February and May a squadron of scouts and cross-checkers and general managers watched D'Antona play. He rarely talked with the scouts, and he forced himself not to think beyond Wake Forest's season. He had sense enough to know that this would likely be his last college season, and that's where he kept his focus. He was still Jamie, of course. Batting against North Carolina State, he joked with Colt Morton crouching behind the plate. He still laughed and made stupid comments during games, still made pyramids of beer-can empties in the apartment, shot stray rabbits out the back window with a BB gun. But the trash talking and clowning quieted, and it was hard to know if D'Antona's growing maturity was behind it, or Wake Forest's disappointing season. For whatever reason, he appeared more serious as his professional career crept within view.

Inside the world of baseball prospects, a player's standing emerged slowly and changed slowly. Statistics and performance revealed true meaning only over time. D'Antona's stock had eroded during that long last summer before the draft. His reputation from the Cape, fairly or unfairly, had followed him south. He needed every bit of success in the spring to move opinions back around.

He signed on with Barry Meister and Bob Lisanti, agents who often worked together in representing pro athletes. Meister had come to D'Antona on his own, not through the Scott Bradley–Princeton connection that had led him to Scott Hindman (and, as it turned out, also to Thomas Pauly). The agents, talking with clubs about D'Antona's standing and "signability"—the money he might command—guessed that D'Antona would go somewhere between the end of the first round and the end of the third. That wide spread meant the difference of, potentially, hundreds of thousands of dollars.

After Wake Forest's season ended, D'Antona drove from Winston-Salem down to Atlanta for a private showcase at Turner Field, and crushed the ball with everyone in the Braves front office watching. Out of thirty-five swings, he hit twenty baseballs out of the park. He flew out to Phoenix the following day and took batting practice in 113-degree heat. D'Antona launched one ball into the desert air of the Diamondbacks' Bank One Ballpark that caromed off a T.G.I.F. restaurant in the upper deck, an awesome shot. "I wasn't really that surprised," said D'Antona afterward. "I've always hit B.P. pretty well." He loved the way the ball carried in that park, and he thought the pool beyond right-center field was the best.

In the days heading into the draft, Meister and Lisanti had conversations with a number of clubs. The Atlanta Braves, Arizona Diamondbacks, Oakland A's, and San Francisco Giants seemed the most eager. But Meister had been through this process before, and knew how hard it was to call. "Once the draft actually starts," he said, "it takes on a life of its own."

The accolades Tim Stauffer received on the Cape had a lot to do with his reputation going in. He pitched well enough in Chatham to enhance the reputation he'd gone in with, but primarily he'd confirmed what scouts already believed; he'd added mass to the momentum he was already carrying toward his junior season at Richmond.

That spring Stauffer focused on his own ambitious goals, even though the numbers of scouts following his every start rivaled those watching Kyle Sleeth at Wake Forest. A lot of twenty-year-old guys would have basked in the attention, let it change them. Stauffer remained level-headed. He showed the same discipline that had brought him this far—in him it seemed innate—and blocked out the background noise. He'd pitched in front of a ton of scouts before. He needed only to remind himself not to overpitch, not to try to do more than he could, not to risk his future for the sake of one outing.

To anyone who had watched him pitch, the results of his Caliper profile were both revealing and surprising. The test highlighted Stauffer's strengths of self-discipline and work ethic. He scored in the test's ninety-fifth percentile for intelligence. But on conceptual, "ideational," thinking, Stauffer scored just two out of a possible hundred, and, shockingly, he measured poorly on leadership and competitiveness. Both Schiffner and Ron Atkins, Stauffer's coach at Richmond, used terms like "bulldog" and "battler" when talking about Stauffer, and pointed at a fastball that jumped a couple of miles per hour with runners on base, or at how Stauffer brushed back hitters who crowded the plate, or at the way he pitched deep into every game he started. But the Caliper test sketched a profile of an overcautious young man afraid to make mistakes, who performed to please others. His coachability was of the "Yes, sir," "No, sir" variety; he lacked D'Antona's self-esteem. In his official summary, Herb Greenberg scored Stauffer at a neutral "4" and wrote, "Mr. Stauffer should be pushed as fast as possible. On a professional level, he should be assigned at a level one above where his current talent would ordinarily suggest that he be. In other words, he should be forced to compete in order to succeed."

From the outside you couldn't tell what drove a twenty-year-old athlete. A pitcher absolutely determined not to walk someone could look as focused and competitive as one who was hell-bent on not disappointing his father. A batter determined not to strike out was fundamentally different from a batter who was out there to kick some pitcher's butt, even if they looked the same in the batter's box. The psychological tests tried to identify motivations that the players themselves were barely aware of. But anybody who knew Stauffer saw something different and altogether more positive than the Caliper test did: a competitor who was also a nice guy; a determined athlete who also happened to be quiet.

Like D'Antona, Stauffer had a team around him to absorb the heat of the spotlight. The Richmond Spiders had ridden Stauffer's right arm to a Super Regional appearance and national ranking in 2002. In 2003, with most of Richmond's starters returning, expectations soared. But almost immediately the team strained to find the chemistry that had helped propel it a year earlier. Nothing seemed easy, not even the weak opponents. Soaking rain and cold weather up and down the East Coast canceled game after game. Stauffer pitched well—at times better than he had a year earlier, with even more command. The team around him, though, played tense games, scored few runs in support, never quite gelled. Stauffer carried multiple pressures with him when he went out to the mound each weekend. He worked harder for his wins.

His numbers—146 strikeouts in 114 innings, with nineteen walks and an earned run average of 1.97—were comparable to what he'd put up the previous year. But he allowed five earned runs in his first start against lowly Drexel, and six earned runs against North Carolina in a 10–0 loss. On May thirtieth, four days before the draft, with a blister on his throwing hand, Stauffer pitched eight innings in his final college game, and allowed eleven hits and five runs (three earned) in an NCAA Regional loss to Cal-Riverside. After the game, Richmond coach Ron Atkins said that Stauffer was probably tired. He'd thrown a ton of innings.

Stauffer's final record of nine wins and five losses appeared as a letdown from the previous year's astounding 15-and-3. In all of the published reports and talk swirling around Stauffer that spring, though, only one commentary—on the Web site of an organization called Team One Baseball—included anything less than glowing praise of his prospects. That one report, filed by a staff member who scouted for himself, questioned why no one seemed concerned about the fall-off in Stauffer's velocity, from ninety-two and ninety-three on the Cape to eighty-eight and ninety less than two months before the draft. The report included a note on an apparent stiffening in Stauffer's shoulder in the later innings, which showed more strain than the easy delivery all the professional scouts had described.

Everyone else in the know, though, said it came down to Stauffer and Sleeth or Sleeth and Stauffer at the top of the draft. A couple of position players had a shot of going ahead of them. Halfway through the season, scouts across the majors acknowledged that Stauffer would be gone by the tenth pick. Those clubs picking lower stopped scouting him altogether, choosing not to waste resources on a lost cause. The clubs at the top of the draft intensified their scrutiny. The dream inched closer.

Stauffer and his parents chose as their adviser Ron Shapiro, a selective Baltimore-based agent and negotiator with a reputation for integrity. Shapiro handpicked only one or two new clients each year, athletes who impressed him with their character and values as much as their ability. He represented Brooks Robinson, Eddie Murray, Jim Palmer, and Cal Ripken, Jr. Shapiro believed that for Stauffer it would come down to one of the first six picks: Tampa Bay, Milwaukee, Detroit, San Diego, Kansas City, or the Cubs. Stauffer, though he didn't admit it in public, allowed himself to imagine what it might be like if one team or another picked him. Those were the weakest teams in the majors, the ones who needed the most help the fastest. A couple of the organizations projected Stauffer in the big leagues as early as September of 2004. Of the six, only the Detroit Tigers received the report from Caliper.

The regional tournament kept Stauffer's imagination from getting ahead of him. The host team eliminated Richmond on June first, three days away from the draft. That night Stauffer had trouble sleeping for the first time all year.

THOMAS PAULY'S DEMEANOR changed when he returned to Princeton in the fall. His romance with Ingrid blossomed. He carried a 3.66 GPA in his major, and he carried himself more confidently on the baseball field. It was a subtle thing, the difference between knowing you belonged somewhere and not being quite sure. He felt the way he had imagined the big-program guys had felt in Chatham—easy, with no worries about how they looked or how they fit in. If he noticed a teammate struggling now he said something to pick him up, not make him laugh. He had put on thirty pounds of muscle since he'd arrived as a gangly, long-limbed freshman. He was deeper across the chest, chiseled. He had crossed the line Scott Bradley talked about, the one between boys and men. He assumed the role of team leader, even as a junior.

He felt uneasy, though, about turning pro after his junior season and leaving his teammates behind, about giving up a chance to be team captain. He couldn't quite believe the next level beckoned, but he and Scott Bradley started talking about agents, what the transition to pro ball might be like, how to deal with guilt Pauly would feel about leaving. Bradley had been there before, and he knew what to say. "You say you want a chance to pitch in the big leagues?" he asked Pauly. "This is the right time. You're ready . . . There are seven chemical engineers graduating in your class. How long will it take those others to put away a half million dollars? . . . You'll be able to negotiate the schedule to finish up classes, and your parents, I'm sure, will appreciate a club paying for your last year at Princeton... Half of your team will probably strangle you if you don't take this chance." And Pauly grew comfortable with the idea.

Princeton's spring trip included a stop at the University of North Carolina, Bradley's alma mater. Pauly posed for a picture with Jeremy Cleveland and Daniel Moore, his Ivy League uniform right alongside their Tar Heels. When Princeton played at N.C. State he wandered over during stretching and said hi to Colt Morton and Chad Orvella. The gestures—the larger club he was now a part of— set him apart from his Princeton teammates, gave him stature.

He made his first appearance of the year against Tim Stauffer in Richmond in front of seventy-five scouts. The brutal spring weather had kept Princeton's team inside until that first game. Outside, on a real mound, against Stauffer, with all that attention and adrenaline,

Pauly overthrew and felt pain for the first time since he had been playing—bursitis in the scapula behind his right shoulder. (He gave up a run in a 3–1 loss.)

The inflammation was minor, not a serious injury. As a freshman, Pauly would have sulked, or hit something, or pretended to ignore it. But he said, "Hey, I overdid it. I'll rest it for a week. It's not the shoulder, not the elbow. It will be fine." He pitched again, and gave up a game-winning home run. Even a year ago, the home run would have thrown him into a spiral, brought out the mask, the voices in his head. Now, he looked his coach in the eye and said evenly, "I made a decent pitch. Get me out there again." And then he went out and blew away the Ivy League. Pauly closed one win after another. With the Ivy League championship on the line, Bradley started Pauly twice, and twice Pauly pitched complete-game victories, including the clincher against Harvard in front of dozens of scouts. He finished the regular season with six wins and a loss, the third-lowest earned-run average in Division I (1.25) and the fourth-highest mark (13.1) for strikeouts per nine innings.

In March, based in large part on his summer on the Cape, Thomas Pauly had ranked eighty-eighth on *Baseball America*'s early draft preview list. By June he'd shot up to fifty-fifth, and there was talk of the first round. He was flying higher than local radar now.

ON TUESDAY, JUNE 3, the 2003 Major League Baseball First-Year Player Draft began at one o'clock in the afternoon at the corner of Park Avenue and 46th Street in New York City. A dozen executives from the Major League Baseball office sat in a nondescript conference room on the thirty-first floor, surrounded by papers, charts, computer screens, and a phone line connected by conference call to the draft rooms of thirty big league ball clubs. This was a virtual meeting, nothing like the public, Madison Square Garden, made-for-TV spectacle that now celebrated the NFL draft. The amateur players whose names would be called were not yet national celebrities. They weren't stepping through a window directly onto an NFL training field, an NBA rookie camp. In the NFL draft the previous year, quarterback David Carr had received a $10 million signing bonus and a six-year professional contract worth more than $47 million from the Houston Texans. In baseball, even the best prospects were two or three years of obscurity away from The Show and big money like that.

During the baseball draft, teams announced their choices over the conference call, which was streamed through Major League Baseball's Web site, mlb.com, into computers in living rooms and apartments and baseball coaches' offices around the country. Roy Krasick, the senior director of operations, worked the central phone as general managers and scouts announced the names of their teams' selections. Clubs chose in the inverse order of the previous year's win-loss records, alternating between the American League and National League. Some clubs that had lost valuable free agents were awarded additional picks in a "supplemental" portion of the rounds. When every club had made a selection, the order would repeat. The process would continue over two days through fifty rounds.

Tampa Bay, with the worst record in baseball, picked first and took high school outfielder Delmon Young. Milwaukee followed by taking the NCAA player of the year (and Team USA star), infielder Rickie Weeks of Southern University. In Richmond, Tim Stauffer had trouble getting the Internet feed in his dorm, so he'd hustled over to a friend's apartment, where a dozen teammates gathered around a computer. He knew it would be Detroit or San Diego, him or Sleeth. He knew that Major League Baseball had recommended bonus levels for the first rounds of the draft, and that "slot money" for the Tigers' third-round pick was $3.2 million, and for the Padres' fourth-round pick, $2.8 million. Those were just ballpark figures. Stauffer knew that negotiating determined the final number. He hoped to go to San Diego, for the weather, for the new stadium that was in the works, for the chance to swing a bat in the National League.

In the Mission Valley section of San Diego, in a low-slung office building a mile from the current stadium, the Padres' scouting depart-

ment had arranged their "draft board": two white magnetic panels to-
taling thirty-five feet in length. Six hundred color-coded magnets with
the names and schools of the Padres' prospects were arranged by position, in the club's order of preference. Mike Wikham, the assistant
scouting director, removed and rearranged the magnets as the draft
unfolded and players were lost to other teams—a straightforward process in the early rounds, with two minutes between selections and
many of the prospects contacted ahead of time to settle issues of
money. The later rounds got crazy, with just a minute between choices,
and the room's three land lines and a bunch of cell phones in constant
use as Padre scouts felt out other teams, contacted agents, congratulated draftees. Tim Stauffer's name appeared on a red "college" magnetic strip above that of Kyle Sleeth. The decision had split the Padres
camp, but in the end they'd leaned toward the safer bet and polish of
Stauffer over the chancier but potentially bigger payoff of Sleeth.

At 1:06 P.M. a Tigers representative came onto the line and announced that Detroit was taking Kyle Sleeth from Wake Forest. In
Richmond, Stauffer grinned, breathed in, not entirely sure, but excited about going to San Diego. His heart raced. His entire life—as
long as he could remember—had been pointing toward this moment.

In San Diego, after the cheering quieted down, scout Jason
McLeod said into the speaker phone: "San Diego selects re-draft
number zero-one-two-five, Stauffer, Timothy, right-handed pitcher,
from the University of Richmond, hometown of Saratoga Springs,
New York." With those words it was official, and the apartment in
Richmond exploded with noise. Stauffer beamed and turned and
high-fived his teammates one after another after another. *Baseball
America's* Jim Callis gave instant analysis over the Internet broadcast,
lost in the noise of the cheering in the apartment: "No surprise there.
A guy with no mechanical problems in his delivery. Polished. Starter-
type for definite future at the major league level." Stauffer's cell phone
rang almost immediately—Tripp Keister on the line, the Richmond-
area scout for San Diego who had presented him to the front office—
and the congratulations didn't stop for forty-five minutes. His parents

252 o The Last Best League

called, his sisters, cousins, aunts and uncles, friends. Newspaper and radio stations from Saratoga Springs and Richmond and San Diego. All of them wanting to know how it felt, to share in the good feeling, share in the pride and the triumph, to touch greatness. Stauffer kept smiling, kept thanking everyone, kept listening to the march of selections. Every few rounds another cheer went up in the apartment, another Richmond player chosen—thanks really to Stauffer, who everyone knew had put his teammates on the board, and Stauffer loved seeing them get a shot, too. In the second round, San Diego picked Daniel Moore—D. Moore! From Chatham!—and then Colt Morton in the third, and then R.J. in the thirteenth and Zane Carlson three rounds after that! A Chatham reunion! All those guys with one team. When had *that* ever happened? And Stauffer felt awesome, light, giddy. For one brief, glorious afternoon, Tim Stauffer had died and gone to baseball heaven.

AT HIS OFFICE in suburban Chicago, Barry Meister looked hard at the teams picking between numbers forty-seven and sixty-seven. Several clubs in that range, the bottom half of the second round, had expressed interest in Thomas Pauly or Jamie D'Antona, or both. Some teams had already talked money, getting a feel for what it would take. Meister made one last pitch for Pauly, playing the Princeton card with both the Red Sox president, Larry Lucchino, and the Indians' general manager, Mark Shapiro, both Princeton alums. "You're not going to let these other guys get a *Princeton* player, are you?" he asked them both in last-minute phone calls. But Cleveland passed over Pauly at forty-seven, and Boston passed at forty-nine. Meister looked ahead to fifty-four, where Boston had a second pick coming. Pauly, at home in Florida with his mother and brother, William, listened to the Internet feed without a clue. After Princeton had lost in the Regionals at Auburn, Pauly had gone home to Florida to hang at the beach and get in some lifeguard training. Pauly hadn't believed Meister's prediction of the second round. "C'mon. You're bullshitting me," Pauly had told him. "You don't have to do that with me." But now he believed that his name would eventually get called.

At pick number fifty-one, Cincinnati came out of nowhere, shocking Meister and Pauly both. The team hadn't had a formal conversation with either of them.

AT HOME IN Trumbull, Connecticut, Jamie D'Antona and his parents struggled to get online. His mom was a wreck, pacing between the living room and kitchen, not knowing what to do with the nervousness. They finally connected during the supplemental portion at the end of the first round.

Around the fifty-eighth pick, D'Antona got a call on the house phone from Diamondbacks scout Howard McCullough. Arizona had the sixty-sixth pick, in sixteen minutes, and was wondering if D'Antona would sign for $500,000. D'Antona hung up and relayed the number to Bob Lisanti at Barry Meister's office, where Meister was already talking numbers with Oakland, and was on hold with the Braves. The teams were all attempting to make a "predraft deal," where a player and a club agreed in advance on the signing bonus—the club guaranteeing money and a pick, the player, in essence, promising the club it could meet his demands. Generally, predraft deals worked in favor of the clubs, who dangled the sure thing of less-than-slot out there in front of the player, at no risk to themselves. If the player said no, teams dangled similar offers in front of other prospects. But the 2003 draft would see a correction of the steadily inflating bonus figures of the past decade. Signing bonuses would fall 10 to 15 percent from 2002, and many of the 2003 predraft deals turned out to favor the players.

Lisanti and Meister conferred, called the Diamondbacks, and settled on a number: $560,000, plus $40,000 for school. McCullough called D'Antona back; D'Antona had him on the regular phone and Lisanti on the cell phone. D'Antona said yes. When D'Antona's name came over the Internet a couple of minutes later, at pick number sixty-six, to Arizona, it was already a done deal.

Analyst Jim Callis said, *Okay. Large frame, durable build. Similar to Matt Williams. Generates tremendous bat speed. Aggressive cuts, plus raw power. Strong hands. Must hit a ton to live with third-base defense. First-base more likely.*

Karin D'Antona jumped up and down at the announcement, tried to hug Jamie, hug Joe. "She was running all over the place like it was a big deal," Jamie said later. The next morning, two different scouts from the Atlanta Braves called to congratulate him and wish him well. They'd put him on their board at sixty-seven, praying he'd last that long.

THE STIFFNESS IN Tim Stauffer's shoulder had appeared right after his final start. The shoulder ached only slightly, but Stauffer knew something was wrong. He'd never before felt pain after pitching. The pain was still there when the Padres set their initial offer at $2.6 million.

Stauffer returned home to Saratoga Springs, hoping that a couple of weeks' rest might be all the shoulder needed to return to normal. Rick and Becky Stauffer made plans to fly out to San Diego for the imminent signing. Becky bought a new dress for the celebration. For the first time, Rick and Tim talked about the money. Stauffer wanted to help his dad cut back at the supermarket, to work more in baseball, something Rick had long wanted to do.

But the pain didn't go away. It grew sharp when Stauffer moved his arm in just the wrong way, even putting on a shirt, brushing his teeth.

In July he had his first MRI. His agent, Ron Shapiro, arranged it with the team physician of the Baltimore Orioles. Outside of Stauffer's agent, the doctor, the trainer at Richmond, and Stauffer's family, nobody knew about the problem. The pictures showed a shoulder joint dangerously weakened from wear on the labrum and rotator cuff. The damage had apparently been caused, gradually, by the number of pitches a twenty-one-year-old arm had been commanded to throw over the past several years.

Stauffer had Ron Shapiro call the Padres and tell them that, in good conscience, he couldn't accept their offer.

The calls and congratulations continued pouring in. Stauffer smiled and sounded cheerful, and kept the news quiet. He was scared. The Padres ordered their own examinations. More MRIs followed. Stauffer got his running in at home, worked his legs and his wind. For the first time since he was two years old, he didn't throw a ball all summer. The Padres' doctors recommended a rehab program that would be painful and uncertain, but wouldn't require surgery. With luck, they said, Stauffer might throw hard again at spring training in 2004. But all bets were off.

In August, Virginia-based scout Tripp Keister drove to Saratoga Springs with the contract. There would be no trip to San Diego, no celebration. Stauffer's mother and father sat with him in their kitchen as Tim signed a contract that should have been a crowning achievement but instead almost broke their hearts. Becky's new dress hung upstairs in a closet. She didn't even think to bring a camera out. The bonus promised $750,000, plus school—but for Stauffer it had never been about the money.

The papers in San Diego put a positive spin on the signing. A stand-up kid with old-fashioned values had saved the Padres a bundle. He'd not been obliged to tell them about his shoulder. Most fans in San Diego and around the country reacted to the news, if they saw it, with only a passing thought. They had no idea. The amateur draft was, for most, esoteric, the stuff of agate type. The names of drafted players surfaced briefly, ran together, disappeared until a handful reemerged, years later, in the bright sunshine of a major league ballpark. But within college and professional baseball and down through an elaborate, invisible, interlocking network of baseball pyramids, the news stunned.

It was impossible not to wonder, not to play "What If?" Wonder if there was something unknown inside Stauffer's shoulder that had marked him from the very beginning. Wonder what a kid who did everything right could have done differently. What if he'd been less of a team player, more out for himself, and hadn't agreed to all those innings? What if the intensity hadn't started at such a young age? Was it just bum luck? In the end, was it all just luck?

Stauffer reported to the Padres' instructional league in Arizona in late August. The arc of his playing life had just abruptly changed, but it hadn't ended. Private as ever, he said, "We'll just see how it goes."

THE CINCINNATI REDS played in Tampa Bay the week after the draft. Thomas Pauly drove down from Jacksonville to meet the manager and pitching coach and players, and put on a major league uniform. Everything was happening fast now. And Pauly pulled out the old mask. "I wanted to get Griffey Junior's autograph, just to prove I was there," he told people. He asked, "Cincinnati is in the National League, right?" A fan saw him walking by and yelled for his autograph. "You don't want my autograph," Pauly yelled back. "I'm not a real player. You don't even know who I am."

"Yes, I do," said the fan. "You're Thomas Pauly, the Reds' second-round pick."

Pauly signed the ball for him. That night it went up on eBay for $9.95. His new life was starting.

Pauly and the Reds quickly settled on a bonus of $660,000 spread over two years, plus $40,000 for school. He'd already received permission from Princeton to graduate with two fall semesters. He planned to front-load his chemical engineering courses in the first fall, so he could finish the program with the small group he'd gone through with, all of them drinking from the same firehose together. Pauly insisted that the Reds schedule his press conference when his brother, William, could make it, and the two of them turned the event into a road trip. Under bright lights, in front of cameras, Pauly pretended he was the seventeen-year-old brother and William, the draft pick. He was assigned to Cincinnati's low-A team in Dayton, Ohio, bypassing the club's two rookie-league teams, where most drafted players started their journeys. He immediately felt lonely, said he wondered if he belonged there. You still couldn't tell if the guy was sandbagging.

Of all the people in the Reds organization, Al Goldis, a special assistant to the general manager, was perhaps most impressed by Pauly. "He could be the next Orel Hershiser," said Goldis, referring to the big league pitcher who'd won more than two hundred games. Goldis had talked with Pauly at a game in Princeton. "Do you have a girlfriend?" he'd asked. Pauly said, "Yeah, she's here. She's the prettiest girl in the stands over there. You can pick her out yourself."

"That showed me a lot of attitude," said Goldis later. "I loved his confidence."

JAMIE D'ANTONA REPORTED to the Diamondbacks farm team in Yakima, Washington, in the short-season Northwest League. Right away, the coaches told him that Arizona wanted him to continue playing third base. They started flattening his swing, just as big Joe had told him to. It was wood from here on. D'Antona would be splitting time between two host families, one with a small golden retriever mix and the other with a big German shepherd. He'd have a borrowed Jeep Wrangler for the summer and a little time to get out on the trout streams west of Yakima. Wake Forest was already blurring into Chatham into Alaska and a thousand other moments that were all in the past. He had a lot of work to do in the batting cage, now, and life was undeniably sweet.

AFTERWORD

One Year Later

On a bright Saturday in November of 2004, Jamie D'Antona, Tim Stauffer, and a number of former Wake Forest and Cape Cod League baseball players made their way to St. Christopher's Church in Chatham for the wedding of Carrie Aitken and Dave Bush. The couple had met through the Chatham A's, Bush as a college pitcher and Aitken as one of the team's student trainers. For Bush, the event felt something like a homecoming and a coronation. Less than three years after pitching for the A's, he was returning to Chatham as a major leaguer — the first of Schiffner's '01 team to make it to The Show. He'd won five games that summer as a starter for the Toronto Blue Jays.

Jamie D'Antona had been back to Chatham a couple of times in the two years since he'd played there. He and his dad had made a trip out for some striper fishing late one summer. And he and **Jeremy Cleveland**, his former teammate on the 2002 A's, both coming off triumphant first years as pro ballplayers, had driven out after their seasons had ended and delivered a new computer to Nick's so Mimi could follow her boys on the Internet. But D'Antona wasn't fishing or roadtripping much these days. He'd bought a house twenty miles outside of Tucson, near the spring training complex of the Arizona Diamondbacks, so he could train year-round in warm weather. After leading the Northwest League in home runs in 2003, he'd punished pitchers in the high-A California League, hitting .315 and driving in fifty-seven runs in sixty-eight games before being promoted to Double-A El Paso.

Tendonitis in his right biceps had ended his season early in El Paso, but the injury wasn't career-threatening. D'Antona had adjusted his workout routine to better strengthen the small muscles in his throwing arm for the new demands of the long season. He had been taking a ton of infield practice. He was showing his critics something: he was still playing third base.

D'Antona was climbing the Diamondbacks' ladder in lockstep with two other marquee college players, Conor Jackson and Carlos Quentin. The three of them hit four-five-six in their teams' batting orders. Scouts said no minor-league trio had as much raw power. Making it to Triple-A and then the big team together, D'Antona thought, would be awesome. The crowded infield situation ahead of him in Arizona, though, complicated D'Antona's immediate prospects. But as far as anybody was concerned, and by any measure, he was on track.

Tim Stauffer had arrived at the San Diego Padres' spring camp in 2004 without having thrown hard off a mound in nearly a year, praying that his rest and conditioning program had done what the team expected it to. He'd gone out and pitched beautifully, and without pain. The Padres assigned him to their Single-A club in the California League, the farm team closest to the doctors in San Diego. Stauffer had toyed with the competition. After just six starts, the Padres sent him to Double-A Mobile, in the Southern League, and Stauffer had kept it going, his fastball darting again, his pitches painting the corners. In July he pitched a dazzling inning in the prestigious "Futures Game," a showcase of the best minor-league talent in the country. After eight starts in Mobile, the Padres pushed him to Triple-A Portland in the Pacific Coast League, just a step away from the majors, and Stauffer had responded by winning six games and losing three. He'd finished his summer there. His velocity, a couple of miles off his earlier speed back in his one-day-a-week rotation at the University of Richmond, registered between eighty-eight and ninety-one miles per hour after a full season in a professional four-day-rest rotation, exactly where it had started originally in the spring. He had pitched 168 innings without pain. He hadn't missed a start. An article in the *Wall Street Journal* cited the comeback from his arm injury as evidence against the accuracy of psychological profiles. Two weeks after the wedding in Chatham, Tim Stauffer would fly to San Diego to accept that club's award as its minor league pitcher of the year. The banquet honored the Padres' best major-league players, as well. Stauffer's dream, once again, was not only within sight, but within reach.

Paul and Laurie Galop were at the wedding. Charlie Thoms was, too, of course, with Ginor. Bush's coaches from Wake Forest and Chatham, George Greer and John Schiffner, were there. After his twelfth year as manager in Chatham, **John Schiffner** had become the third-winningest coach in Cape Cod League history. But his A's had finished out of the play-offs again in 2003 and 2004. He had the sinking sense that the Internet had taken away the recruiting advantage he'd held through years of cultivating contacts. George Greer, after his own run of disappointing seasons, had retired from coaching at Wake Forest. The two old friends didn't have to think about such things at the wedding. They looked over the gathering and, in Schiffner's words, "felt like proud papas."

❁   ❁   ❁

For the graduates of the 2002 Chatham A's, the marathon of professional baseball had begun right away, with the daily grind of at-bats and pitches and more pitches that inexorably wear down bodies and expose weaknesses. By the end of the 2004 season, it was hard to remember that most of the guys who had been teammates on Cape Cod were still only twenty-two years old.

Thomas Pauly, after a streaky, inconsistent debut at low-A Dayton in the Midwest League, completed his chemical engineering classes at Princeton. He went out the following year and, after a rough start, came on strong and led the high-A Carolina League in strikeouts. (And returned promptly to Princeton to finish his degree. He was one of the few A's to take advantage of the "school" portion of the signing bonus.) Another organization might have moved him along more quickly, giving him a taste of the competition at double-A. But the Cincinnati Reds were patient. "I'm actually glad they left me in Potomac all year," Pauly said. "Pitching here reminded me of how I pitched in Chatham. Having some success is so important for my confidence. I think they know that about me."

Others were getting caught in the grind. **Zane Carlson**, at twenty-four an elder member of the A's fraternity, had turned down his selection by the San Diego Padres in the 2003 draft, returned instead to Chatham for a third summer (setting a Cape Cod League record for career saves in the process), then pitched at Baylor for a final season as a fifth-year senior. He'd been re-drafted by the Kansas City Royals, and pitched twenty-two innings in the rookie Pioneer League before shutting his season down for another arm surgery, this time a Tommy John procedure on his right elbow.

Pitcher **Scott Hindman**, in the midst of a promising start in the Anaheim system, finished up his Princeton degree with a major in history and dual certificates in American studies and African-American studies. His thesis on umpiring in the old Negro leagues had been selected for the archives at the National Baseball Hall of Fame Library. After starting out in the minors' bottom rungs in Provo, Utah, and Mesa, Arizona, he threw thirty-four innings at low-A Cedar Rapids, Iowa, in the spring of 2004 before undergoing surgery again—this time on his shoulder, for a partial tear of the rotator cuff, fraying of the labrum, and scar tissue. ("The trifecta," he called it.) He was hanging in there, uncertain of his future but determined to play to the end of the string, wherever that might be.

Chatham teammates **Daniel Moore** (sore arm) and outfielder **Ryan Johnson** (injured shoulder and sore back) were rehabbing and doing the same.

The **Universal Soldier** was struggling. Catcher **Colt Morton**, healthy and as impressive as ever behind the plate, had already played at three different levels in the Padres' system, having been promoted twice and demoted once over two seasons. He ended his

2004 season where he'd finished a year earlier, back at Eugene in the Northwest League, where he hit seventeen home runs but struck out seventy-five times in sixty-six games. Scouts were still in awe of his power. It was still an open question, however, whether or not he'd ever learn to hit a major-league curve ball.

The big surprise was Orvella. In his senior year at North Carolina State, **Chad Orvella** occasionally walked in from shortstop to pitch the final inning of a tight game. He pitched just a dozen innings that spring, but he showed great command and a surprisingly good change-up. He'd take infield practice on Saturday and Sunday and play shortstop in back-to-back doubleheaders and come in and throw gas — fastballs at better than a hard ninety, even in a dirty, sweat-soaked uniform. Tampa Bay signed him for $2,500 in the thirteenth round of the 2003 draft, not for his glove and bat but for his arm. In less than two full seasons in the minors, Orvella burned through short-season Single-A ball, low-A, high-A, and Double-A, finally landing in Triple-A at the close of the 2004 season. His numbers were gaudy, almost un-believable: in eighty-five innings over two summers he struck out 131 and walked just eleven. He threw three pitches with pinpoint control and a fastball that had jumped to ninety-seven miles per hour. Schiffner's classic East Coast shortstop had blossomed into one of the premier pitchers in the minor leagues. Baseball is a funny game.

In the 2003 and 2004 major-league drafts, nineteen players from the 2002 Chatham A's were given a shot at careers in professional baseball, an extraordinary number even for a John Schiffner team. It made the losing season feel even stranger.

A twentieth player, **Blake Hanan**, cried at the end of the '04 draft when he learned that he wasn't among them. He cried again a few minutes later when the phone rang and scout Jim Howard told him that the Baltimore Orioles wanted to sign him as a free agent. A crack in the door. At Aberdeen in the short-season New York–Penn League, Hanan hit .256 in sixty-six games, stole seven bases, and played the best shortstop of his life. The Orioles had invited him back to spring training. Against all odds. Hope was alive.

Ten Years Later

A decade after the final names were called in the 2003 amateur draft, the publisher of *The Last Best League* phoned, asking if I'd follow up on those players whose lives, back then, had just begun. A decade is a long time in the publishing world. Most books quickly go out of print. Da Capo Press surprised me by proposing a new edition, including this new final chapter, to bring readers up to date.

In baseball years, a decade is an eternity. At the highest levels of the sport, the average twenty-something progresses from prospect to player to has-been in the time that careers in other professions are still launching. Minor leaguer ballplayers—annually pressured by younger talent coming up behind them—are allowed only a scant few seasons to keep advancing, or else they're cut loose. Injuries, especially to pitching arms, routinely end the careers of players not conditioned or constructed for the unforgiving demands of a seven-month season. Starting at the bottom of a new ladder, professional baseball players perform in obscurity, their ambition tested by interminable bus rides and endless crappy restaurants and cheap motels; by long weeks or months recovering from strained muscles and torn ligaments; by terrible pay, frustration, disillusionment, and the sinking feeling that they might not quite have what it takes to make it, after all. A few love the whole adventure. More come to realize its extraordinariness afterward.

Of every ten who start the climb, only one steps from the final rung into the brilliant light at the pyramid's major league pinnacle.

Half of those who do make it don't last long enough to play a fifth season. In every player's story, a moment arrives when the dream is finally over.

For the wave of athletes sweeping onto Cape Cod full of hope in 2002, the question haunting the soft summer air was, *Who would make it?* And the more complex one: *Why those and not the others?*

Of course I was interested in the view from ten years later.

During the 2013 baseball season and deep into the fall, I traced the arcs of stories I had seen as they began. And more—I had the chance to explore questions that no baseball player at age nineteen or twenty has the perspective to answer, questions I'd rarely seen asked in baseball literature: What does it mean for a young adult to have devoted his life to an almost-impossible goal, and to have made it? Or, more interestingly, to almost but not quite have made it? What were the choices and the costs? What does a dream look like in retrospect?

How does the game itself look different?

I revisited Chatham, a place I had revisited several times during the past decade, and where in 2006 I had finally seen for myself one of the fogged-out games for which Veterans Field was famous.

I caught up with John Schiffner during his thirty-first year in a Chatham uniform. He'd had two heart procedures during the prior eighteen months and had retired from teaching after thirty-three years at Plainfield High School in Connecticut. But on the field he looked the same. He was adapting to a new competitive landscape. It had been almost completely leveled by the explosion of detailed prospect-information, accessible to anyone, not just those who had spent a career building contacts and relationships. He had, as a result, begun looking away from the ball—to find less-heralded stars in the mid-major conferences and strong Division II programs—to fill his roster in Chatham. In 2013 he led the A's to the best record on the Cape and made it to the play-offs for the first time since '01, and was unanimously voted manager of the year by his peers. Among the scores of congratulations he received by text message was a one-liner from his former 2002 pitching coach, Bobby Myers. Myers had finally tired of piecing two and three assistant-level jobs together to make ends meet, and had taken a job with the American Automobile Association. He was out of the game without ever getting a shot at a head job. It wasn't only the players on the Cape who'd had dreams.

Schiffner had steered through some choppy water behind a change of command in the Chatham organization. Long-time fan Bob Sherman had recently taken on the job of general manager. He'd become a somebody. (Sherman's son, Matt, a former A's batboy who grew up with the game while watching these players, had gone on to become one of the youngest scouts in the business, doing area work for the Cubs. More dreams.) Schiffner's team had a new name, as well. In 2009, Major League Baseball's legal department—alerted by a trademark application submitted by the Chatham A's—had threatened lawsuits against Cape League teams who used the names of Major League franchises without purchasing their uniforms and merchandise though MLB licensees. The Chatham A's, loyal to their local suppliers and savvy about keeping control of their own product lines, had kept the "A's" but made it stand for "Anglers." Merchandise revenues, which had fallen off during the turnover, had rebounded. The 2013 totals were 40 percent above what they'd been in 2002. The league's annual budget, meanwhile, had climbed from $350,000 to half a million dollars. All ten teams were live-streaming simulcasts over the Internet and employing squads of media interns. The all-star game, which had moved to Fenway Park for a few years, was now televised. The wooden bats and free admission were still there, preserving at least the illusion of old-fashioned simplicity.

Schiffner's long-time assistant, Matt Fincher, now coached a Division I team—a position he'd long hoped for, but one that demanded too much of his summer for him to continue coaching on the Cape. The A's had retired his number. The two friends no longer spent their summers together, but still spoke by phone two or three times a week. I watched Schiffner pull down the nets of the batting cage in August 2013, a day after Chatham had lost the Eastern Division Championship to Orleans, and knew he felt the pang of another season passing, especially without Finch there to help him put the field to bed.

The old ball field, with yet another turf improvement, a new permanent concession stand, and a tidy brick backstop, looked great. The place still had a shine on it.

I talked to scouts and college coaches. Elliott Avent was still sending his best North Carolina State players to Chatham. Mike Gillespie had moved from USC to UC Irvine, bringing the Chatham pipeline with him. The players coming into the league, everyone told me, included fewer blue-chip starting pitchers, whose college coaches (with increasing influence from the pitchers' "advisors") were shutting those precious arms down over the summer to reduce the number of pitches they threw. Some of the aces were allowed just two or three starts on the Cape before being called back. All of the Cape League coaches had to shuffle their rosters in response.

The intensity and commitment of the players coming into the league had continued to escalate. In addition to the expanding travel schedules and marquee showcase events during the high school years, serious players were now expected to hone their game year-round through private baseball academies, skill-specific instructors, and new technologies, all of which created more opportunities and more pressure. Players entered the chute younger, or risked being left behind. Schiffner said that few players on the Cape worked day jobs any more—they were too serious about baseball to let anything distract them from their goal. Peter Troy, who still helped the A's with fund-raising, felt that something special in the relationship between the community and the team had been lost as a result, and that something fundamental had shifted in the memories and life lessons the new players carried home with them from the Cape. Nick's Deli had closed.

But the Cape Cod Baseball League was still the best wooden-bat summer league in the country. Its stars continued to add their names to the long list of those rising to sparkle in the majors. One of

Schiffner's former players, Matt Harvey, was the National League's starting pitcher in the 2013 all-star game.

The dream was the same. That hadn't changed.

I tracked down the players I'd come to know during a time in their lives when everything still felt possible. Ten years on, the end of their baseball stories can, for the most part, now be told.

Chris Iannetta

Forty-seven of the elite college prospects who played baseball on Cape Cod in the summer of 2002 eventually climbed all the way to the major leagues. Five of them were Chatham A's. If part of the fun of the league was picking out the future big leaguers, another part was being startled by what you never saw coming. Schiffner often remarked that it was hard to see what was inside someone.

Schiffner hadn't invited Chris Iannetta back to Chatham for the summer of 2003. He'd thought Chris was way too hard on himself—the catcher had been one of the players Schiffner had joked about being on suicide watch. At one low point, watching him play tight and let several low pitches skip past him, Schiffner had ragged him in the dugout, saying, "Chris, maybe you could try catching the ball the next time it comes by."

I asked Iannetta about that summer, and he told me, "I was already motivated when I got to the Cape, but after that, I was super-motivated." Schiffner's sarcasm had touched home. Iannetta said, "I heard his voice in my head all that fall when I went back to school. It was fuel on the fire."

No other Cape team had wanted Iannetta back in 2003, either—a tough message for him to absorb. He landed a last-minute spot, instead, in Newport, Rhode Island, in the New England Collegiate Baseball League. His coach there, Terry Rupp, from the University of Maryland, took him aside and worked with him all season. "I ended up having a lot of different coaches at different levels," Iannetta told me. "Not all of them were geared toward improving players for the next level. Terry was. He was a huge help to me."

Iannetta returned to North Carolina and attacked the game with a determination that seemed extreme, even to his teammates. I had the chance to ask Daniel Moore what he remembered. "The kind of focus Chris had didn't leave a lot of room for other people," Daniel said. In Chatham, I had watched Iannetta sitting apart from the other A's in the dugout, muttering to himself, smoldering, beating his bat against his helmet, wrapped up in his own struggle even as his teammates put on rally caps and cheered for each other. Even on a team full of hardworking, focused players, Iannetta's intensity had stood apart. I had wondered, then, about selfishness, confidence, about the "not too high, not too low" mentality that was supposed to keep baseball's inherent failure from consuming someone alive. Insecurity was a powerful but combustible fuel. I hadn't considered what might happen if its slow burn could incessantly drive a player who already had the size and build of a major league catcher and had major league talent inside him.

Iannetta pounded ACC pitching in the spring of '04 and was picked in the fourth round that June by the Colorado Rockies. He drove himself past an early slump at high-A Modesto, and then hit .321 the next season for the Rockies' AA team in Tulsa. He refused to let himself think ahead or look beyond his current level. The Rockies moved him to Triple-A in Colorado Springs, where he hit .351. Iannetta, still whipping himself, finally let himself imagine that he might actually play in the big leagues. "I knew which way Denver was," he told me. "And once in a while I'd look in that direction. That was the only place left for me to go."

In August 2006, buddies from the New England Collegiate Baseball League were chatting with Iannetta on the field after a road game in Salt Lake City when manager Tom Runnells sauntered over. The buddies started razzing Runnells for not having Chris in the lineup that day. The manager cut them off and said, "You won't get a chance to see him play tomorrow, either," and Iannetta felt a spasm of fear.

"He's just been called up," Runnels said. "He needs to get out to Denver."

Iannetta started for the Rockies against San Diego two days later and got a single off Jake Peavy in his third major league at-bat. The following year he helped the Rockies win a National League championship. Seven seasons later, he's still in the big leagues, his story not over yet. In 2012 he signed a three-year contract with the Los Angeles Angels for $15.6 million. He was still pushing. Toward the end of a subpar 2013 season, he had himself fitted for contact lenses. The prescription was minimal (he still had 20/20 vision), but with the contacts in, Iannetta felt his eyes relax, and his body relax. His play picked up. "Maybe they'll make a difference," he said.

I wondered how the spotlight had changed him. He showed up now on the same SportsCenter highlights that the A's had cheered on the big screen at Nick's Deli. A "Chris Iannetta Sucks" Facebook group had popped up on the Web. Interested women, clueless about his having married in 2009, gossiped about his private life on a quasi-stalker discussion forum called "Chris Iannetta's Girlfriend." I had tried seeing him once in Denver, on short notice, between games of a doubleheader at Coors Field, and he hadn't returned my call. Now that he was in the big leagues, I'd assumed he was big leaguing me. I had mistaken focus for self-importance.

This time, I waited until the season was over, then I called him at home in Rhode Island. He was friendly and thoughtful and seemed like he had all the time to talk that I could ask for. "I'm still the same person I was," he told me. "I think that I'm terrible at baseball, and that I don't deserve to be here. I'm still taken aback when someone recognizes me and asks for my autograph. I think, *Really? Me?*"

Chad Orvella

The other major leaguer that no one saw coming was Chad Orvella. He played with Tampa Bay from 2005 through 2007—not as a short-stop, which had been his dream, but as a pitcher. A different kind of fuel also set him apart. He seemed more laid-back than Iannetta, but laid-back college players didn't play hard all summer with a broken finger, as Orvella had on the Cape.

Orvella still had a scrap of fortune-cookie fortune he'd gotten when he was thirteen years old. It said, *The best thing in life is doing what others say you can't.* (He had taped the little strip of paper near the light switch in his old bedroom back at home, so he would see it every day.) After being drafted by the Devil Rays, he was determined to prove that he was better than the thirteenth-round pick they thought he was. The team had told him that his only shot at the majors would be as a pitcher, and offered him a paltry $2,500 to sign. Orvella carried that chip on his throwing shoulder as he blazed up through the Tampa Bay system.

Another motivation drove him, as well, one he didn't talk about at the time. His arm hurt every time he pitched. "I knew my body," he told me over lunch on a rainy day last fall in Bellevue, Washington. "I knew I wasn't going to have a long career. I had only so many bullets in my arm." He ignored the lousy pay and the hard life of the minors and focused on getting to the majors as fast as he could. Every new city was an exciting step closer. In AAA Durham in 2005, a step below the majors, he heard ex–big leaguers at the ends of their careers talking about what they might do after baseball, about their Plan B, and he walked away from them, not wanting to hear it. He refined a changeup to go with his mid-nineties fastball and near-perfect command. He was called up while the Devil Rays were playing a series in Oakland. Manager Lou Piniella greeted him in the hotel lobby: "Congratulations, son. You're in the big leagues, now. Do something about those shoes. And get a new pair of pants."

Orvella, his arm still hurting, had some early success with Tampa Bay but learned just how wide the gap was between perfect and near-perfect command. In the minors, he'd throw that hard fastball three or four inches outside, to a catcher setting up the target just off the plate, and routinely get strikes called by the umpire, or weakly hit balls by the batter. In the major leagues, he threw the same pitch one or two inches off the plate, but batters wouldn't even bite at it, and umpires called it a ball. It was impossible to measure how much more effective he would have been with a sound arm, or if the difference was simply a matter of ability. Between 2005 and 2007, he bounced several times between the minors, where his electric stuff dominated, and the majors, where it did not. The game had a label for players like him. AAAA.

Each time Orvella dropped back to Triple-A, he was pissed, and he pitched with a complex of motivations. He knew he was good enough to pitch in the majors, now, and he attacked hitters with that confidence, mixed with the anger of not throwing against actual major league hitters. But the excitement of new guys in the locker room and the different minor league cities had worn off. He resented the nighttime bus trips, could no longer get comfortable stretching out and sleeping in the aisle between the seats, the younger players refusing to shut up the noise all around him. He'd started to see the game with a broader perspective, saw it as a business for the first time. He was bothered by the special treatment and second chances he saw the club giving highly paid prospects, by roster moves made because of contract status and finances rather than performance. He began regretting all the family birthdays and friends' weddings he'd missed during the summers when making it in baseball was all he could think about. At some point, standing around before a game with some of the older players, he started talking about a Plan B.

It's hard to walk away from the major leagues, though. Orvella finally had shoulder surgery in 2008, and the Rays gave up on him. The Kansas City Royals gave him a look, but released him. The Los Angeles Angels gave him one more shot. At the start of the Angels' minor league training camp in Tempe, Arizona, in March 2010, Orvella made his first appearance in a game, against the Seattle Mariners. He felt strong and fluid throwing his fastball, without pain. He set down the first two batters he faced—and saw the manager trotting out of the dugout toward the mound. "Chad, we've got you at eighty-four, eighty-five. You feeling okay?"

"Yeah," said Orvella. "I feel good."

"Okay, then. Great," the manager said, and patted him on the arm that could no longer throw with major league speed. "Go get 'em."

A week later Orvella found a pink slip of paper in his locker. The final moment in his story arrived. He cleared out his gear and walked across the complex to a lobby where he and other players with pink slips needed to fill out their "retirement paperwork." Some of them vowed they'd be back. "I'm done," he told them. He was out of bullets.

For a few disorienting months, Orvella felt lost. He slept in. He watched television. His girlfriend finally kicked him off the couch and told him to get going on Plan B. He started working for a niche medical-supply company founded by his former roommate from State, selling pediatric nebulizers to hospitals and clinics. By the time I had lunch with him, Orvella had opened more than two hundred accounts across Washington, and was doing fine. He'd put away a nice nest egg. He'd married his girlfriend. He sounded excited about the new life. "The fact is, I was ready to be done," he told me. "I never loved pitching. I loved playing shortstop. Once I started pitching, baseball became work. I'll never forget what a thrill it was striking out Marco Scutaro, the first batter I ever faced, or pitching in Yankee Stadium in front of 60,000 fans. But as far as baseball goes, I had a *ton* of fun playing in college and on the Cape. It would be a different story if I were still playing shortstop. I'd be scrounging for anything I could get. I'd never want to stop." He'd recently hooked onto a local softball team. He was their shortstop.

Colt Morton

Orvella's teammate from North Carolina State, Colt Morton, had been motivated by those who said his six-foot-five-inch frame could never stand up to the abuse that catchers took playing everyday professional baseball. Two big-league organizations stayed with him for seven years, excited by his defense and betting that he'd learn to hit a breaking pitch consistently—a skill that he never did master. They'd finally concluded what John Schiffner could have told them in 2002: Colt Morton could not hit a curveball. The more nuanced understanding involved the key mental component of "strike-zone discipline" and the anticipation and eye-blink recognition-and-adjustment skills that Morton's long swing required when attacking a darting, dipping, curving, deceptively fast or deceptively slow ball coming from a pitcher's expected or unexpected arm angle. Morton told me, "It wasn't that I couldn't hit a breaking ball. It was that I couldn't consistently make hard contact. I swung at the wrong pitches. My pitch selection was bad. It's a really hard thing to be what a major league hitter needs to be, which is patiently aggressive."

Morton did make it to the majors, getting two hits in fifteen at-bats over two brief stints with the Padres. He made his debut at the end of the 2007 season against the Rockies and his former Chatham A's catching counterpart, Chris Iannetta. When Morton stepped up to the plate, Iannatta called time and trotted out for a quick conference on the mound. Morton dug in, knowing that a September call-up would almost surely see at least one fastball. He waited for it—as the players put it, looking "dead red." The game was tight. Cold-hearted Iannetta called the pitches, and Morton saw, instead, two roundhouse curveballs that froze him for strikes. On the third pitch he instantly recognized the spin of a straight ball coming at him—but registered too late that the pitch was a changeup. He couldn't make the slight timing adjustment to the interlocking mechanics of legs and hips and arms, and lofted a lazy fly ball to left field off the end of his bat for an easy out.

He spoke with his former A's teammate after the game and said, "Seriously, Chris? My first major league at-bat and I couldn't even get one fastball?"

Iannetta just shrugged.

Morton worked on his hitting through two shoulder surgeries and five teams at four levels between 2008 and 2012. At the end, playing in Tennessee for the Sugar Land Skeeters in the independent Atlantic League—one of the motley unaffiliated leagues that embodied the last dying breath of major league hopes—Morton talked with a psychologist, who asked him, "When you go home after a game, what do you think about?" Morton ticked off sequences from the game that he replayed over and over in his head: *How did I miss that pitch? Why did I roll over on that fastball? Why did I pop up that curve?* The psychologist pointed out that Morton had been imprinting negative behavior onto his subconscious—probably for years—in a game whose speed insisted that a player react subconsciously. "Why don't you visualize instead," he asked, "the successful swings, the ones that produced great contact?" The question hit Morton like a revelation. He felt a change in his psyche, and at bat. Two weeks later, diving back to first base after a hard single, he dislocated a shoulder that had been held together by five anchors, and the final moment of his dream arrived.

"It ended too early," he told me on the phone. "But that's true no matter who you talk to—whether it ends in high school or after a Hall of Fame career. It's a kid's game, and none of us wants to grow old."

He still wondered what might have been different if he'd talked with that psychologist near the start of his career. But he had no doubt that the years of work and sacrifice had been worth it. When the Padres sent him back to the minors for the last time, Morton remembered not the demotion but that one of the coaches—a former scout who had doubted that Morton's tall frame would ever hold up—stepped in and said, "Colt, you may be going down today, but you are a big league catcher." Morton felt proud and validated. He had savored every sip of his short time in The Show. "If I ever write a book," he told me, "I'm going to call it *The Greatest Cup of Coffee in History.*"

A year and a half after leaving the game, he was slowly adjusting to a new sense of himself. "Transitional quicksand," he called it. Outside his religious faith, he had devoted more than half of his life to a single purpose that no longer existed. He had grudgingly moved on to the next chapter, doing motivational speaking for a time, and then working on a 4,000-acre ranch in south-central Missouri for Beyond Organic, a vertically integrated company that produces and distributes natural foods, nutrition supplements, and skin care products. But he wasn't completely over the game. Attending Chad Orvella's wedding in 2012, Morton had been the only one of sixty wedding guests who chose not to attend the Mariners game that Orvella had sprung for.

He still couldn't watch games on TV. The emotion was still too raw.

Jamie D'Antona

Jamie D'Antona's career stalled in the minor leagues, though he'd never stopped hitting. In 2008, long after his fellow draftmates Conor Jackson and Carlos Quentin were on the big-league stage, D'Antona hit .365 and drove in seventy-nine runs in 110 games at AAA Tucson in the Pacific Coast League. He was selected to play in the all-star "Futures Game" at Yankee Stadium, where he won the Triple-A home-run derby. Arizona finally called him up that July to fill in for Justin Upton, who had been sidelined with an injury. D'Antona was twenty-six years old—already over the average age of the young Diamondback regulars around him.

The deal breaker was defense. Over six seasons in the minors, D'Antona committed 119 errors. The Diamondbacks stayed with him at third base most of that time, hoping that his feet would catch up with his good hands and his great arm. They tried him at first base, and catcher. Then there was nowhere left on the field to try him. D'Antona lacked the range and foot speed to compete at the major league level. Over two call-ups with the Diamondbacks, he batted seventeen times, all but one as a pinch-hitter.

He asked for his release at the end of the 2008 season, and signed a two-year deal worth 73 million yen plus incentives (over $750,000, more than he would have made in two seasons at the major league minimum salary) with Tokyo's Yakult Swallows in the Japanese Central League. Batting cleanup and playing first base, he hit thirty-six home runs in 216 games, and had one sustained streak when the pitches slowed down for him and he won the league's player of the month award.

During those two seasons with the Swallows, D'Antona picked up taxicab Japanese and a taste for the culture. He loved the respectful fans and the festive atmosphere at the ballparks. He loved the food. He loved staying up all night in Tokyo and wandering down to watch the Tsukiji Market tuna auctions at three A.M., then eating unbelievably fresh fish at four-table, hole-in-the-wall restaurants an hour and a half later. He loved taking teammates out tuna fishing during spring training in Okinawa, and bringing home the catch for the kitchen staff at the hotel to fillet and cook up for the entire team. "It was the best time I had in organized baseball, by far," D'Antona recalled.

He'd been hoping to land another contract and stay in Japan, to stay in the game for five more years. But he'd been playing with increasing pain and stiffness in his knees, regularly taking cortisone injections just to keep on the field. He'd had surgery on both knees, had a scare with blood clots in his lower legs, and had lost most of the strength in his atrophied left quadriceps. He was doing his running in a pool. The Swallows let him walk.

The Florida Marlins invited him to minor league spring training in January 2011. D'Antona was twenty-nine years old and his legs were shot. The Marlins released him after just a month. The Texas Rangers called, kicking tires, really, and D'Antona had to tell them he couldn't play. By the end of that calendar year, he'd undergone three more surgeries, had early-onset arthritis and only half of the cushioning cartilage that knee joints should have.

After eight years as a professional baseball player, D'Antona returned to Wake Forest to finish his degree—on his own savings, as the time limit on the "school" part of his signing bonus had expired. He had been frugal with his paychecks; he'd matured since his earlier days as a student, when he'd bounced checks and run up his credit card. He hung around the baseball office and tried to help out where he could. "But it's ridiculous," he said. "I walk like a friggin' old man, carrying a stool with me because I can't stand on my feet for more than an hour. I can't even demonstrate batting."

He had no clue what he'd do after he finished his degree. He tried to imagine a career that kept him in the sport, but found he'd had enough of living out of suitcases, didn't like the stress of college recruiting, and didn't know how much use he could actually be on the field. He still enjoyed watching the game ("Baseball is a brotherhood," he told me.) and marveled at the young players coming into the majors. "The new guys are so much stronger and more athletic," he said. "You see something every day that used to be impossible. I'm not bitter. I think it's awesome."

He still talked fast, still lived in the moment. He could recall his jobs in Chatham, and Mimi and Nick's Deli, but he remembered very little else of his summer on the Cape. For him, Chatham and Wareham and Hyannis blurred into Yakima and Lancaster and El Paso and Knoxville and Tucson and all the other towns in all the leagues he'd played in. He'd bought a townhouse on a 12,000-acre lake in Tega Cay, South Carolina, where he kept a "flats" fishing boat and his light tackle. He occasionally got down to Florida with his dad, Big Joe D'Antona, and fished in salt water. He had joked with a reporter that having his own fishing show on TV was his real ambition. But fishing had always been a release, an outlet from the pressure of trying to succeed at a hard game. It never matched the joy he felt hitting a leather baseball with a wooden bat. Without that sweet spot anchoring the center of his life, D'Antona, in the present moment, felt at sea.

The brotherhood D'Antona spoke of included not only major leaguers, but everyone who knew firsthand what it took to make it to the top. This brotherhood shared a bond that was difficult to replicate outside of the game. Like all of the other former ballplayers I talked to, D'Antona said he missed most the camaraderie of the clubhouse and the friendships he'd formed. After they'd lost their long daily routines, most members of the fraternity needed time to find something else as important. D'Antona, if he thought about such things, could at least take comfort knowing that most ex-players, sooner or later, found their legs again.

The baseball parts of the stories were all variations on a theme. You could look them up on web sites such as www.baseball-reference.com or www.fangraphs.com and see that **Mike MacDonald** pitched 1,165 innings in the minors and made it to Triple-A five times with four different teams, but never made The Show. He was one of the rare exceptions who'd had life breathed into his career from the deathbed of the independent leagues, returning back to affiliated ball to pitch in the Red Sox farm system in Portland and Pawtucket before finally calling it quits.

You could see that **Ben Himes** had spent four seasons in the Reds and Yankees organizations and never gotten beyond the starting rungs of A ball. It would take a little more digging to learn that the Universal Soldier had found his land legs back in Texas, first as a private hitting coach and fitness instructor, then as the founder of an elite training facility called Sharp End Athletics. He still had the broad shoulders and rippling muscles of a cyborg—D'Antona could have used some of his parts.

Left-hander **Fraser Dizard** topped out in 2006 at AA Birmingham in the White Sox system. He returned home to the Pacific Northwest and coached high school ball. On the "About" part of his Facebook page, he mentioned only one association with baseball: the Chatham A's.

Greg Conden retired after three years with a minor league career pitching record of eight wins and thirteen losses. He made it as high as AA Mobile in the Southern League. At the end of the line, in 2005, he appeared in four games in the independent Canadian-American Association for a "traveling" team called the Grays that didn't even have a home ball field.

Blake Hanan played just that one season in Aberdeen, Maryland.

Those online reference sites only hinted at the deeper stories. How could the record show that Hanan had hated the cutthroat attitude he found in A ball, that the game felt different when so many teammates were hoping others would fail? He told me that he'd felt burned out. He said the Orioles were surprised when he asked for his release—he was still in their plans. The worst part, Hanan said, was having to face his family and all the others who had sacrificed and supported his dream for so many years. He felt that he had let them down.

It would take him several more years and a lost marriage to realize that his greatest asset as a baseball player—his narrow, single-minded commitment—came at a higher personal cost when he no longer had family and others investing in his future right along with him. He woke up on a business trip in North Carolina, alone, his online restaurant catering company, Mealeo, launched and on its way, and realized there wasn't a single person in his life with whom he could share the excitement of his growing enterprise. He returned early from that trip back to New England looking for balance.

He started a second company, Givebug, which sold apparel, donated proceeds to charity, and connected him to a world of need beyond his own. He reconnected with friends, worked to repair relationships. He continued lifting—he'd gotten into competitive CrossFit training, in fact—but he no longer lifted alone.

Daniel Moore had recovered from shoulder surgery and was pitching in single-A Fort Wayne when he tore the flexor tendon in his left elbow. He felt a twinge of pain, and then a little more pain with each ensuing pitch, and ten pitches later he felt the bottom half of his arm travel to home plate with the ball. The Padres brass, some of whom had publicly questioned Moore's toughness, gave up on him. He intended to go through all the rehabbing again and try to hook on with another organization. But baseball in the minors hadn't been nearly as fun as it had been in Chatham and Chapel Hill, and meanwhile he'd gotten his degree and gotten married. "I don't remember ever actually deciding I'd stop playing," Moore told me over the phone from his home in North Carolina. "But when I told my wife that fall of 2004 that I didn't think I was going back, I felt this lightness come over me. I know that for some guys, losing that identity of being a baseball player is really hard, but I suddenly felt like I could do anything. It was freeing." He earned a master's degree in accounting and became a finance analyst in a pharmaceutical company.

He held an especially vivid memory from the Cape. During the Fourth of July parade, he had written on only one Styrofoam ball, penning the words I LOVE YOU. In the throng of spectators lining Main Street, he picked out his girlfriend, Sara, who was visiting Chatham for a few days, and he threw her a pitch. "I guess I was pretty accurate," he said. They still had the ball on a bookshelf.

Jeremy Cleveland washed out at age twenty-six after six years in the minors. Not ready to leave the game, he got a job scouting for the San Francisco Giants and had the unsettling experience of understanding from a scout's perspective why he hadn't made the grade as a player: no team was going to pay major league money for a 190-pound corner outfielder who didn't have enough speed to steal bases or enough power to hit home runs. Like so many good prospects—like John Schiffner decades before him—he had been caught in between the skill sets that defined specific positions. After three years of three hundred–plus nights on the road scouting in four states plus the District of Columbia, though, he'd tired of the motels and low pay. He turned to a career that ex-athletes seem especially well suited for: a job in sales and marketing. It's no coincidence that the "psychological profiles" given to prospects were variations on tests originally designed for success in sales. Sports and sales both rewarded the same traits of competiveness, self-confidence, and discipline—not to mention that former professional ballplayers had instant credibility and easy conversation in a job where personal impressions counted. Pro ballplayers carried the aura with them, and it helped.

In the summer of 2002, Cleveland had dated a pretty blonde trainer for the Brewster Whitecaps named Alison Stewart. The two of them had made one return trip to the Cape—for their wedding at the Chatham Wayside Inn. Schiffner was there. D. Moore was there. R.J. was there. Cleveland said it felt like old times.

Zane Carlson returned to Chatham in November 2009 with his parents and in-laws to attend the Cape League's hall of fame induction ceremony at the Chatham Bars Inn. His plaque at the museum in Hyannis beat his "Thunder-and-Lightning" counterpart Dave Bush's to the hall by two years. It was a crowning moment for Carlson. His major league dreams had ended three years earlier, playing out the string in independent league ball for the Fort Worth Cats. "When I was having success on the Cape," he told me, "the majors felt very close. On the fourteen-hour bus ride from Texas to Sioux Falls, South Dakota, surrounded by a bunch of thirty and thirty-five-year-olds, the majors felt like a long way away." At the end he was just looking for a reason to shut it down. "With two weeks left in the season, the team told me that they'd traded me to Corpus Christi, and I said no they didn't. I quit."

He works for his father-in-law in Texas selling line pipe, tubing, and casing to the oil and gas industry. I talked to him in the fall. He had three kids in the house under two-and-a-half years old, with no crowds to cheer on that kind of hard work. We talked about injuries and bodies and talent, and he said something that has stuck with me. "Anyone who makes it to the major leagues," he said, "is a freak."

Ryan Johnson made the trip to Chatham to watch Zane's induction (he stayed with John and Martha Schiffner while he was there). He talked about his own brief career in medical terms. "I had my labrum done back when players didn't know what a labrum was. I damaged the facet joints in my back, lost some feeling in my legs, learned the difference between sports surgeries and surgeries that are normally done on old people. In the minors I learned more about medicine than I did about baseball." He was done playing at twenty-three. "If you'd asked me then, I would have said I was a failure. A few years later, I felt proud of how far I went."

He eased out of playing by landing a job in advertising sales for *Baseball America*, where he had a box-seat view of the changing game. He saw new technologies such as Pitch F/X and TrackMan push into the burgeoning scouting tool kit. The devices captured quantitative analyses such as a batted ball's average launch angle and exit velocity, and a pitcher's spin rate and angle of curve ball. A decade after Michael Lewis's book *Moneyball* highlighted the power of statistical analysis for evaluating prospects, scouts were sifting through blizzards of minutely sliced data on hundreds of top prospects. Organizations struggled figuring out how to use all that information—or which parts of it were even useful. Johnson saw video cameras behind home plate at Cape League games becoming as ubiquitous as radar guns and stopwatches had been in his day. He witnessed the expansion of the sport's largest for-profit showcase organizer, Perfect Game, which attracted more than 40,000 amateur players in 2013, alone.

In the databases, Johnson saw a difference in the emerging prospects. "Back when I was at Wake, Coach Greer said, 'You'll be playing in Chatham next summer,' and I said, 'Great. Where's Chatham?' I never swung a wooden bat before I got to the Cape. Today, kids go to wood-bat showcases in high school. They not only know about the Cape, they know what bonus slot amounts they'll be looking at in the draft after they're done on the Cape. They're a lot more aware." Some teenaged baseball players were skipping their high school seasons altogether, preparing, instead, for their AAU travel teams and summer showcase circuit. The parents of prospective pros took on the same stressful worry as those who wanted their kids to get into an Ivy League university—with plenty of opportunistic businesses emerging to profit from the worry. The investment and career-mapping were starting earlier and earlier, and had moved beyond young men, to boys.

As D'Antona had mentioned, a lot of the young players who'd come up through the intensifying baseball mill were indeed awesome. (The Nationals' Bryce Harper was a poster child. He'd gotten a GED after his sophomore year in high school and then played a single sixty-six-game season at a junior college in a wooden-bat conference—all so he could accelerate his career through a couple of loopholes and enter the major league draft as a seventeen-year-old. He signed a five-year, $9.9 million contract right out of the chute, and became a major league all-star two years later.) Still, enough late bloomers and low-draft-pick surprises (and impoverished Dominicans and Cubans) were keeping the question open about whether or not the intensifying baseball mill was the make-or-break difference. A major league player still had to possess an unusually high percentage of fast-twitch muscles and strong vision and natural foot speed and preternatural processing speed, no matter where he came from. The mill helped with preparing and sorting. But it also raised questions: How many young kids who had major league ability in them had opted out of the escalating arms race? How many reluctant or uncertain kids were forced into the chute by parents or coaches? How many would-be major league stars burned out because the game stopped being a game so early? Research was emerging that suggested intense year-round focus on individual sports as children—with the exceptions of gymnastics and diving—didn't correlate with future success.

In the end, the questions weren't strictly about baseball. The pursuit of excellence—in any sport, in ballet, in music, in acting—included the high costs of trying your hardest. How much were you willing to pay or forgo? What opportunities were you willing to miss in the pursuit? It was the costs that were rising.

On my way up as a high school player in New Hampshire in the late 1970s, I was considered unusually dedicated because I went off to a two-week baseball camp in the summer and because I stopped playing basketball after my freshman year to focus on lifting weights and getting ready for the baseball season a few months early. I wanted to play professional baseball more than anything—but not so much that I didn't find the time to become an all-state soccer player and get good enough grades to get into Dartmouth. Still, by the standards of the time, I was giving it my all.

At Dartmouth, as it became clear that I simply didn't have professional ability in me, I became achingly aware of what I was missing. The final moment in my story arrived after our final home game in my junior year, in the locker room in the basement of Davis Field House. I told my coach I wouldn't be coming back for my senior season. I wanted to experience too much else at college, and I had only one year left.

All of that came back as I chatted with **Steve LeFaivre**. LeFaivre had felt closest to the major leagues when he was lightning in a bottle at his small high school outside of Atlanta and college recruiters were all over him. After his 2002 season in Chatham, he was ignored in the draft. He struggled through a miserable, unhappy season back on the Cape in 2003 as a temp and then a replacement player in Bourne and Falmouth. "At that level," he recalled, from his accounting office in Ottawa, "baseball needed to be an obsession. And I think I just never really fit into that culture. It's funny. Looking back, baseball seems like such a small thing."

He returned to play his senior year at Wake Forest, where he led the team in home runs and runs batted in. Before the season even started, though, he had already made plans to finish his final two classes across the Atlantic, in Paris, during the summer, with his girlfriend and future wife, Catherine Fortin—whether he was drafted or not. The cost of the chase had risen too high, and he had a life to live.

Pitcher **Aaron Trolia** had also weighed the costs of the game against his life. Following his summer in Chatham, Trolia had transferred from Clemson to Washington State. The Seattle Mariners took him in the 2004 draft. In the summer of 2007, after impressively striking out nearly a batter an inning for the AA West Tennessee Diamond Jaxx, Trolia got the call to join the Mariners' Triple-A club in Tacoma.

Two hours later, he cut his pitching hand in a freak accident at home, pushing trash down in a can. He severed a ligament and a nerve. He permanently lost feeling in the top half of his thumb, and lost his feel for the ball. He never pitched at Triple-A.

Following the accident, he staggered through a couple of losing seasons for backwater independent-league teams in Illinois and Canada. The final moment of his playing career arrived in June 2010 in British Columbia, lying on the field of the Victoria Seals, clutching his hamstring.

For years, he told me, he had been living a self-absorbed existence, "selfishly and arrogantly" resisting failure at the only thing that had mattered to him. He had married and had two children, but he was a terrible husband and father and an absent friend. As the failure had drawn nearer, his fear had mounted, and he'd started drinking heavily. He felt the hamstring go, and he knew it was over.

Trolia returned home to Washington, to Tacoma, where he was reminded every day of how close he'd been but would never be. He had started a little side business of providing pitching instruction, to augment the low pay he'd gotten in independent ball. But he admitted it was half-assed. "I'd be out there in the rain giving pitching lessons on some tennis court," he told me. "I didn't even have a place to work. I wasn't even making enough money to support a family." His life, spinning around such a tenuous center, spiraled out of control. The dream, if it ever had been real, had vanished. Its void left something ugly.

He couldn't let it go, and he had nothing to hold on to. On March 12, 2012, at three in the morning, he found himself standing on the rail of the Tacoma Narrows Bridge, ready to jump.

He had known a lot of guys in pro ball who had lost themselves, who'd battled addiction, who'd alienated the people who loved them. *And for what?* Trolia had become one of them, and he couldn't answer the question.

He described what happened next as "the Lord stepping in" and giving him something that forced him to stop. Stop what he was

288 o THE LAST BEST LEAGUE

about to do. Stop the empty, fearful life he'd been living. Gave him
something to hold on to.

With a newfound faith, Trolia threw himself at the opposite of the
false god he'd worshipped—not the game, but the consuming pursuit of the major leagues. He looked at his baseball coaching business, and tried to find a new way to teach an extraordinarily difficult
game to kids who wanted to reach a high level—not only a way to
give them the skills to succeed, but a framework that changed the
definition of success. He created a nonprofit to give private instruction within a team setting. His new business cut against the culture
in two ways: it reduced the cost to families who felt the profit-driven
sting of the sport's escalation; and it shifted players' emphasis away
from the fear of failing to the joy of working hard for teammates who
worked hard for you in return. For instructors, he reached out to former professional players whose spirits had been broken by the game,
and gave them a chance to stay in it, on new terms.

His AT Baseball center was part skills academy, part leadership
school, emphasizing confidence, sportsmanship, and integrity over
winning, and especially over the goal of advancing to a distant pinnacle that only a tiny percentage of players would ever reach. He took
his message and his workshops on the road to church groups, school
classrooms, and military bases. He added specialized training programs in softball, in strength and agility, and was expanding across
the country. He was gearing up to add a new program in football. His
message resonated. He'd found an answer to the question, *And for
what?*

And found that he'd touched a nerve.

Thomas Pauly refused to quit. Named minor league pitcher of
the year in the Reds organization, he tore the labrum in his pitching
shoulder—not while throwing with that gifted, resilient arm, but
while lifting weights in the off-season. He spent most of the next
three years following the Reds' advice and working with the Reds'
medical team and trainers. His parents thought their son was loyal to
a fault. Pauly's mother, Marta, told me, "Thomas refused a second

opinion and went ahead and had his shoulder operated on by a team surgeon, who butchered it."

As he rehabbed, Pauly grew close to his trainers, and mentored the younger players around him. To kill the down time, he dabbled in online poker. He went back to a reunion at Princeton and discovered that a bunch of his classmates were doing more than dabbling: they were gambling and making real money. Pauly soaked up as much as he could from them, then read everything about poker that he could find. This was back in 2005 and 2006, before the Party-Poker online site moved overseas ahead of tighter regulations, back when a lot of math-challenged online players with mouse-click access to money made easy marks for a guy like Pauly. Before he knew it, his online hobby grew into a second job, eight to ten hours a day—more hours than he could spend working on his legs and his strength and his pitching shoulder—medium stakes, large stakes, three to six tables at a time. Some days his swings would be in the six figures. He won big.

He worked hard in the weight room and did all that was asked of him, but he wasn't improving on the mound. He worked still harder, through growing frustration, and pitched worse than he had as a still-green freshman at Princeton. He couldn't get right. But there was no way he was going to let his trainers and his teammates down by walking away from the Reds after all they'd done to support him. Back on the mound in 2007, he got lit up. He started tugging at his uniform again, pulling the brim of his cap lower and lower to hide his face, in embarrassment. Finally, on a sunny afternoon as he drove away from the baseball complex in Sarasota, Florida, the Reds called him on his cell phone, and told him he was done. He felt relieved. He was happy knowing he'd given it everything he had.

He continued playing poker through that spring and summer in the underground gray-area beneath Florida law. He played high-stakes games in country clubs, houses, condos, dimly lit office buildings, four nights a week, seven or eight P.M. until dawn. The crowd was an interesting mix: high-rolling businessmen, high-quality lawyers, hustlers and drug dealers and scumbags, all of them known only by nicknames. They called Pauly "Baseball." He made a ton of money. But after six months, he folded, not liking the edge of the path he was skirting.

He put his math skills to use as an energy-sector analyst for Raymond James in Houston and then brought that experience and his unusual risk-reward gene back to Jacksonville, to long/short hedge funds managed by Water Street Capital, which controlled more than $3 billion, much of it from educational endowments and charities. On his LinkedIn profile Pauly included previous experience as "Pitcher/Rehab Specialist" with the Cincinnati Reds. Still goofing. He had played competitive dodge ball in Houston, competed in a couple of Half Ironman events, and had recently taken up boxing. A writer couldn't make this stuff up.

He didn't dwell on the past, and he had great memories of playing on the Cape. He'd had the time of his life there. He wasn't convinced, though, that his surprising summer in Chatham had made his shot at pro ball possible. "There were a lot of inflection points in my path to the pros," he said. "The Cape was a fun one, and it happened to be documented. But it wasn't the only one."

His teammate from Princeton, **Scott Hindman**, had skirted a different path and ended up in a different place. Hindman looked in the mirror in March 2005 and saw a twenty-three-year-old pitcher with a damaged shoulder and a pathetic 7.00 ERA in A ball. He called his Princeton coach, Scott Bradley. Then he called the Angels, and said he was moving on. "It felt like a quick decision," he said, "but it was probably eight months in the making. I guess I could have tried more—but I wasn't on the fast track to the majors and I knew I had other opportunities."

He cruised into investment banking and worked for J.P. Morgan during the three best years in Wall Street history. Schiffner would have thought, *Of course he did.* The money was insane. *Of course it was.* Hindman couldn't sleep on his left side because of the shoulder, and the pain kept him from playing even a round of golf at the club, but those were trivial annoyances. Professional baseball now gave a cool little facet to his résumé, and by all appearances he was a prototype blue chipper with a good face who had grown up in a privileged family and gone to an Ivy League school, the path in front of him rolled out smooth.

At some point he looked in the mirror again. On the Cape and in pro ball, he willingly acknowledged, he'd been the kind of player who was out for himself. He had grabbed what he could reach, and he'd taken as much as he could from the system. It wasn't clear if he saw that same self-serving person in the mirror, but he saw someone who looked exactly like everyone else around him. He was happy and comfortable doing investment banking, but he found himself asking, *You only get one life, right? Is it finance for me?*

He stepped to the edge of the smooth path, and found an eleven-year-old boy he could spend time with in the Big Brothers program. For the first time in three years he threw a baseball—and loved playing catch with his new little brother. He wondered what else he might do to make a difference.

By 2013 Hindman had gone to Stanford for a combined MBA and master's degree in education, and received a Broad Residency fellowship aimed at transforming urban education. He moved to inner-city Memphis and took on a daunting challenge. Tennessee had been awarded a $500 million federal "Race to the Top" grant to create a brand-new school district that would raise the state's bottom 5 percent of schools to the top 25 percent within five years. Fifteen of the sixteen schools in the new Achievement School District were in Memphis. The Broad fellowship helped identify the talent that would make it happen—the emerging leaders with private-sector experience who could manage radically new educational organizations. Scott Hindman was hired as the finance director and charged with building the infrastructure.

He was working harder and making a fraction of the money he'd made on Wall Street. "I wanted a different path than the one I was on," he told me. "I wanted to do something that had a chance to move the dial. I thought a lot about the inequity we have in this country in education and opportunity. It's really the issue of our time."

His discovery wasn't a life after baseball. It was that life was so much bigger than baseball. He said he didn't talk much about his playing career—he had little time to bore people with stories about a game.

Simon Williams, the Maine outfielder, showed up at the Cardinals' rookie league team in Johnson City, Tennessee, and was immediately instructed to get rid of his batting crouch. Midway through his second summer, he was promoted from low-A Davenport ("The Swing of the Quad Cities") to high-A Palm Beach, where he tweaked a leg muscle during a doubleheader. It wasn't a bad injury, but he felt pressured to come back from it before the leg was ready, and the soreness hampered him through the rest of the season and into the fall instructional league. Speed had been his one bona fide major league tool. The short leash given to eleventh-round draft picks got shorter. He was pushed out by the new tide coming in with the 2006 draft.

Unlike other players who bitterly clung to one last shot at the dream in the independent leagues, Williams found a spot back in New England with the independent-league Brockton Rox, and had a ball simply playing the game. He had fun moving to left field from center, and he enjoyed the team, which actually felt like a team, without players jockeying for position or constantly being moved up or down by the big-league club. The next year he went with a friend out to the Frontier League, a different independent league, and played in Kalamazoo. The dream was technically still alive—as long as he was playing, he told himself, anything was possible, even if he were playing only for fun in Kalamazoo. But after hitting twenty homers and stealing fifteen bases and getting zero interest from any major league teams, he knew it wasn't going to happen. He decided to play one last season in 2008, to see, unofficially, how it would feel to help with the coaching and working with the younger players. Maybe a new career.

In Kalamazoo, the players lined up on the field after every game to sign autographs for kids. Williams noticed that the kids were happy meeting the players whether the team had won or lost, and no matter how the player had performed. It made him realize how much they meant to the kids simply by being who they were. He enjoyed joking around with the youngsters, talking with them. His girlfriend told him he was an absolute natural with children, and something in him clicked. For the first time in his life, he could actually see himself doing something outside of baseball.

He joined the Peace Corps and spent two and a half years in a small village in central Ukraine. He taught English and health and baseball to elementary school kids, pulled a string back in the United States to get some athletic equipment donated, and helped raise $5,000 to build a soccer field for the school. He ate soup and drank vodka and became friends with nearly every one of the five hundred people who lived in the village.

After Ukraine he went to Thailand and completed a yoga training program. He returned to Portland, Maine, in August 2013, just in time to start his new dream job—kindergarten teacher. I talked with him in November. "Teaching is a blast," he told me. He'd also recently begun helping out down the coast with the Bowdoin College baseball program as an unpaid assistant. He sounded exhausted and happy. He told me he had loved playing baseball, and that the last four years—the ones without baseball at the center—had been the best years of his life.

Tim Stauffer

There is one other story to tell.

In every draft year, some 1,500 players are given the chance to see which half-dozen will emerge as undeniable major league stars, and which twenty or thirty will survive as legitimate professional ballplay-ers. Those are the numbers. Once considered a can't-miss prospect, Tim Stauffer's early arm trouble reset the odds against him becom-ing a member of either group.

He was back in New England in 2013, on a Fourth of July that was as hot in Boston as it had been in Chatham in 2002. At 10:30 A.M. in the visitors' clubhouse at Fenway Park, players for the San Diego Padres drifted in and kicked back in the cool of the A/C and checked their cell phones and iPads or listened to Peter Gammons on Sports-Center on the big-screen TV. Off to the side, next to the trainer's room, Mark Kotsay loosened his legs on a stationary bike. Kotsay, in the twi-light of a long career with several teams, had played on the Cape, in Bourne, way back in 1994. He remembered filling grocery bags for Peter Gammons at his day job at the local A&P supermarket. He was a dinosaur in a room full of chiseled, tattooed twenty-somethings.

Across from Kotsay, along the wall of blonde wooden lockers, the Padres' traveling gray uniforms hung neatly on hangers. Stauffer's "46" was still hanging in there. At thirty-one, Stauffer had perse-vered. No one had been with the Padres longer.

He'd posted a 1.85 ERA over thirty-two games in 2010 and had been the ace of the staff down the stretch as the Padres narrowly missed catching the Giants for the division title. He was the team's Opening Day starter in 2011. He had come all the way back through shoulder trouble and surgery and minor-league rehab stints and was on the cusp of reaching the star power that had been projected when he'd been the fourth player chosen in the 2003 draft. (Kyle Sleeth, the Wake Forest pitcher taken just ahead of him, never threw a pitch in the major leagues.) But the Padres were horrible in 2011; Stauffer had nearly the lowest run support of any National League starter. His numbers at the end of the year were only so-so. In 2012, elbow tenderness shut him down for all but one game.

He methodically worked his way back from the injury, and in 2013 had established himself as a workhorse in the Padres bullpen. The team valued his dependability. He could spot-start or pitch on consecutive days, or in long relief. As his arm strength returned to what it had been before the elbow flared up, he could come into tight games late and set up the closer, or be called to close himself. Whatever they wanted.

He walked into the clubhouse at Fenway Park a few minutes before eleven A.M., carrying a baby's car seat in one hand and the stature of a veteran leader. He quietly greeted Kotsay and the other players, then dressed and went about his pregame business. In the sweltering sun in front of Fenway's Green Monster, Stauffer completed his light sprints and grapevine drill, the backward running, the trunk rotations and leg stretches, the soft throwing that gradually stretched out to a hundred feet. He looked professional, efficient, no-nonsense. On every throw, he carefully replicated his old-school hands-over-the-head pitching motion, and followed through completely.

He had changed as a pitcher. He no longer attacked every batter he faced, no longer tried to be perfect with every pitch. He had learned to throw his slider to both sides of the plate, and had developed a cutter that he could mix in with his two best pitches, his fastball and hard curve. He had watched the Padres' Trevor Hoffman continually experiment with grips and arm angles, and it made an impression: a perennial all-star refusing to be complacent. Stauffer learned what his body could handle, how to pace himself for the long season, to trust that he could "throw to contact" and get outs on fewer pitches than strikeouts would require. He wanted to be a starting pitcher again, but his versatility was a higher value to the club. He had become one of the twenty or thirty lucky ones from the 2003 draft: a legitimate professional player.

Back when he was still a prospect, the damning "Yes, Sir. No, Sir" part of his Caliper psychological profile could have been interpreted as an impediment to making the majors. But that same trait did wonders for job security once Stauffer was there. The Padres valued character. They had never forgotten that Stauffer voluntarily returned all that bonus money after he'd discovered the damaged shoulder.

In the stands behind home plate at Fenway, Becky and Rick Stauffer sweated in ninety-five degree heat and watched the Red Sox pull ahead early. Tim sat with the other Padres' relievers, baking in full sunshine in Boston's cement bullpen beyond the right-field fence. The Red Sox had been Tim's favorite team growing up; in the backyard throwing to his father, he'd imagined himself hundreds of times pitching right there, at Fenway Park.

His sister Erin and her daughter, visiting from London, sat with Rick and Becky. His wife, Roseanne, and thirteen-month-old son, Noah, sat with them. They'd all stayed at the Ritz.

The camera, widening, would pan sideways to show Stauffer's stucco ranch in Cardiff-by-the-Sea, which looked out over the deep Pacific Ocean, mirroring the ocean-view houses his Chatham team-mates had once teased him about; would zoom in on the ball on which he'd written his phone number and handed to a young woman after a game in San Diego in 2005, not knowing she was the niece of the Padres' owner, or that she'd one day become his wife. (Like Daniel and Sara Moore's, the ball sat on display in their home, on the mantel above the fireplace.) And flashing back: to the memory of the Cape League's 2002 showcase in that beautiful ancient ball yard, when Stauffer had been emaciated and sick with strep throat and all the A's had slipped inside the Green Monster and signed their names on the wall; and to when he'd first walked across that immaculate green grass with the other all-stars of the Cape Cod Baseball League and saw his name flash across the center-field scoreboard, so close he wanted to touch it.

And there he was, on another red, white, and blue-sky day on a hot Fourth of July in New England. Baseball. America. The family all together, watching. In the top of the fifth inning, the Padres pushed across a run to make it four–two, Boston. Striking distance. Stauffer would be ready if they called him. He stood and stretched his throwing arm. Shadows lengthened across a perfect diamond. It was all there. It wasn't a dream, but it was.

APPENDIX A

CHATHAM A'S SELECTED IN THE 2003
MAJOR LEAGUE BASEBALL FIRST-YEAR PLAYER DRAFT

ROUND	NAME	SCHOOL	CLUB	BONUS
1	Tim Stauffer	Richmond	San Diego Padres	$750,000
2	Daniel Moore	North Carolina	San Diego Padres	$800,000
2	Thomas Pauly	Princeton	Cincinnati Reds	$660,000
2	Jamie D'Antona	Wake Forest	Arizona Diamondbacks	$560,000
3	Colt Morton	North Carolina State	San Diego Padres	$500,000
3	Matt Chico°	Palomar Junior College	Arizona Diamondbacks	$365,000
6	Ryan Braun°°	Nevada–Las Vegas	Kansas City Royals	$1,000
8	Jeremy Cleveland	North Carolina	Texas Rangers	$85,000
9	Ben Himes	Oklahoma City	Cincinnati Reds	$40,000
10	Fraser Dizard	Southern California	Chicago White Sox	$153,000
13	Chad Orvella°°°	North Carolina State	Tampa Bay Devil Rays	$2,500
13	Ryan Johnson	Wake Forest	San Diego Padres	$1,000
16	Zane Carlson	Baylor	San Diego Padres	did not sign
18	Greg Conden	George Washington	San Diego Padres	$1,000
20	Brad Ziegler°°	Southwest Missouri State	Philadelphia Phillies	$1,000
40	Pete Soteropoulos°°°°	Connecticut	St. Louis Cardinals	$1,000

° On original 2002 Chatham A's roster. Academically ineligible.
°° Member, 2001 Chatham A's.
°°° Selected as right-handed pitcher.
°°°° Member, 2001 Chatham A's. On original 2002 roster. Injured.
Note: Signing bonus amounts don't include school reimbursements.

CHATHAM A'S SELECTED IN THE 2004
MAJOR LEAGUE BASEBALL AMATEUR PLAYER DRAFT

ROUND	NAME	SCHOOL	CLUB	BONUS
1	Chris Lambert	Boston College	Cardinals	$1,525,000
3	Jeff Frazier	Rutgers	Tigers	$500,000
4	Chris Iannetta°	North Carolina	Rockies	$305,000
4	Ross Ohlendorff	Princeton	Diamondbacks	$280,000
5	Ryan Klosterman	Tennessee	Blue Jays	$180,000
5	Anthony Raglani	George Washington	Dodgers	$180,000
6	Tim Layden°	Duke	Cubs	$155,000
8	Neil Jamison	Long Beach State	Mets	did not sign
8	Marshall Hubbard	North Carolina	Mariners	$85,000
8	Kyle Bono	Central Florida	Red Sox	$432,000
11	Simon Williams°	Maine	Cardinals	$1,000
16	Mike MacDonald°	Maine	Blue Jays	$1,500
18	Michael Moon°	Southern California	Padres	did not sign
20	Tim Lahey	Princeton	Twins	$1,000
27	Zane Carlson°	Baylor	Royals	$1,000
27	Aaron Trolia°	Washington State	Mariners	$1,000
37	Tim Rice	Richmond	Pirates	did not sign
37	Glenn Swanson	California-Irvine	Red Sox	did not sign
44	Zane Green	Clemson	Cubs	$1,000

° Member 2002 Chatham A's
Note: Signing bonus amounts don't include school reimbursements.

INDIVIDUAL STATISTICS THRU GAMES OF : AUG 6

Chatham Athletics

W/L RECORD : 19/ 23

NO	BATTERS	B	T	HT	WGT	BRTHDATE	CL	HOMETOWN	COLLEGE	AVG	G	AB	R	H	2B	3B	HR	RBI	BB	SO	SB	CS	E
30	Cleveland, Jeremy,1B	R	R	6/2	190	9/10/81	04	Alexandria, VA	UNC/Chapel Hill	.250	43	164	14	41	9	0	2	12	16	52	0	1	3
33	D'Antona, Jamie,3B	R	R	6/3	205	5/12/82	04	Trumbull, CT	Wake Forest	.235	43	153	19	36	8	0	5	19	18	48	0	1	11
1	Hanan, Blake,2B	R	R	5/9	165	6/20/82	04	Clifton Park, N	Siena College	.176	25	68	5	12	1	0	0	3	5	23	1	1	2
20	Himes, Ben, OF	L	R	6/5	220	3/09/81	03	Austin, TX	Texas A & M	.192	8	26	0	5	0	0	0	3	1	12	0	1	
19	Hubbard, Ryan,OF	S	R	5/10	170	9/06/80	03	Huntgtn Bch, CA	Wake Forest	.000	1	3	1	0	0	0	0	0	1	2	1	0	
24	Iannetta,Chris,C	R	R	5/11	192	4/08/83	05	Providence, RI	UNC/Chapel Hill	.222	34	108	7	24	3	0	2	9	14	34	0	1	1
44	Johnson, Ryan,OF	L	L	6/2	215	1/11/81	03	Laguna Hills, C	Wake Forest	.200	35	120	15	24	6	1	3	10	16	21	4	1	1
11 2	Layden, Tim,OF	L	L	6/3	190	1/22/82	05	Deer Park, NY	Duke	.159	26	82	4	13	3	0	1	7	6	26	1	1	1
11 T	Layden, Tim,OF	L	L	6/3	190	1/22/82	05	Deer Park, NY	Duke	.170	30	88	4	15	3	0	1	7	6	26	1	1	2
7	LeFaivre, Steve, OF	L	R	6/2	200	12/09/81	04	Winston/Salem,	Wake Forest	.229	41	140	16	32	5	0	5	14	12	37	2	0	5
36	Moon, Michael,2B	L	R	5/10	175	8/27/81	04	Alta Loma, CA	Southern Cal.	.263	42	152	21	40	11	0	2	14	11	28	4	1	5
41	Morton, Colt,C	R	R	6/5	220	4/10/82	04	Loxahatchee, FL	NC State	.187	38	123	12	23	5	0	6	18	14	59	0	1	2
5	Orvella, Chad,SS	R	R	5/10	183	10/01/80	03	Redmond, WA	NC State	.173	42	156	12	27	4	0	0	4	17	51	4	5	11
14	Udvarhelyi, Travis,OF	L	L	6/1	185	11/18/81	02	San Diego, CA	Grossmont Coll	.140	23	50	3	7	1	0	0	1	3	25	2	1	0
27	Williams, Simon,OF	R	L	6/2	200	6/30/82	04	Portland, ME	Maine	.184	28	87	8	16	3	0	1	9	8	38	4	1	4
	TOTAL/ALL BATTERS									.209		1432	137	300	59	3	27	122	142	455	18	20	41

NO	PITCHERS	B	T	HT	WGT	BRTHDATE	CL	HOMETOWN	COLLEGE	W/L	ERA	G	GS	SV	IP	H	R	ER	BB	SO
17	Carlson, Zane	R	R	5/10	175	8/11/80	03	Desoto, TX	Baylor	2/2	3.13	23	0	12	23.0	16	13	8	11	36
46	Conden, Greg	R	R	6/3	225	7/24/80	03	California, MD	George Wash.	1/2	4.91	9	3	0	22.0	27	13	12	12	21
31	Dizard, Frasier	L	L	6/0	185	8/06/81	04	Edmonds, WA	Southern Cal.	2/1	1.59	6	6	0	28.1	24	5	5	14	37
16	Everson, Eric	R	R	5/11	170	6/20/82	04	Spokane, WA	Gonzaga	0/0	4.10	15	0	0	26.1	19	13	12	18	29
30	Gramolini, Dennis	R	R	6/2	205	5/07/81	04	Wakefield, MA	Geo. Washington	0/0	4.50	2	0	0	4.0	3	2	2	0	6
42	Hindman, Scott	R	R	6/3	210	3/06/81	03	Inverness, IL	Princeton	2/1	3.21	5	0	0	14.0	9	6	5	9	12
11 T	Layden, Tim	L	L	6/3	190	1/22/82	05	Deer Park, NY	Duke	0/0	0.00	1	0	0	1.0	0	0	0	0	2
9	MacDonald, Mike	R	R	6/1	180	10/29/81	04	Camden, ME	Maine	1/2	5.14	4	4	0	21.0	23	14	12	7	20
25	Moore, Daniel	R	L	6/6	200	6/24/82	04	Spencer, NC	UNC/Chapel Hill	2/5	3.50	10	10	0	54.0	45	25	21	21	51
22	Pauly, Thomas	R	R	6/1	198	7/28/81	04	Atlantic Beach,	Princeton	4/0	3.26	14	1	0	47.0	36	21	17	11	47
6	Shea, Chris	R	R	5/10	175	12/26/80	03	Bangor, ME	Bryant	0/0	7.36	2	0	0	3.2	4	3	3	5	7
26	Stauffer, Tim	R	R	6/2	190	6/02/82	04	Saratoga Spring	U. Richmond	3/2	2.59	9	9	0	62.2	50	20	18	17	67
8	Trolia, Aaron	R	R	6/3	210	10/01/81	02	Tacoma, WA	Edmonds CC	1/5	3.95	9	9	0	41.0	39	19	18	31	34
21	Yates, Adam	R	R	6/3	200	2/16/82	04	Jackson, TN	Mississippi	1/3	2.85	21	0	2	41.0	35	17	13	12	39
	TOTAL/ALL PITCHERS									19/23	3.39	137	59	44	388.0	330	171	146	168	406

NOTE: 2 INDICATES STATISTICS WITH SECOND TEAM ONLY; T INDICATES TOTAL LEAGUE STATISTICS

APPENDIX C

SCOUTING REPORTS

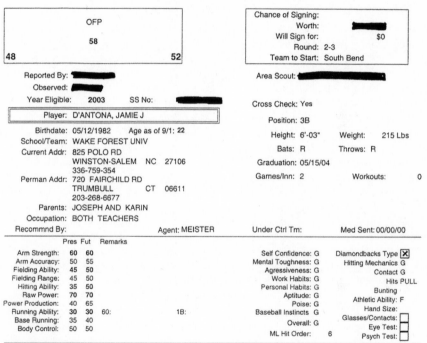

	OFP
	58
48	52

Chance of Signing:
Worth: ████████
Will Sign for: $0
Round: 2-3
Team to Start: South Bend

Reported By: ████████
Observed: ████
Year Eligible: **2003**   SS No: ████

Area Scout: ████████

Cross Check: Yes

Player:	D'ANTONA, JAMIE J

Birthdate: 05/12/1982   Age as of 9/1: **22**
School/Team: WAKE FOREST UNIV
Current Addr: 825 POLO RD
WINSTON-SALEM   NC   27106
336-759-354
Perman Addr: 720 FAIRCHILD RD
TRUMBULL   CT   06611
203-268-6677
Parents: JOSEPH AND KARIN
Occupation: BOTH TEACHERS
Recommnd By:

Position: 3B
Height: 6'-03"   Weight: 215 Lbs
Bats: R   Throws: R
Graduation: 05/15/04
Games/Inn: 2   Workouts: 0

Agent: MEISTER   Under Ctrl Tm: Med Sent: 00/00/00

	Pres	Fut	Remarks		
Arm Strength:	60	60			
Arm Accuracy:	50	55			
Fielding Ability:	45	50			
Fielding Range:	45	50			
Hitting Ability:	35	50			
Raw Power:	70	70			
Power Production:	40	65			
Running Ability:	30	30	60:	1B:	
Base Running:	35	40			
Body Control:	50	50			

Self Confidence: G
Mental Toughness: G
Agressiveness: G
Work Habits: G
Personal Habits: G
Aptitude: G
Poise: G
Baseball Instincts: G
Overall: G
ML Hit Order: 6

Diamondbacks Type ☒
Hitting Mechanics G
Contact G
Hits PULL
Bunting
Athletic Ability: F
Hand Size:
Glasses/Contacts: ☐
Eye Test: ☐
Psych Test: ☐

Physical Description:
BIG STRONG PLAYER,LUIS PUJOLS

Abilities/Weaknesses:
POWER, ARM STRENGTH 3B, BOTH PLUS ABILITY, HAS TOOLS FOR POSITION, LIFT TO SWING PRODUCING HOME RUNS.SP[ECIAL LIFT, ATTACKS BASEBALL, CAN PLAY 3B.NEEDS TO USE WHOLE FIELD MORE.

Summation:
FITS 3B PROFILE HAS POWER TOOL AND USING THAT TOOL, WILL BE OKAY AT 3B, BATTLES, INTELLIGENT PLAYER.LIFT YOU CANT TEACH NATURAL POWER, WOOD WILL NOT AFFECT.

2002 CAPE COD ALL-STAR GAME

EAST

Pos	Name	Team	B/T	Class	School	HIT	POWER	RUN	ARM	FIELD	COMMENTS
11 C	Ryan Hanigan	Orleans	R-R	2003	Rollins Col	20/40	30/70	36	50/55		*(handwritten comments, illegible)*
40 1B	Wes Whisler	Y-D	L-L	2005	UCLA						
14 2B	Chris Snavely	Harwich	L-R	2004	Ohio State						
4 SS	Matt Maniscalco	Orleans	R-R	2003	Miss State						
44 3B	Brett Cooley	Y-D	R-R	2003	Houston	20/45	20/56		50/60		*(handwritten comments, illegible)*
3 DH	Cesar Nicolas	Harwich	R-R	2004	Vanderbilt						
23 OF	Adam Bourassa	Y-D	L-L	2003	Wake Forest	29/65	20/..	55	45/50	40/55	*(handwritten comments, illegible)*
4 OF	Jayce Tingler	Brewster	L-L	2003	Missouri	20/55	20/30	50	45/50	48/55	*(handwritten comments, illegible)*
5 OF	David Coffey	Orleans	L-R	2004	Georgia						*(handwritten comments, illegible)*
30 IF	Jeremy Cleveland	Chatham	R-R	2004	UNC-Chap Hill						*(handwritten comments, illegible)*
12 C	Mitch Maier	Harwich	L-R	2004	Toledo	20/50	30/85	40	55	40/55	*(handwritten comments, illegible)*
2 OF	Anthony Gwynn	Brewster	L-R	2004	San Diego St	25/70	20/40	60	46/50	40/55	*(handwritten comments, illegible)*

Pos	Name	Team	B/T	Class	School	FB	CB	SL	CH	CONT	COMMENTS
16 P	Brian Rogers	Orleans	R-R	2004	GA Southern	86-91	74	72-80	71-75	55	*(handwritten comments, illegible)*
26 P	Tim Stauffer	Chatham	R-R	2004	Richmond	89,94 93,94	78,79		81,79	60/65	*(handwritten comments, illegible)*
19 P	Brad Ziegler	Harwich	R-R	2003	SW Missouri St	87-93 84-90	72-91		77-79		*(handwritten comments, illegible)*
30 P	John Hudgins	Y-D	R-R	2004	Stanford	89,86,87 90,86,87	70,69	79	76		*(handwritten comments, illegible)*
14 P	Whitley Benson	Orleans	L-R	2004	UNC-Chap Hill		70,69		77-72-76		
34 P	Taylor Tankersley	Brewster	L-L	2005	Alabama						*(handwritten comments, illegible)*
7 P	Jamie Vermilyea	Y-D	R-R	2004	New Mexico						
22 P	Scott Baker	Orleans	R-R	2004	Okla. State	91,91,91 92,91,93	78,74,77		76		
11 P	Shaun Marcum	Harwich	R-R	2004	SW Missouri St						

Evaluation Report
Published

Timothy Stauffer Evaluation Report 01/06/2004

Name:	Timothy J Stauffer	**Present Pos:** Right Handed Pitcher	**GROUP:**	1
School:	RICHMOND U	**Future Pos:** Right Handed Pitcher	**ADJUSTED OFP:**	62.5
State:	VA	**Height:** 6' 2"	**Evaluation By:**	Trip Keister
Class:	JR	**Weight:** 205 lbs	**RAW OFP:**	62
DOB:	06/02/1982	**Bats:** Right	**Report Date:**	04/07/2003
Age:	22	**Throws:** Right	**Report #:**	3

Entry Level:	AA	**TOPS:**	ML	**ETA:**		**Peak Role:**	#1 STARTER
Date Last Observed:	04/05/2003	**Games Seen:**	5	**Innings Pitched:**	42		

Physical Description:	LEAN, ATHLETIC BUILD, STRONG LEGS, BROAD SHOULDERS, LOOSE ARM
Athleticism:	VERY GOOD - HAS BODY CONTROL ON MOUND, QUICK FEET, FIELDS POSITION
Body Comparision:	
Glasses / Contacts:	None
Medical Issues?:	No
What Type:	
Arm Angle:	HTQ **Deception:** GOOD
Arm Action:	VERY GOOD - LOOSE, VERY QUICK
Delivery:	VERY GOOD - FULL WINDUP, REPEATS, STAYS ON-LINE
Balance:	VERY GOOD - STAYS BALANCED OVER RUBBER, HAS GOOD RHYTHM/TEMPO
Finish:	GOOD - GETS EXTENSION
Outpitch:	SL **Fielding:** VERY GOOD **Release Times:** 1.21, 1.18

Click for Rating Key

Pitches	Present	Future	CMD	Descriptive Remarks
FastBall *	55	60	60	THREW MOSTLY 4 SM TODAY, HAD VELO I'VE SEEN BEFORE, TOUCHING 94 HE STILL HAS CEILING BUT WILL PROBABLY PITCH @ 90-92 IN PRO BALL, LOCATES IN & OUT, UP & DWN, MAKES GUYS MOVE FEET
Movement	55	65		RAISED GRADE TO SOLID +, AS HE THROWS MORE FB IN PRO BALL HE WILL GET BETTER FEEL FOR RUNNING 2 SM AWAY FROM LHH & IN ON RHH, WILL HAVE QUICK INNS W/FB VS WOOD BAT WHEN HE THROWS 2SMR, THREW A COUPLE TODAY THAT EXPLODED ON HITTR
CurveBall *	60	60	55	SHRP CB WILL THROW AT ANY TIME, WILL THROW FOR STRIKES, THROWS HARDER W/ 2 STRIKES, GREAT FEEL, 2 BACKDOOR PUNCHOUTS W/LHH'S, HIS GO TO PITCH WHEN HE NEEDS A CALLED STRIKE
Slider *	60	60	60	USES CUTTER AS SL, NASTY OUT PITCH, GETS HITTERS TO CHASE, THROWS HARD W/ LATE ACTION, WILL THROW TO LHH & RHH
Change *	60	65	60	STILL FILTHY, GREAT FEEL, DOESN'T USE ENOUGH, TIES UP RHH, THROWS BACK TO BACK, THROWS ON 1ST PITCH, GREAT PITCH W/WOOD BAT
Other *				
Control *	60	65		POUNDS ZONE W/ 4 PITCHES, WILL HAVE QUICK INNINGS
OFP	59	62		#1 STARTER W/3 + SECONDARY PITCHES

Gun Readings:

	High	Low	Avg		High	Low	Avg		High	Low	Avg
FastBall	94	89	92	FB-Stretch	94	89	92	Curve Ball	77	73	76
Slider				Change	81	78	80	Other	89	86	87

Make UP						
Poise:	EXCELLENT	**Aptitude:**	EXCELLENT	**Self Confidence:**	EXCELLENT	
Competitiveness:	EXCELLENT	**Habits:**	EXCELLENT	**Desire:**	EXCELLENT	
Aggressiveness:	EXCELLENT	**Hustle:**	EXCELLENT	**Emotional Control:**	EXCELLENT	

Summary:	SEE OTHER REPORTS, WILL PITCH IN BIG LEAGUES SOON, SHOWED VELOCITY THAT I'VE SEEN BEFORE, HE HAS VELO WHEN HE NEEDS IT BUT IS STILL EFFECTIVE W/THE 55 FB, WILL HAVE QUICK INNS IN PRO BALL W/ FB & LIFE, HAS SECONDARY PITCHES IN ARSENAL IF HE NEEDS THEM, CMD/CONTROL, CONTINUES TO IMPRESS, MOST IMPRESSIVE THING ABOUT THIS GUY IS HIS PROFESSIONALISM, VERY METICULOUS IN HIS PREPARATION, VERY FOCUSED, VERY BUSINESS-LIKE, I HOPE HE IS THERE AT #4
Pitchability?:	VERY GOOD - +STRIKE THROWER, WILL THROW ANY PITCH AT ANY TIME IN COUNT
How do you feel you saw player:	VERY GOOD - HAD VELOCITY I'VE SEEN IN PAST, SET CAREER STRIKEOUT RECORD AT UNIV OF RICHMOND
Signability:	VERY GOOD - VERY GOOD WHERE HE WILL BE DRAFTED
College will attend:	**Agent:** RON SHAPIRO

01/06/2004--11:54:30 AM

Acknowledgments

THIS BOOK WOULD NOT HAVE BEEN POSSIBLE without the co-operation and openness of John Schiffner, Peter Troy, Paul Galop, Charlie Thoms, and other officers and coaches in the Chatham Athletic Association. John Schiffner, in particular, was extraordinarily generous with both his time and his assistance. The degree to which I was able to get close to the 2002 Chatham A's is due in large part to the complete access he afforded—to games and practices, team functions, closed-door meetings, living-room conversations, and any other parts of his life where I hoped I might learn more about the experience of players, scouts, managers, and fans of the Cape Cod Baseball League. He has played all of those positions, and his perspectives proved invaluable.

There would have been no story without the willingness of the Chatham A's players to share their lives and thoughts with me. I'm indebted most to Jamie D'Antona, Tim Stauffer, and Thomas Pauly, whose generosity extended beyond the playing field to houses, jobs, families, hometowns, and college campuses. For a journalist, it is gratifying not to be "big-leagued" by athletes so close to becoming big leaguers. I am grateful to them all.

Several of the players' families provided important reflections and insights and graciously welcomed me into their lives. Joe and Karin D'Antona, Becky and Rick Stauffer, Marta and Tom Pauly, and Jim

Hanan, in particular, deserve thanks for their helpfulness and unending patience.

In Chatham, many people provided kindnesses large and small, hospitality, color, opinions, and information. Among them: Martha Schiffner, Ginor Hayes, Laurie Galop, Diane Troy, Penny and Andy Ruddock, Rellan and Susan Monson, Bob Sherman, Eddie and Kay Lyons, Joe Fitzback, Mark Bulman, Chris Diego, Peggy Davis, Gus Schumacher, Dave and Judy Buck (and Dave and Marilyn Johnson). Thanks to Judy Walden Scarafile, Sean Walsh, Missy Alaimo, and John Wylde of the Cape Cod Baseball League.

Coaches George Greer of Wake Forest University and Scott Bradley of Princeton University provided key and candid assessments. I am grateful for the time they carved out of busy schedules. Several major league scouts shared information and insights, including Jim Howard of the Orioles, George Biron and Tom Burns of the Angels, and Tripp Keister of the Padres. Will Lingo and Jim Callis of *Baseball America* provided helpful information. The publication itself was a tremendous resource. I recommend it to anyone looking to follow the fortunes of the country's best amateur and minor league baseball players. I greatly enjoyed dipping into deep pools of baseball and Cape Cod literature. Three very useful books were: *Baseball by the Beach: A History of Baseball on Cape Cod*; by Christopher Price, *Dollar Sign on the Muscle: The World of Baseball Scouting*, by Kevin Kerrane, and *The Nature of Cape Cod*, by Beth Schwarzman. Thanks to Barry Meister and Ron Shapiro for illuminating the world of sports agents. Thanks to Dartmouth College engineering professor Robert Collier for illuminating the world of ball-bat collisions. Thanks to Robert Sullivan for wisdom and advice, Ken Burns for perspective, and Dr. Herb Greenberg of Caliper Human Strategies, Inc. Long-term thanks to Mel Allen, Judson D. Hale, Sr., and Tim Clark of *Yankee* magazine. Thanks to Mike Gauthier and Jeff Smykil. Thanks to Julie Dunfey for her good eye. Thanks to HEM for background. Special thanks to the fabulous Allen sisters, Chelsi and

Melissa. Deep, personal thanks to Wentworth Hubbard and to Jeff Hubbard.

I feel blessed to have Stuart Krichevsky for an agent. (Thanks to Shana Cohen and Ross Harris of the Stuart Krichevsky Literary Agency, as well.) I feel doubly blessed to have worked with editor Amanda Cook of the Perseus Books Group, whose enthusiasm and shaping of the book's narrative were both fundamental. Further thanks and appreciation for good work at Da Capo Press to Ingrid Finstuen, Dan Ambrosio, Amber Morris, Karl Yambert, Sean Maher, Lissa Warren, Kevin Hanover, and John Radziewicz.

Special gratitude to Mark Kramer of the Nieman Foundation at Harvard University. His influence touches every page of the book, and many of the words.

Finally, especially, thanks to my wife Kristen Laine for careful reading, for time, space, and support, for her ear and for her heart.